Critical Synoptics

Critical Synoptics

Menippean Satire
and the Analysis
of Intellectual Mythology

Carter Kaplan

Madison • Teaneck
Fairleigh Dickinson University Press
London: Associated University Presses

© 2000 by Associated University Presses, Inc.

All rights reserved. Authorization to photocopy items for internal or personal use, or the internal or personal use of specific clients, is granted by the copyright owner, provided that a base fee of $10.00, plus eight cents per page, per copy is paid directly to the Copyright Clearance Center, 222 Rosewood Drive, Danvers, Massachusetts 01923. [0-8386-3865-1/00 $10.00 + 8¢ pp, pc.]

Associated University Presses
440 Forsgate Drive
Cranbury, NJ 08512

Associated University Presses
16 Barter Street
London WC1A 2AH, England

Associated University Presses
P.O. Box 338, Port Credit
Mississauga, Ontario
Canada L5G 4L8

The paper used in this publication meets the requirements of the American National Standard for Permanence of Paper for Printed Library Materials Z39.48-1984.

Library of Congress Cataloging-in-Publication Data

Kaplan, Carter, 1960–
    Critical synoptics : Menippean satire and the analysis of intellectual mythology / Carter Kaplan.
       p.   cm.
    Includes bibliographical references (p.) and index.
    ISBN 0-8386-3865-1 (alk. paper)
    1. Satire—History and criticism.   2. Satire—Classical influences.   3. Dystopias in literature.   I. Title.
PN6149.S2 K36   2000
809.7—dc21   00-034764

PRINTED IN THE UNITED STATES OF AMERICA

The magic has endured, and whenever a grammar book comes my way, I instantly turn to the last page to enjoy a forbidden glimpse of the laborious student's future, of that promised land where, at last, words are meant to mean what they mean.

—Vladimir Nabokov, *Speak, Memory*

Contents

Preface   9
Acknowledgments   15

Part I: Menippean Satire and Critical Synoptics

1. What is Menippean Satire?   21
   The Approach from Philosophy   21
   The Approach from Theology   31
   The Approach from Post-Modernism   33
   Menippean Satire As It Is   44
2. Games Critics Play   59
   Critical Games   59
   Text Concepts   61
   Reading Games   63
   The Accurate Reading Game   64
   The Appropriative Reading Game   65
   Appropriative and Accurate Paraphrase—A Practical Exercise   66
   Critical Posture   70
   The Synoptic Surview   74

Part II: Anglo-American Romanticism and the Specter of Intellectual Mythology

3. Hawthorne's Arcadian Reality Test   79
4. Menacing the Good Baker's Oven   91
5. The Question of the Monster   100
6. Grinding the Apophatic Axe   114
7. Originals and Their Antecedents   131

Part III: The Synoptic Analysis of Programmed Texts

8. The Advent of Literary Dystopia   147

9. The Edge of Capital ... 161
   Complexity and the Human Condition   161
   Critical Patterns of Evolution   162
   Order for Free   168
10. Scaling up to the Homeric Question: The Aesthetics of Chaos, Complexity, and Cosmogenesis ... 177
   The Cosmogenic Manifesto   177
   The Aesthetics of Complexity—Complexity as Technique   180
   The Aesthetics of Cosmogenesis—The Cosmogenic Narrative   185
   Generic Cosmogenic Narrative—The Chaos Poet   188
   William Blake Meets the Corsairs of the Second Ether   190
   Performative or Symbolic?   194
   Transformations   195

Notes ... 196
Bibliography ... 206
Index ... 215

Preface

IN THIS BOOK I HAVE TRIED TO PAINT A PICTURE OF THE PHILOSOPHICAL concerns shared by Menippean satire, British common sense philosophy, and twentieth century analytic philosophy. These three traditions meet in the field of inquiry that I call "Critical Synoptics"—a fusion of satire and the descriptive, elucidating philosophy of Ludwig Wittgenstein. Menippean satire joins Wittgenstein in the cause of bringing clarity to our world view by stripping language bare of misleading grammar, illusion, conceptual confusion, and the orthodoxies of intellectual mythology. In writing and rewriting the chapters of this book, I was struck again and again by how the authors I treat here, Herman Melville chief among them, recapitulated not only philosophy's struggle against intellectual mythology, but also the struggles—Wittgenstein's struggles if you will—to transcend classic empiricism and arrive at a bigger and more comprehensive form of analysis. I was fascinated to discover that Melville's struggles with epistemology and metaphysics in *Moby-Dick* have their parallel in Wittgenstein's struggles with logic and metaphysics in the *Tractatus Logico-Philosophicus*. Both works are virtuoso performances of the *reductio ad absurdum*. Both works employ elaborate parody as a critical technique. Then I discovered a parallel between Melville's synoptic essays into contextual analysis in *The Confidence-Man* and Wittgenstein's elaboration of the language game metaphor in *Philosophical Investigations*.[1] These works, both the "second masterpieces" of their authors, analyze their topics through the examination of problematic language game scenarios in which meaning, when it can be determined, can be determined by context. When arrived at in this way, even the most complex meanings are made remarkably clear and unconfutable. For Wittgenstein, these games turn the light of resolution upon classic philosophical problems by dispelling the metaphysics and intellectual mythology upon which these problems are based. In *The Confidence-Man*, Melville's fictitious scenarios—like acts in a hypochondriacal morality play—elaborate and qualify the problem of religious faith, seeking a specific, case-by-case resolution of the risks inherent to the exercise of faith in a "fallen" world inhabited by Homo sapiens. By identifying conceptual errors that lead to philosophical credulousness, Melville dismantles myths of faith and myths of cynicism. Both Wittgenstein and Melville's works are like therapies in that they train the reader to think at a high and remarkably clear pitch—the pitch of synoptic analysis. If our species does indeed possess a collective wisdom, as I playfully suggest we do in the final chapter of this book, then this wisdom is to be revealed in the critical patterns elaborated in Menippean satire and described and practiced by Wittgenstein. This book is an attempt to join philosophy and satire to reveal these patterns and inspire others to seek them as well.

But it is not my intention to compare Wittgenstein to Melville, or to introduce Wittgenstein as a means for exploring Melville's intellectual biography. I leave it to more capable colleagues to grapple with those important undertakings. The emphasis in this book is on Menippean satire and how it can be used as a tool to identify and examine intellectual mythology. I hope to build in these chapters a vision of a new literary criticism predicated on the consideration of satire as an unconventional but nonetheless rigorous tradition of philosophy rooted in the analysis of intellectual mythology. A number of studies treating Menippean satire have been produced in the past fifteen years. As far as I know, this study is the first to draw connections between Menippean satire and Wittgenstein's philosophy. Wittgenstein, in fact, is conspicuously absent from the university student's core experience of critical law givers. This lack of exposure to Wittgenstein and his work is surprising when one learns that Wittgenstein is unequivocally the most important and influential philosopher of the past century. I wonder if my readers might reach the conclusion that this lacuna in the university experience is due to the fact that we critics have been busy creating and elaborating (indeed, bowing before) various critical mythologies. And that while we celebrate our differences among ourselves, obviously a system of analysis designed to expose our mythologies and the conceptual shortcomings of our propositions is bound to evoke a passive *demur*. These are entertaining notions, but it is probably more accurate to attribute our philosophical shortcomings to the culture at large which is remarkably indifferent to such issues. Representative artifacts of modern superstition—the big bang, astrology, reincarnation, relativism, cynicism, survival of the fittest, shamanism, dialectical materialism, cyberspace, mind/body dualism, the inner-child, the ego, the id, and the superego—suggest that intellectual mythology is a characteristic of contemporary civilization no less significant than reservoirs, prisons, superhighways, and power lines.

This book is divided into three sections. The first section essays a definition of Menippean satire by approaching it through four orientations: analytic philosophy, theology, post-modernism, and history. The section concludes with a parody of itself, defining a new theory of textual reading in terms of synoptic analysis. The outcome of this new theory, not surprisingly, is satirical. The second section surveys satirical works by Nathaniel Hawthorne, Edgar Allan Poe, Herman Melville, and Jules Verne—a group whose political and philosophical relationship to a young America at the threshold of empire brought unique energy and excitement to the Menippean form. The third section carries synoptic analysis forward to the beginning of the twenty-first century and addresses representative theoretical issues within the context of the post-Cold War order: complexity theory, artificial intelligence, and the triumph of ideological capitalism. This final section begins by defining my notion of the "programmed text" and its relationship to the literature of dystopia. The burden of the third section is given over to two case scenarios which demonstrate the central role synoptic analysis must play in addressing the philosophical questions raised at the beginning of the new millennium by emerging information technologies and global systems of administration.

My ambitious title, *Critical Synoptics*, does little to reflect the bleak and oftentimes frustrating enterprise of promoting a philosophy and a body of literature that seeks to rob people of their mythologies. The path is strewn with the bodies of those who, having been struck and blinded by repeated thunderclaps of apocalyptic insight, have succumbed to the twilight dullness of misanthropy. The myth hunter's soul reward is a tiny but inviolable sensation of "doing good." Of course, there are plenty of laughs along this route too, and laughter is a pretty fair consolation for anything. But I hope my readers will not be too amused when I say that the pages that follow represent an attempt to promote the ideals of enlightenment. With the re-emergence of realpolitik amidst the decline of nation states and democratic military institutions, analytical philosophy and satire might well emerge as the most effective tools that intellectuals have for analyzing and mitigating the interrelated dynamic of euphemistic language, corporate hegemony, and the ascendancy of global oligarchies. Recent utopian theories—postmodernism, relativism, deconstructionism, identity-politics—have exhibited effects variously repressive, divisive, and diversionary. And the practitioners of these systems have already or are currently in the process of being assimilated by a system that cannot tolerate—let alone recognize—the once respected arts of self-criticism, self-determination, subjective appraisal, and nonmaterial enrichment. It is my hope that this book can give clear voice to the insights represented by these arts.

One final note on sources: Wittgenstein's early thought is presented in the *Tractatus Logico-Philosophicus*, a study of language that exploded modern logic and classic British empiricism, and ushered in the revolution of analytic philosophy that came to dominate the first half of the twentieth century. The greatest significance of the *Tractatus* is its ushering a shift in philosophy from an emphasis on metaphysics and deep logic to an emphasis on language. Forcing deep logic through an analysis of itself, Wittgenstein exhausted the subject and removed it from the philosophical agenda. Russell gave up his study of logic after the *Tractatus*. Indeed, so did Wittgenstein. What the *Tractatus* did was prepare Wittgenstein (and the twentieth century) for his final assault on metaphysics and intellectual mythology. Much of Wittgenstein's latter thought survives through notes taken by his students and in manuscripts which he never thought ready for publication. Fortunately, much of this corpus has been published. And of course there is Wittgenstein's second masterpiece, *Philosophical Investigations*, quite possibly the most important work in philosophy since Plato. Students of Menippean satire would do well to begin their own investigations with a perusal of this central work. Peter Hacker's *Wittgenstein's Place in Twentieth-century Analytic Philosophy* is an accessible introduction to the topic. A thorough commentary on the *Investigations* can be found in Hacker's (and Gordon Baker's) multivolume *Analytical Commentary on the Philosophical Investigations*. Ray Monk's biography, *Wittgenstein: The Duty of Genius,* is an invaluable source for material on Wittgenstein's dynamic, charismatic, and heroic character. Monk provides ample evidence that the trajectory of Wittgenstein's persona, like that of our greatest poets, is nearly as interesting and instructive as his work itself. Students should also consult Maurice Drury's *The Danger of Words*. Drury, himself a student of Wittgenstein, applies analytical techniques to psychiatry. Drury had in fact been steered into psychiatric medicine by Wittgenstein, who in this and other ways exerted a profound influence over his life. Monk suggests Drury's book "is perhaps, in its tone and its concerns, the most truly Wittgensteinian work published by any of Wittgenstein's students." Monk says that Drury's work underscores the notion that "there is an important aspect of Wittgenstein's influence that is not, and cannot be, covered in the large body of academic literature which Wittgenstein's work has inspired." Wittgenstein's influence "extends far beyond the confines of academic philosophy." This will continue to be a theme in Wittgenstein scholarship. A reading of Wittgenstein's "poetics" is pursued by Marjorie Perloff in *Wittgenstein's Ladder: Poetic Language and the Strangeness of the Ordinary*. Perloff argues that academic theorists have not understood that Wittgenstein is in fact more poet than philosopher. In Wittgenstein Perloff sees a new poetic aesthetic that reveals the strangeness of ordinary language. Perloff's approach is to read Wittgenstein's works not for what they say, but what they are. Such thinking is attractive, but one has to be very careful with Wittgenstein. The fact remains that Wittgenstein was not a poet and that whatever un- or anti-academic idiosyncrasies he possessed do not negate or mitigate the fact that he wrote for a specialized audience of professional philosophers. If Wittgenstein had believed poetry to be the best venue for his thought, then he would have been a poet. Although he has and certainly will inspire critics, poets, and other creative artists, Wittgenstein remains a philosopher with a commitment to examining language in order to clarify our world view. Wittgenstein was not concerned with the strangeness of the ordinary, but rather with species of philosophical credulous rooted in language that might make the ordinary strange. He did find academic life tedious, he did reject traditional philosophical discourse, but he also knew that the theater of academic philosophy was the best available forum for bringing his discoveries into contact with other disciplines. It is to the young scholars in all fields who respond to the clarion call of Wittgenstein's philosophy that *Critical Synoptics* is dedicated. May they dazzle the world with their revelations.

Acknowledgments

It would be impossible to list all the teachers and friends whose support over the years enabled me to compose this book. I should single out Martha Meek, Michael Beard, and Wallace Martin as the figures who sent me galumphing down the Menippean road. Others who have helped in various ways—through correspondence and conversation—include Charles Carter, Richard Summers, David Hoch, Donald Poochigian, Sister Agnes Vincent Rueshoff, John Bryant, Peter Hacker, Donald Bullough, and Marie Louise Moffett. And I must acknowledge my family, who helped me down a Menippean road of another, richer kind.

Grateful acknowledgment is made to the following for permission to reprint previously published material:

Johnathan Swift and the Anatomy of Satire: A Study of Satiric Technique by John M. Bullitt. Copyright © 1953 by the president and fellows of Harvard College. Reprinted by permission of Harvard University Press.

Excerpt from *Postcript to the Name of the Rose* by Umberto Eco, copyright © 1983 by Umberto Eco, English translation (by William Weaver) copyright © 1984 by Harcourt, Inc., reprinted by permission of the publisher. And (in the British Commonwealth) permission of The Random House Archive and Library.

Fun and Games by Ken Binmore. Copyright © 1992. Reprinted by permission of Houghton Mifflin Company.

Chapter 2 is developed from an article that originally appeared in *SubStance* 81. Copyright © 1996. Reprinted by permission of The University of Wisconsin Press.

Chapters 5 and 8 are developed from articles which originally appeared in *Extrapolation,* Vol. 39 No. 2, pp 139–147; Vol. 40 No. 3, pp 200–212; respectively. Reprinted by permission of The Kent State University Press.

Every effort has been made to obtain permission to quote from the sources used in this publication; where this process has failed, apologies are tendered.

Critical Synoptics

I
Menippean Satire and Critical Synoptics

1
What is Menippean Satire?

MENIPPEAN SATIRE IS THE ENDURING LITERARY FORM OF DESCRIPTIVE OR synoptic analysis. The drawing together of Menippean satire and analytical philosophy demands a cautious and detailed vindication of the use of synoptics—storytelling—as an analytical tool. Such vindication takes place in the examination of those propositions—the grammar and the vocabulary—which language itself offers up to best explain itself as it represents, suggests, and describes the world.

THE APPROACH FROM PHILOSOPHY

In philosophy, Menippean satire is a method for analyzing propositions, clearing off conceptual confusion, and discrediting intellectual mythology.

Parallels to the philosophical orientation of Menippean satire can be found in classic British empiricism, so-called "common sense" philosophy, and twentieth-century analytical philosophy. Analytical philosophy has its roots in British common sense philosophy and British empirical philosophy—intertwining traditions sketched along the lines of Francis Bacon, John Locke, George Berkeley, David Hume, and Thomas Reid. The way these traditions untwine, however, is the remarkable thing. Locke's sense-based epistemology spawned a host of idealized notions concerning mind, body, and sensations that set the Enlightenment up to be intercepted by Berkeley and the German metaphysicians. The notion of Locke being an idealist may cause some to chafe. Suffice it to say at this point that the empiricists "argued that words are connected to the world by the mediation of ideas derived from experience."[1] Hence, from an analytical or common sense perspective, empiricism is actually idealism (see chapter 5). Moving in another direction, Hume engaged in a radical interpretation of Locke's sense-based epistemology that yielded a strident and radical skepticism. Both Hume's skepticism and Locke's "idealism" spawned a reaction represented by Reid and broadly known as common sense philosophy. Jane Austen aptly caught the spirit of the schism between common sense epistemology and sensory-based epistemology in the title of her novel *Sense and Sensibility*. The common sense tradition culminates in the twentieth century in Ludwig Wittgenstein—and not the early Wittgenstein, the Wittgenstein of the *Tractatus*, but rather the latter Wittgenstein, the Wittgenstein of the *Philosophical Investigations*. The notion of a descriptive or synoptic analysis is identified with Wittgenstein's latter stage of philosophy, particularly as it is portrayed in the *Philosophical Investigations*. It would be a mistake to seek a strict congruence between Menippean satire and Wittgensteinian analysis. Being an art, Menippean satire extends into much more idiosyncratic and far-flung realms of subject and activity. However, it is tempting to postulate that further refinement in the practice of Menippean satire will be realized through more closely aligning the genre with the methods and techniques practiced by Wittgenstein.

Synoptic analysis concerns itself with the accurate apprehension of the real world. Wittgenstein considered using Bishop Butler's phrase "Everything is what it is, and not another thing" as an epigraph for the *Investigations*. The world, for Wittgenstein, is as it is. Things are as they are. Rather than speculating on invisible causes that explain the condition of the world—asking *why* the world is as it is—philosophy is a process of identifying illuminating comparisons to get an understanding of *how* the world is as it is. Thus, Wittgenstein sought "the understanding which consists in seeing connections," in seeing how the thing said is related to the context in which the thing is said.[2] Wittgenstein's technique is to tell stories about the ways words are used and understood. This is the process of synoptic analysis. As we shall see, it took British philosophy several centuries and Wittgenstein several decades to arrive at this revolutionary conjuncture.

The five definitions of "reality" offered by the *Oxford English Dictionary* are all predicated, to various degrees, on the definition of "real." An adjective, "real" is the quality of "having an objective existence; actually existing as a thing." In philosophy, "real" is "applied to whatever is regarded as having an existence in fact and not merely in appearance, thought or language, or as having an absolute and necessary, in contrast to a merely contingent, existence." Conspicuously absent from the definition of the adjective is the manifold or plural nature of the world we inhabit. Therefore, the *Oxford English Dictionary*'s third definition of the noun, "reality," exhibits the highest precision and accuracy among available definitions: "Real existence; what is real; the aggregate of real things or existence." What this means for logical process is inductive reasoning. However, intellectual process, which comprises emotions, memory, sensory experience, imagination, skepticism, self-reflexiveness, as well as logic, demands a more comprehensive disintegration.

William Blake argued for the perception of reality as a disparate aggregate, for a reality consisting of "minute particulars" which expressed the distinction and individuality of all things. Blake rejected the neoclassical attempt or practice to get at the essence or first principles of things by homogenizing or otherwise discarding the details. According to Blake, it was these details which comprise the windows into perception. "General Forms have their vitality in Particulars."[3] "Sacrifice the Parts, What becomes of the Whole?"[4] "Minute Discrimination is Not Accidental. All Sublimity is founded on Minute Discrimination."[5] "What is General Nature? Is there such a Thing: Strictly speaking, All knowledge is Particular."[6]

Ludwig Wittgenstein shared Blake's concern for the particular, and championed its ascendancy in philosophy over the general. His early work represents the pinnacle of modern logic. In the *Tractatus Logico-Philosophicus* Wittgenstein argues that the notion of particularity describes the actual physical structure of the world. "Die Welt zerfällt in Tatsachen." Moreover, particulars, states of affairs, or facts are for Wittgenstein independent of each other. The basic disconnectedness of these facts is the true state of the world. According to the *Tractatus*:

1.2 The world divides into facts.
1.21 Each item can be the case or not be the case while everything else remains the same.
2.061 States of affairs are independent of one another.
2.062 From the existence or non-existence of one state of affairs it is impossible to infer the existence or non-existence of another.
5.135 There is no possible way of making an inference from the existence of one situation to the existence of another, entirely different situation.
5.136 There is no causal nexus to justify such an inference.
5.1361 We *cannot* infer the events of the future from those of the present.
    Belief in the causal nexus is *superstition*.[7]

Wittgenstein wanted to eradicate this superstition of causal relationships from the philosopher's mind. By seeing things this way, by seeing facts as they really are, as particular, the philosopher will perceive the world in a highly unusual way. The philosopher will see facts, so to speak, in a frozen frame—essentially unconnected with respect to time, to what comes before and to what comes after. The philosopher will see facts *"sub specie aeternitatis"* or from the "viewpoint of eternity." Wittgenstein says, "viewing the world *sub specie aeternitatis* is the good life." Facts perceived in this manner lose the explainability which they have when they can be related to other facts. "Such facts transform into objects of a profoundly disinterested contemplation."[8]

Influenced by these early ideas of Wittgenstein, Bertrand Russell writes:

> I shall set forth . . . a certain kind of logical doctrine, and on the basis of this a certain kind of metaphysic. The logic which I will advocate is atomistic, as opposed to the monistic logic of the people who more or less follow Hegel. When I say that my logic is atomistic, I mean that I share the common sense belief that there are many separate things; I do not regard the apparent multiplicity of the world as consisting merely in phases and unreal divisions of a single indivisible Reality.[9]

The skeptic philosopher David Hume also expressed doubt for the notion of a causal nexus, and so undermined science by dissolving the concept of law. From the time of Bruno and Galileo, science and philosophy had been predicated on the notion of "natural law." Natural law was a belief in the role of "necessity" in the sequence of cause and effect. Hume observed, however, that we never perceive causes or laws; but, more precisely, we perceive events and sequences and from them merely infer causation and necessity. There is no guarantee that sequences hitherto observed will reappear or reoccur in future experience. It is not law, but custom that we observe in the sequence of events; and there is no "necessity" in custom. For Hume, only mathematical equations and formulae possessed necessity. One plus one necessarily equals two; ten times ten necessary equals one hundred. Hume concluded that science "must limit itself strictly to mathematics and direct experiment." Reality could not be realized through unverified deduction from necessary "laws." Hume writes:

> When we run through libraries, persuaded of these principles, what havoc must we make! If we take in our hands any volume of school meta-

physics, for instance, let us ask, "Does it contain any abstract reasoning concerning quantity and number?" No. "Does it contain any experimental reasoning concerning matter of fact and existence?" No. Commit it then to the flames, for it can contain nothing but sophistry and illusion.[10]

Francis Bacon was sensitive to a tendency in human beings to draw the separate facts, particulars, and events of experience into abstract necessities, general laws, and "natural" mechanisms. According to Bacon in aphorism 45 from book 1 of the *Novum Organum*:

> The human understanding is of its own nature prone to suppose the existence of more order and regularity in the world than it finds. And though there be many things in nature which are singular and unmatched, yet it devises for them parallels and conjugates and relatives which do not exist. Hence the fiction that all celestial bodies move in perfect circles, spirals and dragons being (except in name) utterly rejected. Hence too the element of fire with its orb is brought in, to make up the square with the other three which the sense perceives. Hence also the ratio of density of the so-called elements is arbitrarily fixed at ten to one. And so on of other dreams. And these fancies affect not dogmas only, but simple notions also.[11]

In aphorisms 39 through 44 of the *Novum Organum*, Bacon defines four classes of "idols" which he says "beset men's minds." These four distinctions Bacon calls, first, *Idols of the Tribe*; second, *Idols of the Cave*; third, *Idols of the Marketplace*; fourth, *Idols of the Theater*.

The Idols of the Tribe, says Bacon, "have their foundation in human nature itself . . . [H]uman understanding is like a false mirror, which, receiving rays irregularly, distorts and discolors the nature of things by mingling its own nature with it."

The Idols of the Cave "are the idols of the individual man . . . [M]en look for sciences in their own lesser worlds [—according to their personal nature, the books they read, their education, the friendship and authority of those whom they esteem and admire—] and not in the greater or common world."

The Idols of the Market are "formed by the intercourse and association of men with each other." Because of this association, language is often distorted "according to the apprehension of the vulgar. And therefore the ill and unfit choice of words wonderfully obstructs the understanding." Learned men are often in error in their definitions and explanations because "words plainly force and overrule the understanding, and throw all into confusion, and lead men away into numberless empty controversies and idle fancies."

The Idols of the Theatre are "various dogmas of philosophies, and also the wrong laws of demonstration." These various dogmas are "entire systems . . . principles and axioms in science, which by tradition, credulity, and negligence have come to be received." The demonstrations and proofs for these systems are like "so many stage plays, representing worlds of their own creation after an unreal and scenic fashion."[12]

Like Blake, Hume, and Wittgenstein, Bacon was interested in precisely delineating and eliminating the sources of conceptual error in order to draw a more precise distinction between illusion and reality. In the *Tractatus*, Wittgenstein explains how illusion persists as a condition of superstitious modernity:

> 6.371 The whole modern conception of the world is founded on the illusion that the so-called laws of nature are the explanations of natural phenomena.
> 6.372 Thus people today stop at the laws of nature, treating them as something inviolable, just as God and Fate were treated in past ages.
>
> And in fact both are right and both are wrong: Though the view of the ancients is clearer in so far as they have a clear and acknowledged terminus, while the modern system tries to make it look as if *everything* were explained.

The story of Wittgenstein's struggle to shape twentieth-century analytical philosophy is the most exciting in the history of philosophy. His thought represents the end of philosophy as it was known for at least two thousand years. What Wittgenstein finally introduced as a replacement for philosophy shares astonishing conceptual and methodological similarities with the oldest and most trenchant form of literary/critical analysis: Menippean satire.

Analytical philosophy began with the invention of modern logic by Russell and Frege who were reacting against the tradition of idealism that is rooted, ironically enough, in Locke (see chapter 5). Working with and against nineteenth-century principles of mathematics, Russell and Frege elucidated "the relations between [a deep structure of] logical calculi, language and thought."[13] Logic was conceived as a deep language that could explain fundamental relationships between propositions and reveal the essential character of phenomena. In turn,

Wittgenstein's *Tractatus* was a reaction against Russell and Frege. Through a system embodying something not unlike a parody of formal logic, Wittgenstein disproved the claims that were being made for logic, and analytic philosophy took a "linguistic turn." The *Tractatus* inspired Cambridge analysis, as well as Viennese logical positivism, which embraced miscomprehensions of the *Tractatus*, chiefly verificationism as a theory of meaning and a criterion of meaningfulness. After WWII analytic philosophy came to be dominated by Oxford where, influenced by Wittgenstein's *Philosophical Investigations*, philosophy went through another transformation which lasted another twenty-five years. In the United States the influence of the *Investigations*, "what was popularly and misleadingly known as 'Oxford Linguistic Philosophy' or 'Ordinary Language Philosophy' " was briefly influential.[14] Wittgenstein's later thought had to contend with the flourishing post-positivist tradition that had descended from miscomprehensions of the *Tractatus*.

The *Tractatus* and the *Investigations* present diametrically contrasting philosophical views. Although the *Tractatus* conceived of logic as nonsense, or the metaphysical ends of logic as being beyond sense, it shared logic's desire to employ depth analysis to reveal the hidden essence of things. The *Tractatus* was "possessed by a vision of the crystalline purity of the logical forms of thought, language and the world," and strove for a sublime, unifying form of philosophical insight and procedure. The *Investigations*, however, strove for a " 'quiet weighing of linguistic facts' (*Z* §447) in order to distangle the knots in our understanding . . . [through a] heightened awareness of the motley of spatial and temporal phenomena of language (*PI* §108), [and] the deceptive forms which lead us into conceptual confusion."[15] In the *Investigations* Wittgenstein strove for "no more than the description and arrangement of what is simple and familiar, 'hidden' only because it was always before one's eye and goes unnoticed" (*PI* §129). In these respects, Wittgenstein is remarkably suggestive of the philosophical stance Poe assumes in his mystery stories.

A key difference between Wittgenstein's early and later thought concerns the expressibility of metaphysical propositions. According to Wittgenstein's early thought, metaphysical contraptions do exist, but language cannot describe them. Metaphysics lies beyond the limits of language. Metaphysics cannot be described, but we know that something is "out there." Thus, according to the most quoted slogan from the *Tractatus*: "7. What can be said at all can be said clearly, and what we cannot talk about we must pass over in silence." In contrast to this, Wittgenstein's later thought rejects the notion of the inexpressible entirely. If it cannot be expressed, then it does not exist. Indeed, there is nothing that language cannot express. "For there is nothing that cannot be said, and there is nothing beyond the bounds of sense save nonsense."[16] Metaphysics is nonsense.

In the *Investigations* Wittgenstein broke free from the vision of a single, unifying form of philosophical insight and procedure, and replaced it with a method in thinking that moved upon many levels and was aware of the "prodigious multiplicity, diversity and inexhaustible richness of things, and . . . describe[d] the nature of a vast variety of phenomena for what they are in themselves, without seeking to fit them into one, all embracing unitary vision."[17] Although a refutal of metaphysics and idealism, the *Tractatus* pursued the same illusion of a unified theory (or underlying metaphysics) of logic. In the *Investigations*, however, Wittgenstein came to reject deep logic because it is an act of superstition to pursue "a final analysis of our forms of language, and so a *single* completely resolved form of expression. That is, as if our usual forms of expression were, essentially, unanalysed; as if there were something hidden in them that had to be brought to light" (*PI* §91).

In Wittgenstein's later thought, philosophy is not, as the logical positivists believed, a science. Philosophy "neither explains or deduces anything" (*PI* §128), but "leaves everything as it is" (*PI* §124). Philosophy does not contribute "to human knowledge, but to human understanding."[18] As for philosophical problems, they are simply misunderstandings caused by conceptual confusion. Once these misconceptions are understood, philosophical problems are revealed to be nonsense, but not "beyond sense" or metaphysical—as Wittgenstein had conceived them to be in the *Tractatus*. Philosophical theories are latent, concealed nonsense; the task of philosophy is to transform them into visible nonsense (*PI* §524). In the *Investigations* Wittgenstein introduced a new analysis based on descriptions of the way we use expressions. This descriptive analysis is synoptic in the way context operates as a determining factor in our understanding of the meaning of an expression. From context—or the synoptic overview—the meaning of an expression is determined by (i) its use, (ii) by what is explained by an explanation of its meaning (what is said to be the 'rule for its use'), and (iii) by what is understood when the expression is understood.[19]

Wittgenstein compared his methods of descriptive or synoptic analysis with psychoanalysis (*PI* §225). His technique of philosophical clarification is therapeutic in that it involves a rearrangement of familiar and unfamiliar contexts for the use of expressions that will make the grammar of the relevant expressions surveyable (*PI* §92, §225). It is just this rearrangement of expressions, concepts, and propositions that one finds in Menippean satire. And, again like Menippean satire, the final goal of synoptic analysis is the exposure of intellectual mythology:

> In the days of the Enlightenment, science was rightly seen as being in the forefront of the struggle against religious mystification, superstition and dogma. Today science has replaced religion as the source and authority of truth. Every source of truth must, in the nature of things, also be a source of falsehoods, against which it must itself struggle. But it may also be a source of intellectual mythology, against which it is typically powerless. One great and barely recognized source of such mythology in our age is science itself. The unmasking of scientific mythology (which is to be distinguished from scientific error) is one of the tasks of philosophy. For philosophy is not the under-labourer of the sciences, but rather their tribunal; it adjudicates not the truth of scientific theorizing, but the sense of scientific propositions. Its aim is neither to engage in nor abjure science, but to restrain it within the bounds of sense, to curb the metaphysical impulse that is released by misinterpretations of the significance of scientific discoveries, to restrain scientists and philosophers (who have been beguiled by their myth-making) from metaphysical nonsense.[20]

Rejecting his earlier work, in the *Philosophical Investigations* Wittgenstein shifted his analytical emphasis from realist metaphysics and the logic of propositions to an emphasis upon the clarification of propositions through an analysis of the context in which they are spoken. In this new approach, the use of a proposition determines its meaning. In the *Investigations*, Wittgenstein presents a "therapy" to correct the misapprehension and misuse of language. This therapy, which trains the philosopher in the ordinary and precise use of language, shows many philosophical problems to originate in language rather than in the real world. Wittgenstein draws a distinction between the instrument of language, and the music which is played on that instrument. He exorcises the demons of language—the shadows cast, so to speak, by grammar. He seeks to defuse language's propensity to reify itself, expose the specterous character of abstract nouns, and demonstrate how, instead, language is simply a tool for communicating mutually understood propositions. In therapeutic terms, language is the medium for a communication game. Examinations of contextualized language games reveal conceptual confusion based on the misapprehension of grammar. The purpose of language is to *express* meaning, and careful analysis is required to prevent language itself from becoming a *source* of meaning. Wittgenstein argued that philosophy must seek an analytical dissolution of conceptual confusion; therefore, true philosophy must become an activity of contextual identification and linguistic clarification. This is the activity of synoptic analysis.

Literature and literary criticism can also be made into an activity of linguistic contextualization and clarification. Literature can be made into—indeed *is*—an activity of synoptic analysis. In fact, the tradition of literature itself might be seen as a process of this clarification. Vladimir Nabokov, whose pedagogical technique, like his fiction, emphasized parody, particulars, and sensual details, was convinced of an evolution taking place in literature toward ampler perfection, subtlety, and precision. And this emphasis upon exploring precisely limited reactions to particulars, a desire for precision, and an acute awareness of Baconian-like "Idols," as we shall see, figures strongly in the Menippean analysis of reality, ontology, myth, ritual, ideology, barbarism, philosophy, science, and religion.

This process of clarification in literature is most apparent and deliberate in the tradition of what Northrop Frye calls the "Anatomy," or Menippean satire. Of all the modes of literary or dialectical investigation, Menippean satire is most intentionally and overtly the great human tradition of literary inquiry. Menippean satire is the phenomenon of language inquiring into itself. Menippean satire is the process of language inquiring into a multitudinous, manifold reality. Embracing a broadened program of synoptic inquiry, Menippean satire is a practice whereby a spectrum of particulars, facts, and perceptions of events are brought together to form a uniquely comprehensive and yet particular view of reality. But above all, Menippean satire patterns the process called "the shock of the familiar." Menippean satire is the reexamination, reformulation, and the renaissance of the knowledge and wisdom which have always been the possession of the human race. As Melville says in *The Confidence-Man*, "The grand points of human nature are the same to-day they were a thousand years ago. The only variability in them is in expression, not in feature."[21] The "shock of the familiar" is both the instrumentality and the pattern of enlightenment. In gnostic terms, it might playfully be suggested, this "shock of the familiar" is the resurrection. And now we are brought to a theological discussion of Menippean satire.

The Approach from Theology

In theology, Menippean satire seeks to distinguish genuine theology by pointing out the erroneous aspects of false theology.

Contrasting notions of true and false theology are explored in C. S. Lewis's essay, "Is Theology Poetry?" Through the exercise of defining "theology" and "poetry," Lewis draws an important distinction between humanity's relationship to the godhead, and humanity's relationship to the realm of beauty and imagination. Interestingly enough, Lewis—the author of the heavily moralizing "Space Trilogy" and the Christian Narnia books for children—sees theology as being much more distinct from imagination than one might suppose.

At the heart of Lewis's essay are his definitions of poetry and theology. For Lewis, theology is "the systematic series of statements about God and about Man's relation to Him." Poetry is simply "writing which arouses and in part satisfies the imagination."[22] According to this understanding, if theology is considered as poetry, it will be found to be poor poetry. Lewis cites Greek, Irish, and especially Norse mythology as examples of poetry which are much more satisfying, from an aesthetic point of view, than Christian theology. Big bang theory, emergent evolution, and the Second Law of Thermodynamics and the "heat death" of the universe are for Lewis modern myths that also arouse and to some extent satisfy the imagination. Such myths, however, are representations of a limited world view. Poetic attractiveness and pleasantry present insufficient criteria upon which to base a system of cosmic understanding. The poetical world view relies upon mythological and scientific world views which are narrow and limited. Lewis compares the theological world view to waking life, and poetic world views to the illusions of the dream state.

False theology is poetic and mythological. What then is true theology? From a Menippean perspective, the exercise of pointing out the errors in poetry makes up a large part of theology. This is to say that an important part of theology is teaching us what theology *is not*. Much of what we know about "God" is by understanding what we know "God" not to be. This negative theology is conventionally styled "apophatic theology," or theology by negation. Apophatic theology stresses the inadequacy of human language and concepts for expressing knowledge of God. The process of apophatic theology involves negating concepts that might be applied to God. Since God is not the universe or an object in the universe, he or she cannot be subject to observation or description. The Christian apophatic tradition was influenced by Philo and Plotinus, Gregory of Nyssa, and Pseudo-Dionysius the Areopagite. An apophatic awareness is characteristic of mystical theology and Eastern orthodoxy, and non-Christian conceptions such as the Kabbalistic "ein-sof," or God in his transcendence; the Hindu "neti neti," (not this, not this), and nirguna-brahman (Brahman without qualities), the indescribable, absolute nature of Brahman. The Jewish philosopher Maimonides argued that God could only be known through analogical language. Moreover and more importantly, Maimonides emphasized not the being of God but rather his effects: "All attributes ascribed to God are attributes of his acts, and do not imply that God has any qualities."[23]

It is important at this point to recognize that here there are two notions of theology that may become confused. I call the first type "negative theology" and the second type "apophatic *via negativa.*" Represented by "mystics" such as Meister Eckhart (1260–1327) and Marguerite Porte (d.1310), negative theology has been prominent in books treating postmodernism, Derrida, and theology.[24] Negative theology is characteristically nihilistic, offering neither a graspable picture of reality nor analytical insights into the roots of conceptual confusion. Such a theology is rather a surrendering to conceptual confusion. I would not describe this negative theology as being in the mainstream of enlightened apophatic tradition. The "apophatic *via negativa,*" as I style it, is a deliberate philosophical tool of inquiry meant to discover perspicuous and accurate analyses of false theological conceptions. Indeed, one might wryly suggest that theology has nothing to do with God. Theology is rather the process of clearing away conceptual error in misleading and harmful mythopoetic illusions. Theology is an exercise in exposing abuses and corruptions in learning and religion. Here apophatic theology joins Menippean satire as a tradition of analysis. For enlightened pagans, myth can be turned to the same purposes. For modern pagans, however, theological and mythological discourse presents important shortcomings. Theological and mythological discourse is in some respects ahistorical, unscientific, and valorizes heroes, entities, and archetypes to the neglect of important critics, teachers, patrons, leaders of schools, socioeconomic forces, institutions, races, nations, corporations, ideological movements, and others to whom this valor rightly belongs. The need to engage in analytical activity remains, however. Thus the modern pagan must turn to a "post-modern" discourse.

The Approach from Post-Modernism

In post-modernism, Menippean satire is the revelation of what is already known.

The whole of Homo sapiens culture might be conceptualized in such a way that the great works of history, philosophy, and literature are categorized as being either *dogmatic* or *skeptical*. Such a broad essay seems daunting, but the notion draws attention to an important dichotomy which transcends the countless institutionalized and canonized "isms" which many thinkers, for various reasons, are wont to seek, embrace, embellish, and champion. A dogmatist is one who has hit upon some truth, some dogma, some great approach, some grand design, some celebrated manifesto, and who seeks to measure all phenomena and experience based upon the apparatus of this truth. The dogmatist rejects all phenomena which fail or refuse to conform to this grand design. The dogmatist, in surrendering to the grand design, is in danger of becoming dictatorial, and often succumbs to a compartmentalized and pragmatic resignation. The skeptic, on the other hand, approaches grand designs and fixed approaches with caution. While the dogmatist labors to hammer experience into generalities, the skeptic is a cool observer of particulars. The dogmatist sees black and white where the skeptic sees gray. Most of all, the skeptic does not seek to promote her sensibility through coercion, but through illustration, sobriety, and humor. Ideally, the skeptic is skeptical of her own skepticism, and is ultimately free to choose between optimism and pessimism, while the dogmatist ultimately caves into cynicism. The dogmatic/skeptical dichotomy, I believe, is useful chiefly in the way it can be used to explode other dichotomies and "isms," and cut through mythologies and ideologies to explore the actual, real-world arena of variability and altering relationships. The skeptic approaches the real world not by defining what it is, but by recognizing what it isn't. For example, to the skeptic, the contemporary dichotomy of "liberalism" and "conservatism" is exposed as a divisive hoax perpetrated by unscrupulous politicians, apparatchiks, and mystified neophytes. For the student of literature and philosophy, skepticism identifies those ideas and traditions which seek to encourage wisdom and human felicity by contrasting them with the follies of dogmatism. This is what Swift is doing in *A Tale of a Tub* and other early writings where he parodies the abuses and corruptions of regimentation, ambition, obscurantism, pedantry, and enthusiasm in learning and religion. This is what Swift is doing in *Gulliver's Travels* where by surveying a number of reasonable and yet skewed perspectives of the world, he sets limits to language and reason and draws sharp distinctions between sense and nonsense, sound critical censure and madness. By identifying these limits, Swift can expose misconceived ambitions and projects, as for example in the third book of *Gulliver's Travels* where, through the device of his islands of Laputa and Balinbarbi, with their technocratic governments, he parodies and satirizes the brave new scientific state Francis Bacon champions in the *New Atlantis*. Again, skepticism and common sense are employed as technique by Cervantes in *Don Quixote* when he parodies the false ideals of a lost, halcyon age of epic romance and monumental chivalry, and yet shows that we cannot survive the squalor of the human condition without the presence and operation of such ideals. This is what Rabelais is doing in *Gargantua and Pantagruel* when he burlesques the scholastic, scientific, judicial, and monastical systems of medieval Europe by training upon them the Renaissance in learning that these same systems, despite themselves, helped to ignite. This is what Robert Burton is doing in *The Anatomy of Melancholy* when he attempts to gather together in a single corpus all scientific, philosophical, and religious knowledge and surveys what is sensible and what is mythological in the field of medicine. Of course, these skeptical analyses can also be expressed in ambiguous terms. For instance, this is what Shakespeare apparently does in *Henry V* where he portrays the terrible ambition and glimmering, uncouth demagoguery of a warlord in terms that are jingoistic and complementary. Other writers, of course, refuse to equivocate: Pope in his condemnations of mediocrity and dullness; Byron in his wickedly clever explosions of tedious Tories and ludicrous laureates, particularly in *The Vision of Judgment* and in the introduction to *Don Juan*. Poe, also, refuses to equivocate outside of his parodic purposes as with hilarious scientific zeal he pillories silly dunces, literary cabals, and oily hypochondriacs. Rooted deeply in the common sense tradition, Austen unscrews transparent frauds, prancing buffoons, idling ninnies, rough bullies, and scheming charlatans. The precision of her observations is unfaltering. Her *Northanger Abbey* is a perfect expression of the worldview Wittgenstein would promote a century later with his descriptive philosophy. Unmuddled by inquires into *why* things happen, Austen penetrates into *how* things happen, and so pierces appearances to reveal reality. Her analyses are so supple, her language so appropriate and unhurried that the menace she represents to folly commands legions of followers. As much may be said of Nathaniel Hawthorne, easily the most clever writer produced by America, who in *The Scarlet Letter* puts the lie to the respectable coward and the gossiping mob, and again in the *Blithedale Romance* where he pillories driven ideologues and affected literati. A similar program is presented by Huxley, particularly in *Point Counter Point* where he parades self-dehumanizing intellectuals who seek to dehumanize humanity. Huxley's technique is reflected by Shaw in *Man and Superman* where he exposes the silliness of the vain *Übermensch* who would dare exalt himself above the will of a regenerative universe and the sweeping fruitful embrace of procreation. Shaw takes this theme as a point of departure for exploring the self-deception, complacency and superficiality that lies at the bottom of human evil (see especially the passage on the "Palace of Lies" in "Don Juan in Hell"); point is followed by counterpoint, and ideology is exposed by the particular exigencies and morphologies of unique, real-world scenarios. Conrad, too, exercises a profound skepticism in *Heart of Darkness* where he exposes and vilifies institutions of ambition and bureaucracies of commerce. Skepticism and parody inform Melville in *Moby-Dick* where he parodies Platonic philosophy, transcendentalism, hermeneutic apriority, and the worship of gods that dwell not in the aspirations and actions of human beings, but in stone, in wood, and upon paper; and once again in *The Confidence-Man* where Melville attacks the intellectual imprecision of greedy and grasping traders, crusading reformers, naive enthusiasts, wounded philanthropists, ersatz romantics, lazy intellectuals, backwoods cynics, transcendentalist warlocks, the vain deniers of human error, and the unhappy among us who have lost their faith.

The technocrats, romantics, transcendentalists, reformers, deceivers, and deniers who are targeted by these skeptical writers share a common quality. In theological discourse, this quality is often called lack-of-faith or despair. In secular terms, this quality is often called *modernity*. Unfortunately, the term "modern" carries with it many historical associations and its use is often confused. Here is a way out of this conceptual confusion: The modern quality can also be called a *penchant for dogma*, or fanaticism. The twentieth century has nurtured a good many dogmatists; and at this point dogmatism might be thought of as a kind of rationalized—or methodized—cynicism. Indeed, against the backdrop of the institutionalized mass destruction in the form of the two world wars, it is extremely difficult not to associate the concepts of modernity and dogmatism. They have in this way come to be interchangeable terms. But what constitutes the dogmatism that makes up this modernity?

In the twentieth century, it begins with the triumph of industrialization through the assembly line and mass production, and the resources industrialization yielded for commercial and military development. It begins with the plans of architects, engineers, and social designers to develop and shape those resources. And these plans, voiced in moralizing tones, were as ambitious and giant as the volume of the resources the designers had to work with. Sant Elia's "Manifesto" of 1914 typifies such expressions:

> The formidable antithesis between the modern world and the old is determined by all those things which formally did not exist . . . we have lost our predilection for the monumental, the heavy, the static, and we have enriched our sensibility with a *taste for the light, the practical, the ephemeral and the swift.* We no longer feel ourselves to be the men of the cathedrals, the palaces and the tribunes. We are the men of the great hotels, the railway stations, the immense streets, colossal ports, covered markets, luminous arcades, straight roads and beneficial demolitions.[25]

What emerges in the modern era is an academy of experts, designers, planners, and authorities who take upon themselves the direction and administration of concentrated human effort. According to architectural critic Charles Jencks, in the beginning of our vast, industrially realized modern era:

> the hope of these artists and architects was to substitute powerstations for cathedrals, [and] technocrats for aristocrats. A new, heroic, democratic society would emerge, led by a powerful race of pagan supermen, the avant-garde, the technicians and captains of industry, the enlightened scientists and teams of experts.[26]

These supermen did not limit themselves to public works and skyscrapers but infused themselves throughout the spectrum of human endeavor. Institutionalizing, codifying and compartmentalizing—they provided mytho-academic instructions and guidelines for every conceivable task. Even something as epiphenomenal as the writing of poetry had its heroes, dictators, and gurus. And, like the edicts of the builder of a bridge or a dynamo, the super-poet's prescriptions were embraced and enforced with a dull institutionalized zeal that is still boring us today. Consider savior of civilization Ezra Pound's "Imagism" with its list of enumerated principles, or T. S. Eliot's essayed delineations collected in *The Sacred Wood,* which serve as interesting albeit self-indulgent discussions of the sorts of digressions and contraptions a poet can amuse himself with on a chilly afternoon, but also constitute the pattern and authoritative mandate for a program of aesthetic indoctrination for plebeian neophytes in modern, compartmentalized university institutions. Interestingly enough, Eliot remarked in the 1964 edition of *The Use of Poetry & the Use of Criticism*, that he hoped editors would quit publishing "Tradition and the Individual Talent," so that a student might be able to pass an examination on him without using the phrases "dissociation of sensibility" or "objective correlative."

The modern epoch or moment tracks a cyclic course in history. It is characterized by the process or pattern of a dogmatic authoritative edict, the "mechanical" institutionalization of this edict, and the consequences.

An important modernist assumption is the importance attributed to the stability of industrial structures. Charles Jencks characterizes this assumption in *Architecture 2000*:

> [O]nly by keeping the existing structure constant can we increase freedom through innovation and allow it to occur through choice. That is, only if we accept the limits of industrialization and the various forms of bureaucracy common to all industrial states, can we have the very real freedoms of communication, health and consumption which these limits bring.[27]

In 1967 Buckminster Fuller described the fruits of such stability:

> It seems perfectly clear that when there is enough to go around man will not fight anymore than he now fights for air. When man is successful in doing so much more with so much less that he can take care of everybody at a higher standard, then there will be no fundamental cause for war . . . Within ten years it will be normal for man to be successful—just as through all history it has been the norm for more than 99 per cent to be economic and physical failures. Politics will become obsolete.[28]

Fuller's view is superficially compelling and attractive. However, many such dogmatic utterances are neither compelling nor attractive, and are, in fact, quite terrifying. They exhibit the perfidious vanity of the omnipotent child-tyrant. Le Corbusier says in a 1923 manifesto:

> Industry, *overwhelming us like a flood which rolls on toward its destined ends*, has furnished us with new tools adapted to this new epoch, animated by the new spirit. Economic law *unavoidably governs* our acts and thoughts.

According to Ludwig Mies van der Rohe in 1924:

> *The individual is losing significance; his destiny is no longer* what interests us. The decisive achievements in all fields are impersonal and their authors are for the most part unknown. *They* are part of *the trend* of our time toward anonymity.

In 1936 Nikolaus Pevsner says:

> However, the great creative brain will find its own way even in times of overpowering collective energy, even with the medium of this new style of the twentieth century, which, because it is a genuine style as opposed to a passing fashion, is *totalitarian*.[29]

It might be noted in passing that Mies van der Rohe's claim that great achievement is "impersonal" suggests Eliot's "extinction of personality" from "Tradition and the Individual Talent," while Pevsner's "great creative brain" suggests Eliot's notion of the "mind of Europe."

The "modern" world thus emerges—doctrinaire, rational, authoritarian, planned; where civilization is led by experts who know best how to direct humanity's energies. According to Jencks in *Architecture 2000*, the cynicism of these experts begins with their accepting the overall system, whatever "ism" it might be, "and then applying their very real expertise to technological problems, to making the system more efficient, or humane, or smooth running."[30] Along with the physical structures—economic, bureaucratic, political, educational—of the overall system, the members of the system, the human beings within it, are taught to embrace a particular world view, adopt certain behaviors, and play a variety of roles based on prescribed notions of gender, socioeconomic standing, education, age, and ethnic identity.

Post-modern fiction, encompassing, after a fashion, the cult and techniques of skepticism, is a *practice* which analyzes and ridicules the outer forms as well as the underlying assumptions upon which modern culture is based. The fictional techniques of post-modern skepticism might roughly be labeled *parody, self-referential texts, the hysterical sublime*, and *multiple coding*.

According to the *Oxford English Dictionary,* parody is a

> composition in prose or verse in which the characteristic turns of thought and phrase in an author or class of authors are imitated in such a way as to make them appear ridiculous, especially by applying them to ludicrously

inappropriate subjects; an imitation of a work more or less closely modeled on the original, but so turned as to produce a ridiculous effect.

A shrewd observer of human beings, the skeptic is crucially aware that all orders, directions, specifications, and manifestos are ultimately created by human beings, by authors. The skeptic is aware that great law givers, inspired technocrats, energetic founders of secular religions, notwithstanding their genius, are in the end mere human beings, and that the fruits of their ambition are not mandated by supernatural authority or the will of the cosmos. The ambition of such geniuses, in this sense, is folly. The humor in parody derives from pointing out this folly, and the parody is on a scale funnier, or the humor increases, in proportion to the degree the author being parodied is unaware of his own folly. Parody can be highly vindictive and censorious. This vindictiveness is justified, however, because it illuminates an error that is contributing to the proliferation of vulgarity, waste, or suffering. Parody, despite its humorous effect, is involved in the very serious business of pointing out *that which is to be avoided* in a real world of pain and suffering.

Perhaps the greatest practitioner of parody in recent years has been Vladimir Nabokov. His novel *Pale Fire* is a work in which parody is elevated to an aesthetic principle of extraordinary pedagogical value that is exceeded only by the novel's achievement as a work of art. But it is in his *Lolita* that parody most swiftly and accurately exposes the modern world view and the most basic assumptions about class, sex, and age which perpetuate it. The story is well known and hardly needs to be reiterated here. What is so remarkable about the parody in *Lolita* is the way the technique implicates us in the crimes of Humbert Humbert, the narrator. By sympathizing with Humbert's crime, the reader is forced to examine his or her own assumptions about class, sex, and age. Lionel Trilling describes these dynamics:

> We find ourselves the more shocked when we realize that, in the course of reading the novel, we have come virtually to condone the violation it presents . . . we have been seduced into conniving in the violation, because we have permitted our fantasies to accept what we know to be revolting.[31]

Alfred Appel reaches much the same conclusion:

> What is extraordinary about *Lolita* is the way in which Nabokov enlists us, against our will, on Humbert's side . . . Humbert has figuratively made the reader his accomplice in both statutory rape and murder.[32]

Like the desire to write parody, the post-modern desire to express skepticism through self-referential texts derives from a reaction to an erroneous, cynical, or dogmatic assumption. Self-referential texts are conscious and near-conscious explorations of the roles of the reader and the writer, and the different ways they create and respond to the text. Furthermore, self-referential texts seek to establish the possible functions of the text as art, and the more general role of art in culture. The parodic forward to *Lolita*, penned by suave John Ray, Jr., Ph.D., the fictive editor of Humbert's manuscript, illustrates how a text can ridicule modern assumptions by casting its own self in the dubious light of those same assumptions:

> As a case history, "Lolita" will become, no doubt, a classic in psychiatric circles. As a work of art, it transcends its expiatory aspects; and still more important to us than scientific significance and literary worth, is the ethical impact the book should have on the serious reader; for in this poignant personal study there lurks a general lesson; the wayward child, the egoistic mother, the panting maniac—these are not only vivid characters in a unique story: they warn us of dangerous trends; they point out potent evils. "Lolita" should make all of us—parents, social workers, educators—apply ourselves with still greater vigilance and vision to the task of bringing up a better generation in a safer world.[33]

John Ray, Jr.'s assumptions are as dubious as his professional persona. As alluded to earlier, Humbert's manuscript corrupts the reader in every sense away from the modern, compartmentalized, and dogmatic world view that Ray represents. The notion that the "wayward child, the egoistic mother, the panting maniac" are modern psychological archetypes—indeed, "the panting maniac"—is quite plainly absurd; as is the Philistine league of concerned "parents, social workers, educators," striving bravely together amidst the committee workshop miasma of cookies and coffee to direct the progeny of their communities into the light of provincial pomposity so that—it might be suggested—the true industrially correct infrastructure, *tra la,* might endure.

This same passage can also be seen to contain elements of what Fredric Jameson calls the "hysterical sublime." For instance, "panting maniac" brilliantly exhibits this quality. Such phrases are silly, make the reader laugh, and point out an underlying madness in the author (John Ray) who wrote them, who fundamentally *believed* them without perceiving their humorous dimension.

In his equivocating *Postmodernism, or, The Cultural Logic of Late Cap-*

italism, Fredric Jameson describes how the "hysterical sublime" works to transform the world of urban squalor, for instance, into a "delight to the eyes . . . where even automobile wrecks gleam with some new hallucinatory splendor . . . where the alienation of daily life in the city can now be experienced in the form of a strange new hallucinatory exhilaration." Through the hysterical sublime, "the world . . . momentarily loses its depth and threatens to become a glossy skin, a stereoscopic illusion, a rush of filmic images without density."[34] The excited, stimulated and narcotic nature of the hysterical sublime is illustrated nicely in these lines, but rather than representing post-modern consciousness or post-modern "space," as Jameson suggests, I believe the hysterical sublime suggests the nature of the states of mind that are being parodied when, through the device of the hysterical sublime, the skeptic chooses to illustrate a flaw in the world view and thought processes of a modern (Jameson's hyphen-less "postmodernism" is just such a modern world view; indeed, in many ways his book fulfills the role of a culture product from the comfort industry). Through the hysterical sublime the modern is delivered from physical suffering and the pain of moral conscience and judgment. The hysterical sublime is thus not some aesthetic goal to be aspired to, but rather a narcotic or a soporific that is to be satirized and rejected.

An excellent illustration of the hysterical sublime is found in Brian W. Aldiss' "As To Our Fatal Continuity," a parodic artist biography from a fictitious textbook entitled, "Sculpting Your Own Semi-Sentients: A Primer for Boys and Girls" by "Gutrud Slayne Laboratories." Dayling, whose works are titled after the death bed utterances of famous authors and statesmen, is the artist whose "biography" forms the substance of the story, which concludes:

> It may be, as Torner Mallard has claimed, that these final works of Dayling's mark the demise of a too-long sustained system of aesthetics going back as far as Classical Greece, and the beginning of a new and more biologically-based structure; certainly we can see that, in the Dadaist titles, as well as in the works themselves, Dayling was undergoing a pre-postmodernist purgation of outworn attitudes, and carrying art forward from the aesthetic arena of balance and proportion to the knife-edge between existence and non-existence.
>
> In his reckless sweeping away of all the inessential props of life, Dayling—by which of course we mean Dayling-and-art-computer—takes the bone-bare universe of Samuel Beckett a stage further; humor and death contemplate each other across a tumbled void. Only the grin of the Cheshire Cat is left, fading above Valhalla.[35]

Finally, the role of art itself is challenged, and the student of skepticism is forced to reconsider the mental eye which sees art as redeemer, and the artist—or any author—as social legislator. Along these lines, the following assertion of I. A. Richards is called into question:

> [The artist is most distinguished from the ordinary person] in the range, delicacy and freedom of the connections he is able to make between different elements of his experience. His experiences represent conciliation of impulses which in most minds are still confused, intertrammelled and conflicting. His work is the ordering of what in most minds is disordered.[36]

An irony remains. If the artists and authors don't call into question the claims, assertions, and manifestos of other artists and authors, then who will? And who else can?

According to Jameson, parody, self-referential texts, and the hysterical sublime are the practices or the forms through which post-moderns express their skepticism, perhaps as some prelude to a new leap up the evolutionary ladder, or the Marxist realization of some post-capitalist state marked by an ethos that values euphemism and political expediency (it is not quite clear whether Jameson thinks this is a good thing or no). The categories of parody, self-reference, and hysteria overlap and are interrelated. In the final analysis, self-referential texts and the hysterical sublime are specific forms or effects (or even "sports") of parody. It is all parody: a hall of mirrors and diminishing reflections. We are like the little boy who repeats his name over and over until it loses its meaning, or like a flattened toad on the highway with traces of sensation dwindling into fewer and fewer twinkles. Our concepts are words that refer to nothing but other words. And suddenly our essay itself has degenerated into a meaningless pastiche, an amalgamation of anachronisms underlying some ultra-modern manifesto.

Now we have met the deconstructive crisis.

Our teeth are set on edge. We have fallen into a maelstrom of nihilism, obscurantism, and linguistic self-destruction—words are separated from each other by tremendous voids filled with the echoing clack clack clack of cloven feet. But we must ask ourselves: Is there a conceptual route which can lead us beyond the hallucinogenic splendor of this moment of sublime hysteria?

Yes. We must further refine our notion of the post-modern. Jencks suggests we draw distinctions between post-modernism, late-modernism and ultra-modernism. We are in error when we denominate as "post-modern" works which exhibit late- and ultra-modernity, simply because these works can be construed as expressions of a reaction to modernism. John Barth clarifies this notion:

> My ideal postmodernist author neither merely repudiates nor merely imitates either his twentieth-century modernist parents or his nineteenth-century premodernist grandparents. He has the first half of our century under his belt, not on his back.[37]

For Barth, Jencks, and Umberto Eco, post-modernism involves a consciousness of the past, not merely a reaction to it. Jencks incorporates this concern for historical memory into post-modernism through seeing the practice as a search for plural codings, over-codings, and a multiple communication aesthetic meant to have meaning for a broad cross section of people. Post-modernism represents a sort of eclectic, free-style classicism which celebrates the continua of history and civilization. The avant garde late-modern practice is indifferent to the past, or makes of it an object of abstract contemplation far removed from actual history. The nihilistic ultra-modern practice seeks to destroy the past. But of course the past cannot be destroyed. Umberto Eco makes this very clear in *The Postscript to The Name of the Rose*:

> The postmodern reply to the modern consists of recognizing the past, since it can not really be destroyed, because its destruction leads to silence, must be revisited: but with irony, not innocently.[38]

The cult and technique of skepticism becomes very apparent now. Let us review the three distinctions through examples:

Pale Fire, although it employs Jameson's parodic and hysterical "postmodern" techniques, is late-modern. It addresses the avant garde only, the professional devotees of high art.

The work of William S. Burroughs is ultra-modern. It is nihilist, destructive, and self-destructive. It fails to represent the ironic winking eye of history and so can not communicate to the sophistication of an audience who dwell in a larger, wiser world. Its appeal is limited to sensation seekers, hardened drugsters, and slouching, bad-boy poets.

Finally, *Lolita* can be seen to be post-modern. It communicates to a broad, sophisticated audience, examining the question of love in a context which is aware of our history, our loss of innocence. And yet, in acknowledging our sophistication, *Lolita* drops open the trousers of innocence to invite an examination of the most poignant tissues of human vulnerability, elaborating and affirming love's joy, love's tragedy, love's dignity.

Eco presents us with the classic formulation of post-modern practice:

> I think of the postmodern attitude as that of a man who loves a very cultivated woman and knows he cannot say to her "I love you madly," because he knows that she knows (and that she knows that he knows) that these words have already been written by Barbara Cartland. Still, there is a solution. He can say "As Barbara Cartland would put it, I love you madly." At this point, having avoided false innocence, having said clearly that it is no longer possible to speak innocently, he will nevertheless have said what he wanted to say to the woman: that he loves her in an age of lost innocence. If the woman goes along with this she will have received a declaration of love all the same. Neither of the two speakers will feel innocent, both will have accepted the challenge of the past, of the already said, which cannot be eliminated; both will consciously and with pleasure play the game of irony . . . But both will have succeeded, once again, in speaking of love.[39]

Post-modern practice doesn't assault us with the "shock of the new," as in our conventional sense of an avant garde, but rather assaults us with the "shock of the old" or the "shock of the familiar."

Four and a half thousand years ago a poet described how Gilgamesh went to temple prostitutes for divine revelation and found instead a quarrel; how he suffered the death of his friend Enkidu, the wild man, as if it was his own death; how Gilgamesh sought out Zesudra, the Sumerian Noah and Methuselah, and discovered that his sufferings were part of a greater human tradition. And finally Gilgamesh faced the final irony of coming at the end of his quest to a saloon at the edge of the world where a barmaid concludes his mythic wanderings, in effect saying to him: "Quit crying over the death of the wild man, and assume responsibility for yourself."[40] Parody, multiple-coding, the enlightenment of peripatetic archetypes: the irony we call post-modernism has been around for a long, long time.

Menippean Satire As It Is

In conventional historiographic usage, the story of Menippean satire doesn't begin in ancient Mesopotamia, but several millennia later in classical Greece. As we shall see, however, the generic characteristics of Menippean satire, like those of post-modernism, trace back to the earliest seminars of cosmopolitan conversationalists.

Menippus himself joined the great debate in the first half of the third century B.C. Menippus was born a slave in Asia Minor in the vicinity of Pontus or perhaps Sinope. He made his fortune through usury, bought his freedom, then moved to Thebes where he became a citizen and studied under the cynic Metrocles, a former pupil of Theophrastus. Menippus himself became one of the most caustic of the cynic philosopher satirists. To Marcus Aurelius, Menippus was "a mocker of man's ephemeral existence." Lucian called him "a frightening dog with a treacherous bite." None of Menippus's writings survive, but his reputation endures through the numerous adaptations of his *Descent Into Hades*, *Symposium*, and *Auction of Diogenes*. In his work, Menippus launched mocking attacks against philosophers, philosophical systems, and corrupt institutions. Menippus presented his satires in a wide variety of startling and peculiar settings such as the underworld and the Academy.

He is credited with bringing three important innovations to the business of writing satire. Firstly, he invented a seriocomic method of treating serious philosophical issues in a comic manner. His second innovation was introducing the practice of combining prose and poetry in his monologues. Whether the poetry was quoted or original is unknown, but the practice is of Semitic origin and Menippus probably brought it with him from Syria. Finally, Menippus aimed his work at a broader segment of the population than was the normal practice with such work.

His mixture of prose and poetry—effectively a mixing of genres—is particularly noteworthy as the practice which came to be called "Menippean satire." Quintilian recognized it as a distinct form and it was imitated in Greek by Meleager and Lucian, and in Latin by such authors as Varro, Seneca, Petronius, and Martianus Capella.

In the first century before Christ, Varro, Caesar's librarian and perhaps the most accomplished scholar of antiquity (and nearly the most prolific), wrote one hundred fifty books of related work collectively entitled *Menippean Satires* (81–07 B.C.). Varro intensified Menippus's innovations, increasing the variety and diversity of allusions, quotations, and forms of scholarship; combining, juxtaposing, and developing overlapping themes with greater complexity and frequency. Unfortunately, as is the case with the satires of Menippus, much of Varro's work has been lost.

Lucian, who wrote dialogues in the second century of the present era, includes Menippus as a character in several of his works. In the dialogue *Menippus* the cynic-hero travels to the underworld to visit the inhabitants. Here he finds the dead gods and heroes, and especially the dead philosophers, to be frightful bores of a very intense water. In *Icaromenippus* the cynic-hero, sick and tired of the philosophers, puts an eagle's wing on one arm, a vulture's wing on the other, and jumps off Mt. Olympus. With pumping arms Menippus pierces the blue mantle of the sky and crosses to the moon. He turns to view the Earth and the puny smallness of Man. Then up races Menippus to Heaven. Here he seeks out the gods and tells them what terrible bores the philosophers are. The gods' eyes water at hearing Menippus's report. Their faces grow deathly pale. Thoroughly disgusted, they swear an oath to Menippus that the philosophers shall be destroyed. They take his wings away (not wanting to be disturbed again) and send him back to earth, where he has the delectable pleasure of informing all the boring philosophers they will be destroyed in four months' time.

It is Petronius, however, who is the greatest surviving master of classical Menippean satire. Surviving in fragmented form, Petronius's *Satyricon* possesses an incongruous profusion of invention more characteristic of drama than prose. Petronius's parodies are flawlessly expert, his logic is intrinsic but turned outward toward the real world. The *Satyricon* is perhaps the most biting of satires because its ferocity lies in sensibility, perception, and composition, and not in the language of diatribe and denunciation. It is this same quality in the best Menippean satire which makes it so immediate, relevant, and important.

The variety, improvisational tone, and philosophical program of Menippean satire has its roots in the very origin of satire itself. In Greece, satire derived from the Bacchic festival, and eventually became formalized drama. By the fifth century Aristophanes was writing plays which—through their variety, parody, combination of song, verse, prose, and interlude—very much resemble the complex format of Menippean satire constructed five hundred years later by Varro. Aristophanes's humor in this respect was remarkable, and it is amusing to think of him, for instance, in *The Clouds* when during the parabasis he himself would walk on the stage and denounce Cleon, the warmongering tyrannt of Athens. *The Clouds* is emblematically Menippean, and two hundred years before Menippus. In the play a father, deeply in debt and plagued by creditors, sends his son off to Socrates's school to be educated by the sophists. The reason? The father believes the sophists to possess just the sort of philosophy he needs to argue with and evade his creditors.

The Greek pattern whereby satire springs from Bacchic festival is recapitulated in ancient Italy. During harvest celebrations in Italy, the revelers recited *Fescenine verse*, a sort of rough and licentious incantation of the pleasantries of the vintage and harvest. During these celebrations there was present a *Satura lanx*—a charger or plate piled high with a variety of luscious, ripe fruit. *Saturae* translated means *miscellany*. Now, when you combine Fescennine verse with mimetic action you get a kind of crude drama called *Saturae*, from whence we get the word *satire*. Again, this was very much what had happened in Arcadia during the Bacchic festivals. And this is also very much what informed people do when they gather together in our contemporary age: engage in parodic conversations, declaim, match wits, and mock and denounce vanity, cruelty, and foolishness.

This process is what informs Michael Moorcock's *Cornelius Chronicles* (1968–78) where, against a background of collected scholarship on the harlequinade, he throws vast timeless parties in the San Simeon of his own mind, where characters, avatars, passions in masquerade, and capering reincarnations act out a novelized but seemingly improvised *saturae*. The intellectual force of Huxley's *Point Counter Point* plays itself out in this manner through the portrayal of opulent and diverse parties of fashionable Londoners. Huxley's Mark Rampion (D. H. Lawrence—*Point Counter Point* is a roman à clef) precisely expresses his world-weariness over the vain and crooked faces within the *saturae* and declaims the whole process, naming it "The Conversation."

It is this never-ending conversation in ancient Greece and ancient Italy, pressed into clay as an Epic of Gilgamesh, reproduced in the plot of a medieval harlequinade, in the exhaustion of Huxley's modern London or in the Foucauldian madness of Eco's post-modern midnight convocations of Masons and Knights Templers—it is this manifold farrago of voice, form, and perspective which comprises and defines the "Menippean Moment." It is an insight which elevates life above the level of tragedy, and gives it some of the grace of farce.

According to M. H. Abrams, the major feature of the Menippean narrative "is a series of extended dialogues and debates (often conducted at a banquet or party) in which a group of immensely loquacious eccentrics, pedants, literary people, and representatives of various professions or philosophical points of view serve to make ludicrous the intellectual attitudes they typify by the arguments they urge in their support."[41] Rabelais' *Gargantua and Pantagruel*, Swift's *Tale of a Tub* and *Gulliver's Travels*, Voltaire's *Candide*, Byron's *Don Juan*, Melville's *Moby-Dick* and *The Confidence-Man*, Peacock's novels, including *Nightmare Abbey, Crotchet Castle,* and *Gryll Grange*, Hawthorne's *The Blithedale Romance*, Čapek's *War With the Newts*, and Huxley's *Point Counter Point* are examples which aspire to this practice. Northrop Frye has suggested the Alice books are "perfect Menippean satires;" and read in this light Carroll's tales of Wonderland and the world on the other side of the looking glass take on a startling coherence of curious brilliance.

According to Frye, the Menippean satirist expresses his creative exuberance in what is primarily an intellectual context. The Menippean satirist "piles up an enormous mass of erudition about his theme or in overwhelming his pedantic targets with an avalanche of their own jargon." In some cases this exuberance can take the form of an "encyclopedic farrago." Such is the organizing principle of what Frye claims to be "the greatest Menippean satire in English before Swift," Robert Burton's *The Anatomy of Melancholy*. The idea of an "anatomy" describes the creative practice which identifies this form: a collected dissection or analysis of a vast theme or corpus of knowledge. Frye suggests "we might as well adopt the term 'anatomy' to replace the cumbersome and modern times rather misleading 'Menippean satire.'" It is a provocative suggestion, and indicates a possible course of development for the genre. However, the term "Menippean" will probably remain in use, while the contradistinctions brought forth by contemplating and applying the two terms should provoke much stimulating thought. In my own view, the "anatomy" is a subspecies of "Menippean satire." As Frye himself states, "the encyclopedic compilations produced . . . by Erasmus and Voltaire suggest that a magpie instinct to collect facts is not unrelated to the type of ability that has made them famous as artists."[42]

This brings us to the recent excitement surrounding "Carnival" and Mikhail Bakhtin's contribution to our understanding of Menippean satire. How Bakhtin is perceived by critics, it seems to me, is even more valuable than what Bakhtin has to say, as there is a solid indication here that Bakhtin's concepts lack the precision and clarity that one should expect in light of the great claims of his followers. In *Menippean Satire: An Annotated Catalogue of Texts and Criticism*, Eugene P. Kirk devotes a page and a half (two entries) to Bakhtin. In *Problems of Dostoevsky's Poetics*, according to Kirk, "Bakhtin doesn't insist upon any 'Menippean' characteristics . . . other than the psychological estrangement of the writer from the integrity of his surrounding world, expressed in an extraordinary diction." In *Rabelais and His World*, according to Kirk, Bakhtin mentions "Rabelais' adherence to the Menippean genre briefly, but chiefly argues Rabelais was a proponent of a 'carnival' spirit, an ancient anthropological phenomenon."[43] According to Theodore D. Kharpertian in *A Hand to Turn to the Time: The Menippean Satires of Thomas Pynchon*, "Fundamental to carnival are three themes or 'categories': free, familiar contact; mesalliances; and profanation." Kharpertian further notes that Bakhtin also attributes three original characteristics to seriocomic literary genres derived from carnival: "concentration on the present; a critical relation to legend dialectically interrelated with an experiential and freely imaginative base; and stylistic multiplicity." Next, Kharpertian goes on to elaborate a further fourteen characteristics "which because of . . . [Bakhtin's] categorical repetition and overlapping may be condensed as follows: comedy; fantasy; philosophy; naturalism; trileveled construction (the presence of forms of heaven, hell, and earth); abnormal psychology and morality; indecorous scenes; oxymoron; utopianism; parody and multiplicity; and topicality." In a mystifying inductive leap, Kharpertian concludes that "[u]ltimately, Bakhtin's point is that Menippean satire belongs to a tradition of literature that he terms 'dialogical' and that is opposed to and subverts the 'monological' tradition, one that he associates with institutional forms of absolutism, dogmatism and despair."[44] Joel C. Relihan in *Ancient Menippean Satire* attributes to Bakhtin a list of fourteen characteristics that is similar, though more elaborate than Kharpertian's. Relihan remarks that "Sometimes Bakhtin is careful to distinguish between the genre and things merely influenced by it, but often he is not." This at once established, Relihan formulates the following interpretation: "It seems that the menippea can be viewed as an intellectual attitude adopted toward the value of truth and the possibility of meaning, a particular world view, that may show up in a number of different genres (the pseudo-Hippocratic *Letters*, the logistoricus, the aretaloogy)."[45] In *Chaucer and Menippean Satire*, F. Anne Payne summarizes a similar (and familiar) list of fourteen traits Bakhtin terms "menippea." She adds seven further characteristics of her own which will be of particular interest to the collector.[46] Recent appraisals of Bakhtin and Menippean satire have not been so exhaustive. W. Scott Blanchard in *Scholar's Bedlam: Menippean Satire in the Renaissance* considers Bakhtin not so much as a definer of a genre (Menippean satire) but as an early, perceptive but also flawed commentator on Rabelais. Blanchard emphasizes Bakhtin's "consistent concern with Menippean satire as a subversion of both the heroic values associated with more elite forms of literature and of the hierarchical organization of both classical aesthetics and the social order that classical aesthetic categories mirror." Blanchard points out, however, that Bakhtin overemphasizes Rabelais's use of vulgarity and the grotesque, and Rabelais's attack on decorum. Blanchard criticizes Bakhtin for leaving "his readers with the impression that Rabelais wrote with his glands, ignoring the force of Rabelais's comic conglomeration of learned and recondite materials, and ignoring the simple fact that the Menippean form is often an extremely learned form with a necessarily limited audience."[47] Rabelais might create a subversive "carnival," but how many people can comprehend it? Dustin Griffin in *Satire: A Critical Reintroduction* considers satire in this context as a tool for flattening, reducing and ridiculing "what Mikhail Bakhtin would call 'monological' discourse." Griffin then remarks, "The problem with such accounts is that the satire so identified is finally not very interesting, or very good. At most it induces easy laughter. A better account of the subject would show that satire typically complicates narrative fiction."[48] My own problems with Bakhtin concern the stratospheric medium through which his critical imagination floats.[49] His sensibility is enthused, confused, and it is not difficult in his writings to perceive the image of a scribbling Russian intellectual experiencing *difficulties* as revolution, civil war, a leg amputation, invading Germans, shifty commisars, sadistic bureaucrats, suppressed manuscripts, lost manuscripts, smoked manuscripts (he used one manuscript as a source of paper to roll his cigarettes!) form a backdrop as his political fortunes yo-yo from Russia to Kazakhstan and back again. But more to the point, his desire to identify archetypical notions of subgenre, dialects, and languages that "battle" with one another strikes me as being as absurd as toys coming to life for a teddybear's picnic in the nursery while young master is asleep. Bakhtin's style, too, is very curious. One might easily recall Jane Austen's thoughts on such species of writing as she presents them in *Northanger Abbey*:

> the chances must be against [a sensible young woman] being occupied by any part of that voluminous publication, of which either the matter or manner would not disgust a young person of taste; the substance of its papers so often consisting in the statement of improbable circumstances, unnatural characters, and topics of conversation, which no longer concern any one living; and their language, too, frequently so coarse as to give no very favorable idea of the age that could endure it.[50]

Finally, it is not difficult to conclude that any Menippean satire written since Bakhtin would be skeptical of the notion of carnival and the claims made for its especial social relevance. "Carnival," despite the promise it holds for some academics as an instrument for social reform, remains a place where people go to find cheap thrills and lose money.

One of the difficulties in understanding Menippean satire involves the confusion of purpose and form; in other words, it is easy to confuse form as the criterion for identifying Menippean satire to the exclusion of purpose. This is especially the case in two recent studies that employ the notion of anatomy in connection with Melville's work. In *Melville's Anatomy*, Samuel Otter goes so far as to completely appropriate the notion of the anatomy and recast it in a formula that deflates the notion of Melville being a satirist; he uses Bakhtin to do this. In a brief nod to Frye, Otter describes the anatomy as an "heterogeneous, omnivorous, encyclopedic, rhetorically experimental, stylistically dense form, in which linguistic features—diction, syntax, metaphor—become the vehicle for intellectual inquiry." All this is very well, but what has happened to the satirical purpose? Where is humor? Otter continues, turning the anatomy now into a Hegelian history lesson: "According to Bakhtin," he writes, "these features [—diction, syntax, metaphor—] express orientations toward society, time, nation, and tradition that are laid bare in the literary anatomy." Otter shifts to a very literal and mechanical interpretation of the anatomy, divorcing it (and Melville) from thousands of years of historical precedent, so that Otter's study of "anatomy" transforms into an exercise in the New Historicism. He says, "I use the term anatomy to describe the material analyses of consciousness conducted by Melville in the first phase of his career." The purpose of Otter's work is to investigate Melville's "restless dissecting consciousness," Melville's desire to "anatomize bodies and societies to excess" and expose the "functions of form in the antebellum United States."[51] Thus Otter works a postmodern appropriation of a term used to designate an ancient and widely recognized humanistic literary practice by transforming that term into an impotent euphemism. The term "Menippean satire" is sidestepped entirely, and, indeed, Burton is mentioned in the text only once and without associating his name with the "anatomy." Indeed, Burton's name and *The Anatomy of Melancholy* are conspicuously absent from both Otter's bibliography and index.

Neither is Burton found in the bibliography or index of Jonathan Cook's *Satirical Apocalypse: An Anatomy of Melville's The Confidence-*

Man. In flowing detail Cook describes possible sources for various events and figures in Melville's novel. Cook's study, however, is in large part limited to topical issues in Melville's biography, and rather he makes of *The Confidence-Man* a roman à clef without fully grasping the philosophical agenda that gives the novel its form and purpose. Such are the regrettable closures of the New Historicism, that the dialectical form rather than the purpose and meaning of a work of art is explored and celebrated. It is the theme and activity of critical synoptics that takes Melville's work beyond the roman à clef and makes *The Confidence-Man* a Menippean satire.[52]

This is not to say, however, that Menippean satire doesn't possess characteristic forms, but it is important to understand that these forms are rooted in and are an expression of the genre's analytical purpose. Moreover, Menippean satire is an artistic practice with characteristic syntactic and philosophical features, but these features are not necessarily formal. The chief feature that distinguishes Menippean satire from other categories of analysis is the presence of fictive verisimilitude at some level, or in some capacity. Menippean satire relies upon fictive verisimilitude to properly and comprehensively critique (or anatomize) its topic and promote an accurate vision of a manifold reality. In the perfect Menippean satire, the topic to be analyzed and this manifold vision are brought to the same plane, whereby propositions are placed in a fictitious world, or fictitious propositions are placed in the real world. Such a process dominates the plotting and characterizations in my own novels, particularly *A Novel Rex* and *The Sky-shaped Sarcophagus*. I call the instrumentality of this process "the Menippean list."

According to John M. Bullitt in his *Jonathan Swift and the Anatomy of Satire*, the Menippean perspective is epitomized in the sensibility of Swift who strikes

> at the affectation of those who, by formula and artifice, impose some rigid subjective perception upon the world and then pay honor to this graven image as truth and to themselves as its discoverers. The folly of man's refusal to see things as they really are is thus consistently translated by Swift into symbolic representations of man as a *mechanism*. Inflexible, blinded to external truth by his own conceit, contentious in his assumption of the infallibility of his subjective responses, man becomes a puppet in life's Punch-and-Judy show of artifice, system and self-delusion.[53]

From the Menippean perspective, there is no formula, artifice, or theory that can explain the world or natural phenomena. Such mechanisms are products of folly, an exercise in affectation perpetrated by those who impose some rigid subjective perception or *a priori* theory upon the world and then bow down to it like an idol. The "list" in Menippean satire is an artistic and scholarly practice which deflates the illusions that define and animate this perception of *mechanism* in nature.

Melville engineers just such a deflation in *The Confidence-Man* where, through the accumulated portrayal of a variety of human encounters—a list of scenes, so to speak—he dispels the illusion that human behavior is in any way regular or predictable according to the process of some mechanism. In real life, Melville tells us, one meets with metamorphoses far more astonishing than any found in Ovid.

This process operates in the "Cetology" chapter of *Moby-Dick* where Melville toys with the arbitrary nature and vain conceit of taxonomic mechanisms. Like pagan pantheons, such systems are more in the nature of artifacts which characterize the people who created them than they are descriptions of real nature or its processes.

A startling example of the Menippean list is to be found in the collection of "Extracts" which introduces *Moby-Dick*. Here Melville fractures what we might describe as a series of fixed and rigid subjective perceptions of the world. He accomplishes this through a sample listing of the great variety of perspectives, demonologies, and even experiences of the set of phenomena associated with the notion of whales. The notion of this "set" is construed upon a neutral variable. In the case of *Moby-Dick*, X equals "the whale," whatever that is—and whatever it is, it cannot be reduced, boiled down, or abstracted into the terms of some mechanism.

Now and then these mechanisms capture our imaginations; we admire them, describe them, celebrate, or rail against them. However, the greatest mytho-poetic steam locomotive—like Rome, Carthage, Babylon, Nineveh, or the newest critical theory or trendy academic discourse—falls into disrepair, rusts, decays, and crumbles into a beautiful ruin, many times more interesting than the oily monster that originally came puffing out of the tin shop. Wrack and ruin, therefore, are the material which comprise the Menippean list. Wrack and ruin are the fabric of the Menippean universe—the biggest, brightest, most competent intellectual universe—the one constant, true, and reliable circumscribing sphere where ideologues and theoreticians and the ugly pomp of their arrogant egotism can be put on vulgar display to coax boisterous croaks and guffaws from clever school boys and girls (which further attests to the pedagogical importance of Menippean satire). It is after all only among the wrack and ruin of preceding civilizations where we can find release and freedom from those civilizations; such liberty did not exist when they thrived, nor does it in the midst of modern civilization as it continually mushrooms and consumes the decaying cultures around us. Ultimately, as Michael Moorcock shows us in his novels, it is in the broader context of ruin wherein we find our mothers, our fathers, and the great loves of our lives. Moorcock celebrates this in the title of one of his more ambitious novels: *Byzantium Endures*.

The Menippean list allows us to explore this "Byzantium." Menippean satire—the anatomy—opens the windows of perception between language and our manifold and multidimensional reality and allows us to state the obvious. The list may seem to many an anomaly or crankish conceit lying beyond the pale of accredited learning and academic discourse. I would argue, however, that the list is central to the fountainhead of western democratic thought. As Bullitt explains:

> It is often maintained by historians of philosophy that England has had only one school of philosophy, or rather, that it has had none at all, "for its philosophy is a perpetual protest against Scholasticism." A faith in experimental science, based upon empirical evidence of the senses, and a complementary distrust of scholastic and rationalistic *a priori* speculation, may be said to form the cornerstone of the English philosophical tradition. Although Swift developed no systematic philosophy—this absence, too, seems to be characteristic of the tentative and experimental English mind—a peculiarly English and to some degree Lockean nexus of assumptions underlies one major area of his satiric techniques. This area may be called, on the basis of Swift's own vocabulary, "the mechanical operation of the mind."[54]

"The mechanical operation of the mind" assumes for the Menippean investigator the secular or intellectual equivalent of ultimate cosmic error. This "sin" (the Hebrew word meaning "error") is the human tendency to succumb to illusion through ignorance, conceit, or intellectual laziness. The process of the list reveals the lack of consensus which exists over many of our assumptions, and documents or diagrams the truly varied or multidimensional nature of our true reality—our Byzantium—which itself seems informed by some subtle and humorous—almost supernatural—sense or mood of irony. This same sense of irony which informs Melville and Swift's sensibility also informs the British schools of empiricism and common sense philosophy, and the even more heroic school of synoptic analysis—the philosophy of Wittgenstein. Perhaps this interest in irony may be attributable, both in Melville and in Swift, and in the British tradition, to Keltic cultural antecedents—remnants of an Arcadian pagan humanism and the dying embers of the ancient classical world—existing along the perimeter, first, of scholastic and imperialist Rome, and then later along the lines of contention framed at one time or another (and repeatedly) by Keltic Christians and Roman Christians, Anglo Catholics and Roman Catholics, the sea empire of Britain and the land empires of the continent.

Apophatic *via negativa*, the "Anatomy," the Menippean list suggest to me an aesthetic, a process and a sensibility which apprehend a reality which is self-reflexive, multifaceted, and manifold.

In the lyric to "Packard Goose" Frank Zappa captures the inspiring passion of this ironic, multidimensional reality. Lists might be inductive and elemental, but their elements must also build upon each other, stepping ever upward as from the bottom of a staircase which spirals out of sight. After the singer runs through several verses condemning dialectical analysis and commercial journalistic criticism, a spoken list is introduced:

> Information is not knowledge
> Knowledge is not wisdom
> Wisdom is not truth
> Truth is not beauty
> Beauty is not love
> Love is not music
> Music—is—the best
> "Wisdom" is the domain of the Wiz
> Which is extinct
> "Beauty" is a phonetic corruption
> Of a French cloth neck ornament
> Currently in resurgence—[55]

The lyric is followed by a dissonant musical extemporization marked by the use of shifting rhythms and scales juxtaposed against a regular but syncopated background theme. An electric guitar screams a contrapuntal interlacing or Keltic knot pattern decorating the sentiment of an ever-unfolding resolution. There is an intimation of alarm or warning, and also an intimate familiarity with the strength and the heroic force of human conscience and consciousness. Through musical extemporization Zappa transcends the objects of his loathing: neck ties, professional critics, pop music, corporate America, and the plastic culture which together these elements epitomize.

In the case of "Packard Goose," music is the transcendent aesthetic which can complete our humanistic apprehension of the theme evolving in the list. Observe, however, that music lies outside the domain of human language—or at least certainly outside the domain of "discourse." And because this "discourse" is not in part musical, it cannot apprehend an important dimension of human inquiry and understanding. All lists are as incomplete as the world is manifold, but "discourse," without music, poetry, images, synoptic illustration, presents always an unfinished list in even the most basic categories or modes of perspective. Zappa's poem and the extemporized excursion which follows it pattern the anatomical practice of listing which occurs again and again in Menippean satire: A variety of perspectives, sometimes successively circumscribing, are presented; and—either linearly (at the end of the list) or conceptually as a keynote of Taoist paradox which infuses the list—the list ends and insinuates a half-veiled skeptical irony, or some self-consciously "apocalyptic" chord of multiple voicings. Through a rhetorical, surreal, or synesthetic leap to a contravening mode of expression, the list can create a jarring juxtaposition which evokes either an emotional insight, or a cathartic purgation of melancholic humors. The effect is of a sudden crescendo, the cacophony of leaping from language into the racing carriage of other communicative media: music, painting, sculpture, nonsensical histrionics, or the irony of an officious or legalistic appeal to arbitrary authority.

For example, consider Robert Burton in *The Anatomy of Melancholy*, partition 1, section 2, member 1, subsection 2, entitled "A Digression of the nature of Spirits, bad Angels, or Devils, and how they cause Melancholy." After declaiming for nineteen pages, listing various medical, Catholic, and folk authorities on the symptoms and methods whereby devils possess persons and cause melancholy, Burton suddenly dismisses all such explanations in a seemingly low key and anticlimactic statement, saying that demonic possession "happeneth for a punishment of sin, for their [the victims'] want of faith, incredulity, weakness, distrust, & c."

> A nun did eat a lettuce *without grace, or without signing with the sign of the cross*, and thus was instantly possessed. Durand relates that he saw a wench possessed in Bononia with two devils, by eating an unhallowed pomegranate, as she did afterwards confess, when she was cured by exorcisms. And therefore our papists do sign themselves so often with the sign

of the cross, that the demon dare not enter, and exorcise all manner of meats, as being unclean or accursed otherwise, as Bellarmine defends. Many such stories I find amongst pontifical writings, to prove their assertions; let them free their own credits; some few I will recite in his kind out of most approved Physicians. Cornelius Gemma relates of a young maid, called Katherine Gualter, a cooper's daughter, in the year 1571, that had such strange passions and convulsions, three men could not sometimes hold her; she purged a live eel, which he saw, a foot and a half long, and touched himself, but the eel afterwards vanished; she vomited some 24 pounds of fulsome stuff of all colours twice a day for 14 days; and after that she voided great balls of hair, pieces of wood, pigeons' dung, parchment, goose dung, coals; and after them two pounds of pure blood, and then again coals and stones, of which some had inscriptions, bigger than a walnut, some of them pieces of glass, brass, &c., besides paroxysms of laughing, weeping and ecstasies, &c. And this (he says), I saw with horror. They could do no good by her physick, but left her to the Clergy. Marcellus Donatus hath such another story of a country fellow, that had four knives in his belly, indented like a saw, every one a span long, with a wreath of hair like a globe, with much baggage of like sort, wonderful to behold. How it should come to his guts, he concludes, could only have been through artifice and craft of a daemon. Langius hath many relations to this effect, and so hath Christopherus a Vega. Wierus, Sckenkius, Scribonius, all agree that they are done by the subtility and illusion of the Devil. If you should ask a reason of this, 'tis to exercise our patience; for, as Tertullian holds, virtue is not virtue unless it has a foe by the conquering of which it shows its merit; 'tis to try us and our faith, 'tis for our offences, and for the punishment of our sins, by God's permission they do it, executioners of his will, as Tolosanus styles them; or rather as David, He cast upon them the fierceness of his anger, indignation, wrath, and vexation, by sending out of evil angels. So did he afflict Job, Saul, the lunaticks and daemonical persons whom Christ cured. This, I say, happeneth for a punishment of sin, for their want of faith, incredulity, weakness, distrust, &c.[56]

After lurid accounts of young girls voiding eels, lumps of coal, large stones bearing inscriptions, Burton's simple, subtle and casual explanation— "want of faith, incredulity, weakness, distrust, &c."—seems suddenly arch and ironic—an expression of Menippean sensibility. Burton's use of religion in *The Anatomy* seems always haunted by a sense of irony that is suggestive of the sardonic understatement associated with Chaucer. The theology Burton presents seems just slightly pale, and is voiced in pedantic and perhaps overly simple terms. He is a believer, but the theological dynamic he operates within is much more rigorous and exact than is conveyed in the simple platitudes he smoothly and demurely voices. In one sense, his pose suggests the corny cliché of muddling old fellows haunting high church corridors—vicars falling asleep at the pulpit and so forth—but in another sense the too-simply expressed Christian dogma he espouses hints at a much more complex, heretical, post-gnostic perspective that's best brought out through irony. Burton surprises us by simply stating the obvious. Once again we are confronted with the shock of the familiar

This ironic connectivity is the dynamic which informs my reading of the conclusion of *Moby-Dick*. Ishmael is very much more involved with his universe than the reader is superficially led to believe by the distant and patient tone of the epilogue, notwithstanding the apocalyptic image of the narrator floating around on a cannibal's coffin, surrounded by sharks and sea-hawks, and the melodramatic touch of calling one's self "another orphan" to be caught up in the arms of a square rigged *Rachel*. Melville cannot explore his epiphany in straightforward barbarisms, or in the throbbing gong notes of a Ralph Waldo Emerson; but rather Melville chooses to sketch out a few intersecting paganisms—and then winks his eye. What more happy praise for the familiar shock of rebirth?

2
Games Critics Play

Wittgenstein said, "philosophy is a battle against the bewitchment of our intelligence by means of language" (*PI* §109). It was Wittgenstein's desire to produce philosophical insight by a kind of rearrangement of his reader's mental patterns. Indeed, some philosophers have related his philosophizing to the art of psychoanalysis. Wittgenstein himself says, "The treatment of a question is like the treatment of an illness" (*PI* §255). His philosophy is to be regarded in this respect as a therapy for philosophers, not providing answers to their questions but showing the misapprehensions upon which these questions are based. From Wittgenstein's philosophy we can also design a therapy for literary critics struggling with today's complex theoretical issues: Does language work? Do books have human authors? Are human bodies texts? Does cultural relativism imply that all values are relative? Can a poem be pleasant? Is "art for art's sake" a legitimate proposition? This chapter begins the pattern for such a therapy.

Critical Games

The notion of textual reading games originates in one of Wittgenstein's most important legacies: the game metaphor. Modern game theory is helpful in understanding the use of Wittgenstein's game metaphor. According to game theory, whenever people interact with each other they are playing a game. *Fun and Games*, Ken Binmore's 1992 study of game theory, illustrates the wide range of such games:

> If you drive a car on a busy street, you are playing a game with the drivers of the other cars. When you make a bid at an auction, you are playing a game with the other bidders. When a supermarket manager decides the price at which she will try to sell cans of beans, she is playing a game

with her customers and with the managers at rival supermarkets. When a firm and a union negotiate next year's wage contract, they are playing a game. The prosecuting and defending attorneys are playing a game when each decides what arguments to put before a jury. Napoleon and Wellington were playing a game at the battle of Waterloo, and so were Khrushchev and Kennedy during the Cuban missile crisis.[1]

If all these interactions are games, then game theory is clearly important. Binmore suggests that the social sciences are in fact subdisciplines of game theory. The study of social interactions is the study of games. However, game theory as currently developed focuses mostly on what happens when people interact in a rational manner. So game theorists probably are not the people to consult for answers to the world's problems.[2]

Fortunately for our purposes here, the people who play textual reading games are, for the most part, people who are devoted to cultivating their rationality, their learning, and their critical acumen. Their reputations depend upon how well they learn and play a particular game. In the rational study of literature, these games are called *critical approaches*. The rules for these games are called *critical theory*. Thus as regards any literary text, we have the broad game of sociological approaches. There are Marxist approaches, feminist approaches, gay approaches, sociolinguistic approaches, political approaches, and so on. We have psychological approaches; formalistic approaches; structuralist approaches; aesthetic approaches; game theory approaches; poststructuralist approaches; surrealistic approaches (which are somehow rigorously rational in their irrationality); and late-, ultra-, and post-modern approaches stepping out into ever more obscure realms of intelligibility and abstraction. What unites all these approaches and the rules or theories which govern them is that they are all conducted in carefully monitored and controlled contexts of interaction. They are all games.

One critical game is not superior to another. The assigning of such value is in itself another game based upon its own rules. Any sort of criterion might form a basis for such a game. Very often, both in the academic and trade markets, these criteria are set deliberately by select game masters who, in the broader context of the academic market game, are best informed on "what sells." Fortunately, and I think this speaks well for our level of civilization and the direction of our cultivation, "what sells" is that which does the most good for the most people, and without, we hope, offending the sensibility of particularly thoughtful and sensitive individuals or individuals who, for various historical reasons, have been placed in a position of disadvantage. Still, notwithstanding this, one critical game is not superior to another. Rather, more precisely we say that one game enhances an ideology or set of observations that is more beneficial than another. Who is benefited or who should be benefited is a question outside the scope of this discussion, insofar as the focus here is not on the politics of division, but on what can be determined rationally. As Lauri Carlson explains in her 1983 book *Dialogue Games*, games are rational in that they are goal oriented and must work toward a solution. "The concept of a solution of a game," she says, "can be considered a mathematical explication of the informal concept of *rationality*." Games with purposely obscured or shifting solutions are irrational. "The main virtue (and occasional weakness) of game and decision theory is its ability to explicate this key concept of goal-oriented action."[3]

Text Concepts

As many critical games might be played as can be imagined. One way to understand the scope of this variety is to look at how these various games regard a literary text. Like critical games, there are probably as many ways of considering a text as there are games. However, I have identified at least three of what I consider to be the foremost text concepts: the artifact, the script, and the subtext.

Bibliographical critics look at a literary work as an artifact. They consider its manufacture, the style of its print, the type of paper upon which this print was applied, how these papers are gathered and sewn or glued together. From such investigations these critics can determine where, when, how, and by whom the text was manufactured. Philological critics take note of how words in a particular artifact are spelled, how sentences are punctuated and structured. From these observations critics can make informed sociological determinations about the artifact and the author. Another critic might count the number of words on each page of the text, or each odd numbered page, and average the results. Another might assign numerical value to each letter of the alphabet and through cabalist manipulation produce tables of numbers resembling astrological charts. Artifact games are those games which involve the critic with the physical, phenomenological text itself.

Many critics, and by far the greatest measure of readers, look at the literary text as a script. They consider a literary text as a story or monologue. Such critics read a text focusing on or determining particulars of setting, character, motivation, and plot. The scriptural reader approaches something like experiencing or believing he has experienced the story. The scriptural critic describes these experiences or experience-like beliefs. It is probably through these belief-like experiences that readers and critics have developed the practice we call "understanding authorial intent." Scriptural games are those games which involve the critic with descriptions of setting, plot, characters, and the characters' most overt motives.

Most criticism I've read seems to look at the literary text as a subtext. Probably no scriptural criticism directed at a scholarly audience fails in some way to take the subtext into consideration, sometimes even as a vehicle for understanding the script. Subtextual critics often (but not always) use scriptural and artifact information to support their determinations concerning the subtext. A subtextual critic might consider the political, economic, psychological, or ideological variables in the author's environment that explain why the author consciously or "unconsciously" made certain creative decisions. The subtextual critic might abstract certain textual or scriptural circumstances from a literary text and use these abstractions to illustrate various cultural attitudes toward gender, race, or economic status. A subtextual critic might examine the structure of a literary text and compare it to the structures of other literary texts. A subtextual critic might find in a literary text a "hidden" biographical parallel or antecedent traceable to the author or a figure from history. A subtextual critic might use a textual or scriptural feature of a literary text to illustrate the mechanism of language or argue for the legitimacy of a particular philosophy or ideology. Subtextual games are those games which involve the critic in drawing connections between a literary text and the history, culture, politics, economics, psychologies, and ideologies which either inform it or are informed by it. It is not a value judgment to say that subtextual games comprise the most interesting and dynamic fields of critical effort. Of all critical textual games, subtextual games offer the greatest accessibility and relevance to the publishing academic, and thus the most readily available and meaningful rewards. And for this reason subtextual reading games boast not only the most slipshod, but also the most deft and most energetic expressions of critical effort.

As a postscript to this section, some mention must be made of yet another text concept. The game which forms around the consideration of this text concept is as specialized as the critic who applies himself to it. The antecedents of this text concept can be traced through Čapek, Huxley, Carroll, Melville, Hawthorne, Poe, Peacock, Austen, Byron, Fielding, Sterne, Swift, Rabelais, Cervantes, Varro, Menippus, Aristophanes, The Book of Jonah, and perhaps the Epic of Gilgamesh. Most recently Borges and Nabokov produced such texts, and today post-modernists, utilizing the techniques of parody, pastiche, multiple coding, and self-referential texts are producing what I refer to—or what can be approached as—the supersubtext. If not the intent of the author, the supersubtextual critic comes closest to the ineffable surreality of a text. The supersubtextual text involves the critic in a game played in a hall of mirrors where author, character, setting, critic, ideology, and culture reflect upon one another, and usually to the embarrassment of all involved. If the evolution of letters, the literary-philosophical march of mind, has evolved some semblance of sentience over the past forty centuries, then this sentience reveals itself most clearly to the critic who is playing the supersubtextual reading game. And, particularly if the author is a supersubtextualist critic himself, the voice of the supersubtext, the voice of this ineffable sentience, will invariably ring in the supersubtextualist's ears as unconditional, unabashed, and irrepressible laughter.

READING GAMES

In *Philosophical Grammar* Wittgenstein says that grammar describes the use of words in language.[4] Grammar is like the rules or description of a game. Language thus becomes a game. When we learn a language we learn the rules of this game. In a limited sense, the words and sounds of language are like a deck of cards. We learn to play various games with these cards, and our knowledge of these games is based upon our familiarity with the rules of play. In the action of sitting down to play poker, whist, or any card game, we testify to our knowledge of the game and thus proceed under the assumption that all the participants share a common perception and understanding of what is transpiring during play. As with cards, we play a variety of games with language. There is the receiving-a-bill-in-the-mail language game, the writing-out-a-cheque language game, the explaining-how-to-play-poker language game, the filling-out-a-job-application language game, the writing-an-essay language game, the reading-a-story language game, the discussing-a-story language game, and so on.

From all this it isn't difficult to infer that an infinite number of reading games are possible. However, two are of importance to the literary critic. These are the *Accurate Reading* game and the *Appropriative Reading* game. I sometimes refer to the latter as the *Informed Reading* game. All reading games are of equal value from a philosophical perspective and this nomenclature is arbitrary. The terms *accurate* and *appropriative* are meant to characterize the *posture* of the critic as he or she reads the text, subtext, or script. The posture of a critic refers to the degree of learning, integrity, experience, imaginative curiosity and cold perspicuity the critic brings to bear in a critical reading. The criteria for evaluating a critic's posture will be discussed below. Suffice it to say that as textual reading games are pursued by different schools embracing different postural criteria, it is to be expected that a perspective might evolve where one school might perceive its own reading games as accurate while perceiving the reading games of other schools as being appropriative.

THE ACCURATE READING GAME

Say I place three volumes on the table before you. One is a physics textbook, one is a cookbook, and the last is Washington Irving's *Sketch Book*. I then ask you which of these volumes contains a story. Naturally, you choose the *Sketch Book*. Now I ask you to open to the table of contents. Which of the listed items are stories? Well, you suspect some of the items are essays, such as the piece entitled "The Author's Account of Himself." Most definitely, the items entitled "Introduction" and "Acknowledgements" are not stories. And neither are the items listed under "Editorial Appendix." You know these items are not stories because of your familiarity with the reading-the-table-of-contents language game that you are playing with the editor. Still, the question remains which are stories? I ask you to point out two. Let's say you point out "Rip Van Winkle" and "The Legend of Sleepy Hollow." Why are these stories? Well, we have been taught they are stories because they depict settings, characters, and actions. We expect to read about settings, characters, and actions when we read stories. This is the reading-a-story game. Settings, characters, and actions are what we are reading for when we set out to read a story accurately. Hence, when we play the "let's-discuss-our-accurate-readings" game, we discuss the story in terms of our impressions of the setting, our observations on the relationships and motives of the characters, and our understanding of their actions. When comparing our accurate readings we can either agree or disagree about what is happening in the story. If we disagree, then we refer each other to the text (the script in this case) and argue for our respective readings. If we still disagree over the accurate reading, then we conclude that: 1) one of us is unable to understand the story; 2) that both of us are unable to understand the story; or 3) that the author has mistakenly or purposely failed to describe accurately what is happening in the story.

The accurate reading in this case is concerned with what the story communicates as a story or what happens in the script. When playing the accurate reading game, the reading of artifacts and scripts will prove the least problematic. However, reading games based upon the subtext and supersubtext can be very problematic and often lure the critic into appropriative gaming behavior.

The Appropriative Reading Game

In the appropriative reading game the critic selects either textual features or scriptural figures and events from literary works and attaches to them, in the manner of a cartoonist labeling a caricature, historical, political, psychological, or ideological significance. In the appropriative reading game the critic evaluates and describes an artifact, script, or subtext through a textual reading game which is informed by any agenda or perspective, and in such a way that the appropriative reading conflicts with another reading, either appropriative or accurate. In a sense, all reading games are appropriative. All readings are informed by a perspective and some agenda. However, the designation of "appropriative" necessitates an outside perspective. For instance, sensitive to such literary appropriation, T. S. Eliot observed that in their criticism of *Hamlet*, Goethe "made of Hamlet a Werther," and Coleridge "made of Hamlet a Coleridge." Critics, according to Eliot, "often find . . . [in literary works] . . . a vicarious existence for their own artistic realization."[5]

When playing the let's-discuss-our-appropriative readings game we can either agree or disagree. If we disagree, then we refer each other to the text and, arguing through the texts which inform our readings, reexplain our reading. If we continue to disagree over the appropriative reading, then we conclude that 1) one of us lacks the knowledge or intelligence required to understand the appropriative reading; 2) the appropriative reading itself is either erroneous or contrived; or 3) one or more of the parties playing the let's-discuss-our-appropriative-readings game is operating under or is informed by an agenda which prevents any concession of contrivance or error.

One might observe at this point that if the parties playing the let's-discuss-our-appropriative-readings game agree on an appropriative reading, then that reading is then denominated "accurate"—or at least until a third party comes along and claims it is erroneous. Of course, excluding people from play is an important part of any game, and certain mock-games, within the context of bigger games, are clearly set up so that all the parties playing know (we hope!) who the winner is before the mock-game is even played. Very often in criticism, of course, both sides claim victory. Nevertheless, appropriative reading games are characterized by contrivance as well as description, while accurate reading games can only be descriptive.

Appropriative and Accurate Paraphrase—A Practical Exercise

Washington Irving's "The Legend of Sleepy Hollow" is a tale that has been subject to various forms of critical appropriation. Although these appropriating studies are well informed at many levels, they can be inaccurate in terms of what the story specifically communicates as a story. Loyd M. Daigrepont in his study "Ichabod Crane: Inglorious Man of American Letters" explains that Irving scholarship in the past quarter century has read the tale as a "portrayal of the conflict between civilization (or progress) and the idyllic dream of a new Eden in the American landscape." Most critics, according to Daigrepont, "interpret this conflict in terms of the special concerns of the man of letters or the artist versus those of a practical minded, progressive society."[6] Daigrepont himself appropriates the conflict and focus it, placing "the tale within the context of a specific problem in literary history—the ongoing and increased alienation of the genuine artist from the mainstream of modern society."[7] According to this reading, Ichabod Crane's ejection from the bountiful Sleepy Hollow parallels the alienation of the "genuine artist" (a concept that Daigrepont does not explain) from a rationalized Baconian society seeped in Scottish Common Sense Philosophy and oriented around the production of goods and capital. Then switching the label of "genuine artist" from Ichabod Crane to the antagonist, Brom Bones, Daigrepont makes this further claim: "But just as Brom saves Sleepy Hollow, Irving saves (for himself, at least) the realm of art and letters."[8] This parallels, in the tale's postscript, the storyteller's successful defense against the "tall, dry-looking old gentleman with beetling eyebrows," who has taken the storyteller to task over the authenticity of the tale. The victory vicariously shared by Brom Bones, the storyteller, and Irving is further characterized by Daigrepont in this concluding statement: "But, even in democratic America, art does not depend upon widespread public acceptance, but rather upon the artist's integrity and devotion."[9] As Goethe and Coleridge appropriated *Hamlet*, Daigrepont involves "The Legend of Sleepy Hollow" with the schoolboy myth that economic liberalism—even democracy—discourages artistic and intellectual activity. Like a line of falling dominoes, inaccurate readings lead to inaccurate assumptions, and the genesis of intellectual mythology. The story must be read accurately so that the informed assumptions made about it will be accurate. Hence, Daigrepont's inaccurate formulations involving liberal economic systems and misunderstandings of common sense philosophy can be dismissed so that sharp and accurate descriptions of the provincialisms that Irving is playing off of can be properly formulated. Furthermore, if Daigrepont wishes to level criticisms at the despicable legacy of greed left to us by Reagan and Thatcher, then he should do so directly and accurately without muddling this important issue with an inaccurate reading of Irving's story.

Daigrepont's analysis is clearly and rationally argued. However, while such criticisms may be *informed*, they are not necessarily *accurate*. Indeed, very often an informed perspective can interfere with the delicate balance of worldly experience, imaginative curiosity, and cold perspicuity which plays itself out over the course of an accurate reading. Consider the following informed reading of the syllogism in the tale's postscript, where, I believe, Daigrepont misconstrues the nuances of the nonsensical syllogism:

> The old storyteller constructs a nonsensical syllogism, juxtaposing unrelated morals and facetiously reducing his own tale to didacticism. All situations, he says, have advantages as well as disadvantages; toying with ghosts is a losing proposition; therefore, being refused the hand of an heiress means the satisfaction of ambitions. Ironically, the storyteller's critic is mollified by this purposeful nonsensical imitation of Poor Richard.[10]

This informed reading is misconstrued because it fails to understand what is happening between the characters; it fails to penetrate what the story specifically communicates as a story. Using the story to illustrate important trends in philosophical and economic history has some pedagogical value in the short—very short—term. However, such practice has dubious polemical value, and in the long run is very damaging pedagogically. The informed reading must assume its place *behind* the accurate reading if the text is to be most clearly understood and appreciated. In much the same way, informed assumptions must come after those assumptions which are more purely accurate.

The accurate reading begins with an inquiry into the dynamics and the identity of the characters attending the meeting of "illustrious burghers" depicted in the story's postscript. What precisely is the nature of the exchange dramatized here? In the course of the conversation is there buried a hint of the fate of Ichabod Crane? After his ejection from Sleepy Hollow, could he have fled to the city to pick up the shattered remains of his ego and made a success of himself—albeit a sad one? A reading of the postscript in which the "tall, dry looking old gentleman, with beetling eye brows" is taken to be Ichabod Crane might lead to the answers to these questions.

This character is introduced among the burghers as a rather grave fellow, "one of your wary men, who never laugh, but on good grounds—when they have reason and the law on their side."[11] Indeed, during the telling of the story, which has incited a most mirthful and amused reaction among its auditors, this figure has "maintained a grave and rather severe face throughout, now and then folding his arms, inclining his head, and looking down upon the floor, as if turning a doubt over in his mind."[12] By the reading suggested here, this is Ichabod Crane, many years after his ejection from Sleepy Hollow, ill-amused, befuddled, remembering and, though distanced, still emotionally ambivalent.

The story told, he demands of the storyteller "with a slight but exceedingly sage motion of the head, and contraction of the brow, what was the moral of the story, and what it went to prove."[13]

With an air of "infinite deference" the storyteller responds to the inquiry of Ichabod-cum-burgher in a tone that is both needling and compassionate, suggesting by its general ambience and specific tenor that the storyteller is a sympathetic—though more honest—friend. He answers in the form of a syllogism, observing

> that the story was intended most logically to prove:
> That there is no situation in life but has its advantages and pleasures—provided we will but take a joke as we find it.

That, therefore, he that runs races with goblin troopers is likely to have rough riding of it.

Ergo, for a country schoolmaster to be refused the hand of a Dutch heiress is a certain step to high preferment in the state.

Ichabod "knit his brows tenfold closer after this explanation, being sorely puzzled by the ratiocination of the syllogism"—while being, as the accurate reading suggests, quite aware of the syllogism's sardonic tenor. Ichabod's reaction and response are warmly tragic and the welling of humanity which takes place in him is made plain to the reader through the storyteller, who, sensitive to the emotions stirring within Ichabod, responds with a "triumphant leer." By and by, Ichabod accepts what is brought forth by the syllogism and, his point of view cautiously drawing closer to that of the storyteller, admits "all this was very well, but still he thought the story a little on the extravagant—there were one or two points on which he had his doubts." Of course the storyteller is not to be checked in his pursuit, and the divergent points of view concerning the "legend," which Ichabod, the storyteller, and the reader have held up to this point, are brought together in an arch response which, in the warmth and drollery it evokes, celebrates this union: " 'Faith, sir' replied the storyteller, 'as to that matter, I don't believe one-half of it myself.' "

As with the peculiar syllogism, the unbelievable events of the tale are nonetheless true in terms of the tenor they convey. In this way Ichabod's possible fates, both believable and unbelievable, are equally true as well. Earlier, when ending the tale, the storyteller speaks of a report circulated around the Hollow, that, after his ordeal with the Headless Horseman, Ichabod Crane had

> left the neighborhood, partly through fear of the goblin and Hans Van Ripper, and partly in mortification of having been suddenly dismissed by the heiress; that he had changed his quarters to a distant part of the country; had kept school and studied law at the same time; had been admitted to the bar, turned politician, electioneered, written for the newspapers, and finally had been made a justice of the Ten Pound Court.
>
> The old country wives, however, who are the best judges of these matters, maintain to this day that Ichabod was spirited away by supernatural means.[14]

The metaphysics of these "supernatural" means are suggested by the tale's epigraph:

> A pleasing land of drowsy head it was,
> > Of dreams that weave before the half-shut eye;
> And of gay castles in the clouds that pass,
> > Forever flushing round a summer sky.[15]

The critic is now prepared to accurately paraphrase the syllogism, which might read as follows:

— This story is pointing out the humor in a ridiculous incident of courtship.
— A skinny schoolmaster who competes with a big, double-jointed farm boy for the affections of the daughter of a big, double-jointed farmer isn't likely to fare very well, and runs a serious risk of ending up with pumpkin in his face.
— Being jilted by the farmer's daughter can be just the thing to sharpen up a dreamy-eyed country schoolmaster, and motivate him to go to law school.

Critical Posture

Critical posture refers to the degree of learning, integrity, experience, imaginative curiosity, compassion, and cold perspicuity that the critic brings to bear in a critical reading. Wittgenstein's notion that philosophy should move toward an analytical dissolution of conceptual confusion adds an additional element to be considered in determining a critic's posture. It was one of Wittgenstein's aims to make philosophical inquiry into a therapy and, through an examination of language, purge philosophy of those questions which were based upon illusory concepts, that is, concepts which were parented by a misapprehension of grammar rather than the facts of nature. Wittgenstein was put on this track by Hertz and his grappling with the terms *force* and *electricity*. Hertz writes:

> Our confused wish finds expression in the confused question as to the nature of force and electricity. But the answer which we want is not really an answer to this question. It is not by finding out more and fresh relations and connections that it can be answered; but by removing the contradictions existing between those already known, and thus perhaps by reducing their number. When these painful contradictions are removed, the question as to the nature of force will not have been answered; but our minds, no longer vexed, will cease to ask illegitimate questions.[16]

Critical posture, in its purist sense, refers to a critic's commitment to identifying illegitimate questions and pursuing the analytical dissolution of conceptual confusion. Some reading games obviously contribute to conceptual confusion, while other games seek a clarification of assumptions and concepts. Thus I have polarized the literary tradition of our species into the hypothetical traditions I call (1) *Cat-alytic* and (2) *Syn-aesthetic*. A literary gamester, based upon his actions, might be characterized as tending to either one of these poles.

Cat-alytic is a portmanteau word, a combination of the words "categorical" and "analytic" which suggest the cardinal characteristics of this tradition. The *modus operandi* of the cat-alytic critic is analysis based on the drawing of categories. The cat-alytic critic is also a "catalyst" in the sense that he remains unchanged while transforming the character of what he criticizes. This tendency to remain unaffected produces for him the illusion of objectivity. *Mediocritarian* (Mediocrity + Authoritarian) might also serve to describe this tradition.

Syn-aesthetic is a portmanteau word combining the words "synthetic" and "aesthetic" which suggest the cardinal characteristics of this tradition. The underlying *modus operandi* or, perhaps more specifically, operative motive of the syn-aesthetic critic is synthesis based upon the pursuit of aesthetic realization. The syn-aesthetic critic is a synesthetist in his pursuit of casting familiar objects and patterns in new forms which either reveal or alter their aesthetic values.

The critical mechanism of the cat-alytic thinker is analytical, categorizing, and differentiating. The syn-aesthetic thinker instead seeks to synthesize, revalue forms synesthetically, and denominate objects and patterns figuratively rather than through a process of dialectical alchemy.

The criteria upon which the cat-alytic thinker bases his categorizing is either a conception of a beauty-aesthetic or some scholastic or academic agenda. The syn-aesthetic critic instead embraces a truth-aesthetic and a "believed-in" humanist agenda. Thinkers from both traditions of course are at various degrees sensitive to and are affected by a political agenda.

While thinkers in either tradition may be affected by similar concerns, their agenda of expression remains distinct. The cat-alytical critic is interested in expressing the general and the abstract in institutional terms, in the theoretical language of his or her favorite comrade-in-study and according to the format specified in the *MLA*

Handbook. The cat-alytic critic seeks in his determinations to preserve the authority of his office. His expressions are cumulative in the sense that they integrate with and support the generalizations and abstractions voiced by his colleagues in the institution. On the other hand the syn-aesthetic critic is interested in expressing the particular and the specific in terms of a cultural or cross-cultural orientation. The syn-aesthetic critic seeks in his determinations to reinforce the authority of the feeling individual. His expressions are particular truths and in this pursuit do not hesitate to be revisionary.

Both traditions utilize a vast repertoire of modes and forms of argument. The cat-alytic is expressive while the syn-aesthetic is suggestive. The cat-alytic critic utilizes the manifesto and the critique while the syn-aesthetic critic utilizes the poem, the treatise (obsolete definition), the satire, and parody. The cat-alytic critic can and often does slip into a language of cant and jargon, and to one degree or another veils the weaknesses of his arguments with obscurantism. The syn-aesthetic critic seeks to be understood in terms of an organic cultural or transcultural perspective and so employs ordinary language and seeks to defend the weaknesses of his argument through vivid or even intoxicating illumination.

The Table of Dialectical Traditions pursues the contradistinctions of cat-alytic and syn-aesthetic critics in further detail. It should be observed that the notion of these two traditions is at an early stage of refinement and much work remains to be done in an accurate survey of literature and criticism in order to more precisely codify the notion of critical posture, and further explore its possibilities as a therapeutic apparatus for helping mediocritarian readers. Some mention must be made here, however, of an important hypothetical dichotomy of pedagogical attitudes in respect to these two traditions. This dichotomy involves the attitude of critics toward myth and corporate and cultural institutions. The cat-alytic critic teaches reaction toward myth and institutions while the syn-aesthetic critic seeks or promotes individuals to intellectually and materially transcend the ersatz world of institutionalized myth and tribe. It might be suggested that civilization is the achievement of such transcendence. This, however, doesn't entail abandoning myths and tribes entirely, but only myths and institutions which are reified beyond the mandate of our synoptic methodology, the syn-aesthetic tradition. Our understanding, after all, must rise to the occasion of all our sensibilities. In literature, this means Menippean satire.

Table of Dialectical Traditions

Cat-alytic	**Syn-aesthetic**
Mechanism:	
Analytical	Synthetic
Categorical	Synesthetic
Differentiating	Nominative
A priori	Empirical
Deductive	Inductive
Cause and Effect	Correlation
Observation and experiment serve to illustrate the hypothesis	The hypothesis serves to illustrate the results of observation and experiment.
	Synoptic
	Therapeutic
Criteria:	
Rectitude-Aesthetic	Truth/Beauty-Aesthetic
Intellectual	Moral
Scholastic	Humanist
Agenda of Expression:	
The General/The Abstract	The Particular/The Specific
Institutional	Cultural
Authority of Office	Authority of Speaker
Accumulative	Revisionary
Mode:	
Expressive	Suggestive
Manifesto	Poem/Treatise (obsolete def).
Critique	Satire
Cant/Jargon	Ordinary Language
Obscurantism	Illuminative
Orientation:	
Ideology	Philosophy
Academy	Tradition(s)
Institution	Civilization
Memory	Inspiration
Epistemology	Ontology
Relativistic	Cyclic
Cynicism	Skepticism
Activity	Outcome/Result
Mythology	Science

The sign	The signified
Symbol	Action
Logos	Mythos

Antecedents:

Hellenism	Hebraism
Aristotle	The Prophets
Catholic	Anglo-Catholic
French Revolution	American Revolution
Russian Revolution	K-Mart

Political System:

Universal Helotism with an occasional Carnival	Universal Helotism with an occasional Harliquinade
Power	Authority
Proletarian	Bourgeois
Mediocritarian	Meritocracy

Process:

Pedagogical	Talent/Genius
Upheaval	Parody
Dissemination	Insemination

Motivational Factors:

Coercion	Duty-Service
Survival	Love
Fear	Honor/Conviction
Procreation	Procreation
Ego	Ego
Reduce	Comprehend
Surveillance	Exploration

Example:

Graduate Record Examination	Menippean Satire

The Synoptic Survey

It would seem that the notions of accurate and appropriative games and the incumbent notions of artifact, script, subtext, and supersubtext might form the basis for a system of practical criticism. Like the game metaphor itself, however, the use of such notions is merely therapeutic; the discussion of criticism as a game, though instructive and amusing, is first and foremost a technique for improving the critic's analytical faculties. As we will see in the next chapter, it is often necessary to use an informed assumption as a point of departure for arriving at an accurate reading of a text. Also, the terminology would become cumbersome and awkward—indeed, silly—if each time we discussed a text we had to pull out the apparatus of the game metaphor and discuss formalized issues of textuality, accuracy, and appropriation, nor can I envision critics identifying themselves with either the mediocritarian, cat-alytic, or syn-aesthetic "causes."

Following after Wittgenstein, the purpose of the games described in this chapter and the purpose of the discussion undertaken in the first chapter are not to create a system of criticism. The purpose of these excursions is to teach readers to identify, in whatever guise, the mistaken assumptions which undergird conceptual confusion. We have found that satirical procedures highlight modes of reading that are attentive to context and interconnections; the procedure of satire and synoptic analysis brings us into contact with ever-widening spheres of relations while at the same time emphasizing the attention to particulars that is necessary when words or labels are connected to things. Still, before we can go further we must focus upon some memorable technique for arriving at a perspicuous, synoptic survey of our critical problems.

The term "critical synoptics" can be used to refer to a number of analytical activities. For critics, critical synoptics refers to the examination of the influences of context, scenario, and lexical/syntactical precision upon the meanings of propositions and concepts. The idea is to construct a synoptic overview of a concept or proposition. Any variety of techniques might be applied toward this end. In memorable terms, the basic idea of synoptic analysis is to tell stories about the ways propositions and concepts are used and understood. Such an overview provides a test for determining whether or not the proposition is valid. Once an appreciation for the synoptic overview is part and parcel of the critic's technique, any variety of concepts might be analyzed. The point of the following questions is to realize a synoptic overview:

I. *How is the concept used?* The use of the word, phrase, or proposition determines its meaning.
II. *How is the concept used and understood in other scenarios? What is the accustomed practice of its use?* The meaning of a word, phrase, or proposition is determined by what is explained by an explanation of its meaning, or an explanation of the rules

for its use. (How does the concept reflect the discourse community that gives it rise?).
III. *How is the concept understood?* The way the word, phrase, or proposition is understood is its meaning.[17]
IV. *What does the concept mean in simplified terms?* How would the use of the word, phrase, or proposition be taught to a child?
V. *What are the implications of the concept?* What kind of world must be necessary in order for the use of the word, phrase, or proposition to be correct or legitimate?
VI. *Are abstract nouns used in the formulation of the concept?* Abstract nouns often have no validity outside of (and thus also within) the proposition in which they are used.
VII. *Does the concept represent an* empirical explanation *of a phenomenon, or does it advance* understanding *of a phenomenon?* Does the concept represent what we really want to know about a phenomenon?
VIII. *Does the concept ascribe mechanism to nature?* The universe is not a machine.

More sophisticated synoptic overviews can be constructed through the use of literary storytelling. The idea isn't to tell a story about one proposition, but rather to set up a scenario in which a variety of propositions can be explored and analyzed. The point of these stories might not be purely analytical, but even stories which are written chiefly to entertain might employ critical synoptics as either a technique, a theme, an activity characters are engaged in, or all three at once. A miraculous thing about exploring critical synoptics is that in addition to being useful and instructive it is also very entertaining. For the storyteller, amusement is to be got in formulating entertaining scenarios. For the reader, amusement comes in reviewing and penetrating the various levels of the story and appreciating the story teller's wit. For the critic, amusement comes in telling stories about alternative readings, in contrasting alternative readings, and in refuting readings that are different from one's own. But for the analytical critic and the satirist, these activities and purposes variously converge in the synoptic surview.

II

Anglo-American Romanticism and the Specter of Intellectual Mythology

3
Hawthorne's Arcadian Reality Test

> "Come," said I to my friend, starting from a deep reverie, "Let us hasten hence or I shall be tempted to make a theory, after which there is little hope of any man."
> —Nathaniel Hawthorne, "The Hall of Fantasy"

IN "*THE SINS OF THE FATHERS* REVISITED" FREDERIC CREWS DESCRIBES HIS rejection of Freudianism—as well as any other form of critical dogmatism. Crews came to his rejection of dogmatism through his realization that Freud was narrow, in some cases dishonest, and because many so-called Freudian concepts had actually been explored earlier in various ways by other thinkers and writers. Along with the cult of the theoretical law giver and the academic guru, sectarian, orthodox and dogmatic criticism is irrational and fraught with inaccuracy. Many critics in the academy, according to Crews, also share his distaste for deductive and dogmatic theorizing. For Crews, critical dogmatism is the central issue of current academic contention. He calls the academy "polarized," with the division falling between "apriorists" and "empiricists."

> For apriorists, a theory is worth exercising if it yields results that gratify the critic's moral or ideological passions; no further demands need be placed on it. To an empiricist, however, the justification for a theory must reside in its combination of logical coherence, epistemic scrupulousness, and capacity to explain relatively undisputed facts at once more parsimoniously and more comprehensively than its rivals do. The partisans of these opposed attitudes toward knowledge occupy the same corridors and go though the same institutional motions, but in a profound sense they live in different worlds.[1]

The image of polarized academicians haunting the same college hallways yet living in separate worlds has its comic aspects. However, beneath the absurdity there lies a regrettable tragedy—if, indeed, Crew's observation is accurate. The image of a sectarian "battle of the ideologues" within English departments is demoralizing. It presents a Byzantine distraction for students as well as a negative image which has been seized upon by politicians who are railing against "tenured radicals" and the "elite" before a bewildered public. There are sardonic scorners who point to this schism, as well as the academy, and blatantly assert, as Shaw did in the "Don Juan in Hell" section of *Man and Superman,* that "they are not educated: they are only college passmen."[2] Such drollery hardly does much to remedy what is, after all, a serious condition of intellectual illness that penetrates all levels of contemporary society. What is most frustrating about the situation is the impression that the polarization Crews describes is ground that is already well gone over. In the United States, the pattern for this dichotomy originated over a century and a half ago during the American Renaissance. What makes this problem so trenchant? Contemplating the persistence (or the resurgence) of this polarization prompts me to ask why no one has lifted the scholarly needle, so to speak, from the scratched record? Or is the recapitulation of this polarization within the scholarly community the best way to teach students about the American Renaissance? Or philosophy? Or intellectual freedom? Do the terms of this dichotomy pattern the central problem of civilization? And, as Crews intimates, are our apriorist colleagues mistaken and even cynical in their attitudes toward knowledge?

In *The American Adam*, R. W. B. Lewis suggests, "America, since the age of Emerson, has been persistently a one-generation culture. Successive generations have given rise to a series of staccato literary movements with ever slighter trajectories . . . We regularly return decade after decade and with the same pain and amazement, to all the old conflicts, programs, and discoveries. We consume our powers in hoisting ourselves back to the plane of understanding reached a century ago and at intervals since."[3] This "dull" and "unconscious" repetition assumes an edenic pattern, the myth of the American Adam. In this myth, life and history are just beginning; the world is starting up again under a fresh new initiative where individuals are emancipated from their past and from history, "untouched and undefiled by the usual inheritances of family and race." The "American Adam" occupies a moral position which is prior to experience. Fundamentally innocent, "the world and history lay before him . . . a creator, a poet par excellence, creating language itself by naming the elements of the scene about him."[4]

But on the other side is the awareness of a broader, more complex reality. As Henry James the elder states, "Nothing could be more remote . . . from distinctively human attributes . . . than this sleek and comely Adamic condition."[5] The childish idea of a brave new edenic world suggests an ironical "Stairway to Heaven," a "Celestial Railroad," or a bright emerald city called "Oz."

Lewis tells us that during the American Renaissance Emerson was sensitive to a "schism" in culture between two polarized parties: the party of the *Past* and the party of the *Future*. Historians either accept Emerson's dichotomy or "dualism," or choose "one of Emerson's two parties as constituting *the* American tradition, rejecting the other as either a bleak foreign hangover or as immature native foolishness."[6] Because people like Hawthorne were skeptically sympathetic toward both parties, Lewis further refines Emerson's dichotomy into three parties or voices: 1) the party of Memory; 2) the party of Hope; and 3) the party of Irony.

The party of *Memory* comprised the legacy of Puritanism, and the consciousness of pervasive sin.

The party of *Hope* consisted of the transcendentalists and the new voices of social reform which, when combined, promised the mechanistic re-engineering of human experience and, it was hoped, the human condition. Like the Guardian of the Gates of Oz, they were passing out green sunglasses so that everyone entering the new Utopia saw emerald; and so it is with the apriorist program, where people see *with* rather than *through* their eyes; where ideology proceeds reality; and where a broadcast hermeneutic liberty allows critics to identify confirmations of their assumptions everywhere.

The party of *Irony* embraced a curious, ambivalent, off-beat kind of traditionalism. For these writers, according to Lewis, "an organic relation between past experience and the living moment became a factor in narrative—a recurring theme *of* narrative; and at the same time—most notably in the novels of Hawthorne and Melville—the narrative revealed its design through an original use of discredited traditional materials."[7] This formulae suggests to me Wittgenstein's synoptic analysis and Menippean satire. Synoptic analysis, in the hands of satiric artists like Poe, Melville, and Hawthorne, became a manifold technique for toying with, disassembling, and disintegrating apriorist assumptions, affectations, and mythology.

In Hawthorne's *The Blithedale Romance*,[8] we can see these satirical processes exercised; and we can also follow the maneuvering of a consciousness which derives aesthetic and moral enjoyment through the process of playing with its reader's expectations. The reader of Hawthorne cannot escape the impression that not only is satirizing ideologues and apriorists fulfilling an important intellectual duty—but it is also *lots of fun*.

The dichotomy between apriorist and Menippean perspectives is implicitly indexed in *The Blithedale Romance*. This dichotomy can be explored through the handy, if crude, process of labeling the characters in *The Blithedale Romance* as if they were archetypes in a myth about the apprehension of knowledge. Zenobia we shall label "the world as it really is." Priscilla is "the world as an ideologue or apriorist would like to see it." Hollingsworth is our philanthropic "ideologue" or "apriorist." Our empirical narrator, Miles Coverdale, is our "Hawthorne as he might have been without Sophia Peabody" or, more simply, "Hawthorne: absurd, hypochondriacal bachelor." To what end is this process of labeling? It can only be this: Books may talk about reality, but are not themselves reality. Rather than talk about the unreality of books, human beings have a wise and proven tendency to talk about the reality books are talking about. Outside the academy and the work of a handful of hypochondriacal poets, this tendency is almost universal. In accordance with this tendency or principle, Hawthorne, the "real" author of the novel, we shall deem "shrewd analytical satirist."

Zenobia is an exponent of the world as it really is, bright, manifold, active, and unpredictable. Zenobia's cheeks are flushed with life; she is interactive, committed to her own independent energies and genius. Coverdale describes her as proud, noble, careless, free, frank, fine, haughty, gracious, delectable, courageous, mirthful, glowing, generous, lusty, and shivering. Zenobia possesses bloom, vigor, and health in such abundance that Coverdale claims a man might fall "in love with her for their sake only." Zenobia is as varied, tempestuous, and as charged with vernal potential as the earth she represents. "In her quiet moods she seemed rather indolent; but when really in earnest, particularly if there were a spice of bitter feeling, she grew all alive, to her fingertips."[9]

"I am the first comer," says Zenobia to the freshly assembled brothers and sisters of Blithedale. Coverdale describes feeling an "influence breathing out of her such as we might suppose to come from Eve, when she was just made, and her creator brought her to Adam saying 'Behold! here is a woman!' "[10] Zenobia presents the irresistible effect of a circumscribing perspective, an unfolding and universal wisdom. Upon one occasion, in her deliberate but unconcerned gesture of discarding a flower, Coverdale is moved to observe "the presence of Zenobia caused our heroic enterprise to show like an illusion, a masquerade, a pastoral, a counterfeit Arcadia, in which we grown-up men and women were making a play-day of the years that were given us to live in."[11] Through her conversation, wit, independence, strength, her ability to confront and challenge, even the "dark" rumor that there has been a man in her past, Zenobia express herself outward. Coverdale can muse over her in poetic terms and conceive tropes involving her, but he cannot define her, delimit her, or superimpose a construction over her that she doesn't break through with the life force and her universelike variability. Even her falling in love with Hollingsworth, whose philanthropy appears ludicrous, even odious to her intellectual sensibility, is an expression of her manifold worldlike nature. Whether or not Hollingsworth has corrupted her away from her nature, it is entirely her prerogative to be attracted to the strength and commitment of his personality—properties which are deficient in the refined and intellectually superior Coverdale.

I once heard a dinner table assertion that, through such characters as Hester, Miriam, and Zenobia, Hawthorne demonstrates the greatest understanding of women known to any male author. In *The Blithedale Romance*, this understanding is extended from women to embrace a shrewd survey of the mutability of life-contexts and the human condition.

Priscilla is an exponent of the world as an ideologue or apriorist would like to see it. There is about her no fixture. She is pliant and malleable. Her form and her psyche softly yield to the superimposition of any construction that is put upon her. Priscilla is weak, sickly, pale, passive, quiet, awkward, distracted, inward, devoted, obedient, humble, and insubstantial, "like a figure in a dream."[12] Coverdale's initial description of Priscilla brings to bear the logic of poetic images and fancies to mold and conform her identity. He reflects on her poverty, her plainness, and her sickliness. She is shivering. Coverdale first interprets her cold as fear and nervous excitement. Then he poetically refracts her discomfort into the fanciful image of her shadow vibrating on the fire-lighted wall. It is of course doubtful that a flickering and moving flame could provide the stability required to articulate the image of a shivering figure. Coverdale next creates a pleasing, faery tale explanation for her tatty condition: "The fantasies occurred to me that she was some desolate kind of a creature, doomed to wander about in snow-storms; and that, though the ruddiness of our windowpanes had tempted her into a human dwelling, she would not remain long enough to melt the icicles out of her hair."[13]

Zenobia isn't moved by Priscilla's pathetic condition. She doesn't seek to fill Priscilla's apparent vacuousness with poetical or transcendental conjectures. Much to Coverdale's amazement, Zenobia identifies Priscilla as a seamstress from the city. Coverdale asks how she came so easily to such a conclusion. After criticizing the "obtuseness of masculine perceptions," Zenobia directs Coverdale's attention to the needle marks on the tip of Priscilla's forefinger. From this simple observation Zenobia proceeds to account for Priscilla's debilities: "Poor thing! She has been stifled with the heat of a salamander-stove, in a small, close room, and has drunk coffee, and fed upon dough-nuts, raisins, candy, and all such trash, till she is scarcely half alive; and so, as she has hardly any physique, a poet, like Mr. Miles Coverdale, may be allowed to think her spiritual."[14]

Notwithstanding Zenobia's rational explanations, Priscilla's spiritual aspects are very curious. On one occasion Coverdale extends his hand to her and Priscilla's own hand "moved slightly towards it, as if attracted by a feeble degree of magnetism."[15] Priscilla evinces a very startling effect early in the novel when she visits Coverdale's sickchamber to deliver a letter. Coverdale is amazed by Priscilla's appearance. There is something about her air and the expression on her face which to him suggests his friend, Margaret Fuller. When the letter is passed from her hand to Coverdale's, she completely loses the resemblance. Coverdale asks Priscilla if she knows Margaret Fuller and explains the remarkable resemblance he has just observed in her. Priscilla is confounded by Coverdale's observation, and expresses her desire that "people would not fancy such odd things in me." She then asks Coverdale, "How could I possibly make myself resemble this lady, merely by holding her letter in my hand?"[16]

As the reader discovers later in the novel, Priscilla is a medium. She is the famous Veiled Lady, a clairvoyant often exhibited in Boston. Clairvoyance is treated in *The Blithedale Romance* as something existing between "the birth of a new science" and "the revival of an old humbug." The description Hawthorne provides of this "new science" remarkably prefigures materialistic and mechanistic theories of personality which became dominant in the twentieth century. Indeed, there is something Orwellian in Hawthorne's treatment of clairvoyance. Hawthorne sounds a warning against "scientific" paths to dehumanization. Hawthorne prefigures the scientific totalitarianism portrayed in dystopian novels ranging from Zamyatin's *We* to Anthony Burgess's *A Clockwork Orange*. In this respect, the vulgar, Philistine/neophyte dictatorships Nabokov explores in works such as *Invitation to a Beheading* and *Bend Sinister* strike a particularly sympathetic chord.[17] In *The Blithedale Romance*, Professor Westervelt serves as the exponent of this "new" science and the provincial lecture hall environment in which it is fostered. Coverdale's description of Westervelt's lecture is telling:

> The Professor began his discourse, explanatory of the psychological phenomena, as he termed them, which it was his purpose to exhibit to the spectators. There remains no very distinct impression of it on my memory. It was eloquent, ingenious, plausible, with a delusive show of spirituality, yet really imbued throughout with a cold and dead materialism. I shivered, as at a current of chill air issuing out of a sepulchral vault, and bringing the smell of corruption along with it. He spoke of a new era that was dawning upon the world; an era that would link soul to soul, and the present life to what we call futurity, with a closeness that should finally convert both worlds into one great, mutually conscious brotherhood. He described (in a strange, philosophical guise, with terms of art, as if it were a matter of chemical discovery) the agency by which this mighty result was to be effected; nor would it have surprised me, had he pretended to hold up a portion of his universally pervasive fluid, as he affirmed it to be, in a glass phial.[18]

Earlier, Coverdale had overheard a follower of Professor Westervelt discourse along similar lines. According to Westervelt's follower, the character of a human being is plastic and malleable. Traits such as "guilt" and "virtue" are simply forms which can be arbitrarily molded like soft wax. Religious aspirations are likened to a flame that can be blown up or as easily extinguished.[19] In contemporary terms, human beings are programmable machines.

It is a world peopled by such machines, by clockwork oranges, which our philanthropic *apriorist ideologue*, Hollingsworth, requires to fulfill his monomaniacal mission: the reform of hopeless criminals. Coverdale describes Hollingsworth's appearance as striking, heavy, dark, rude, strong, massive, and brawny. Hollingsworth was originally a blacksmith. His head is shaggy, his beard is "abundant" and his features seem "hammered out of iron." His gaze is inauspicious, stern, and reproachful. And it is through this gaze that, Coverdale tells us, Hollingsworth "first met Zenobia's eyes, and began his influence upon her life." There is in Hollingsworth no polish or courtesy, "although in his gentler moods, there was a tenderness in his voice, eyes, mouth, in his gesture, which few men could resist, and no women."[20] Hollingsworth is a charismatic leader. Coverdale is surprised when he sees this charisma effect Zenobia. Hitherto, he has mistakenly interpreted Zenobia's strength for solidity and continuity, and has denied her variable, worldlike nature. But Zenobia, like the world, like society, is vulnerable to Hollingsworth's fortitude and singleness of purpose.

On one side Hollingsworth is a mesmerist, a dynamic and compelling personality; on the other side he is a tyrannical blacksmith who would thrust men into his forge and, with "blood and iron" fortitude, beat out their souls upon his anvil. As he discovers the full ramifications of Hollingsworth's ambition, Coverdale is appalled: "Mankind, in Hollingsworth's opinion, . . . is but another yoke of oxen, as stubborn, stupid, and sluggish, as our old Brown and Bright. He vituperates us aloud, and curses us in his heart, and will begin to prick us with the goad-stick, by and by. But are we his oxen? And what right has he to be the driver? And why, when there is enough else to do, should we waste our strength in dragging home the ponderous load of his philanthropic absurdities?"[21]

Our discussion of Coverdale begins in surveying the biographical characteristics which Frederick Crews has formulated after many years of studying Hawthorne. Among these characteristics, Crews emphasizes Hawthorne's

> fear of passion; his tendency to reduce historical issues to a psychomachia between impulse and inhibition; his antiradicalism, combined, however, with a radical's distrust of authority and institutions; his misogynistic streak; his self reproach as a voyeuristic bystander, and his association of art with that guilty role; his clinical coldness, which works at cross-purposes with his endorsements of affection and community; his yearning toward a Phoebe- or Hilda-like blandness to swallow up his morbidity; and as a result of all this, his profound loneliness and premature world-weariness . . . his sardonic but never altogether sincere self-denigration, his poison-dipped satirical humor, and a certain impenetrable ceremoniousness that hints at aristocratic disdain for the coarse Jacksonian world.[22]

Crews draws a figure which we identify closely with Hawthorne; but I would stipulate that specifically in this character sketch Crews presents us with a figure of the "Hawthorne Mystique." That mystique might more properly be the property of Reverend Dimsdale or Miles Coverdale than Hawthorne himself. In the act of writing about one's self, the properties hitherto involved with the personality are transformed into mere phases and divisions. They have become exterior and malleable objects of a strange contemplation. Coverdale is that bachelor poetic force in Hawthorne which weaves the webs Hawthorne perceives himself weaving. Coverdale is Hawthorne's daydream of himself as an artist. In discussing his daydream of himself as he writes *The Blithedale Romance*, we might easily picture Hawthorne say: "I must have fallen asleep, and had a dream, all the circumstances of which utterly vanished at the moment when they converged to some tragical catastrophe, and thus grew too powerful for the thin sphere of slumber that enveloped them."[23]

Mirroring Coverdale's confusion and mystification in trying to understand the strange reality of Blithedale and the dynamics of the inter-relationships among Moodie, Westervelt, Zenobia, Hollingsworth, and Priscilla, the reader is frustrated to understand the importance or meaning of the novel's circuitous and self-reflexive implications. For instance, consider the forest meeting of Westervelt and Zenobia, the implications of which are focused into this mystifying statement. Zenobia responds to Westervelt: "With what kind of being am I linked? . . . If my Creator cares aught for my soul, let him release me from this miserable bond!"[24] In grappling with the narrative, the reader, like Coverdale, is confounded to know to whom Zenobia is referring. With equally plausible and fantastic implications, it could be Hollingsworth, Westervelt, Priscilla, or Coverdale. And then there is the resurfacing of this scene in odd and suggestive particulars when Zenobia tells her "legend" in chapter 13; and, from the same chapter, Zenobia's prefiguring the unveiling of Priscilla and her rescue by Hollingsworth. There is the grotesquely comic return of Miles Coverdale to Blithedale depicted in chapter 24, "The Masqueraders," which works to reflect the theme of illusion, mystery, and affectation which is by slight of hand, as it were, hidden, spoken to, and conjured elsewhere in the novel. The highlight of this scene occurs when the costumed revelers perceive Miles Coverdale hidden in the trees and laughing at them. One of the masqueraders calls out: " 'The voice was Miles Coverdale's,' said the fiendish fiddler, with a whisk of his tail and a toss of his horns. 'My music has brought him hither. He is always ready to dance to the devil's tune!' "[25] There is in chapter 26, "Zenobia and Coverdale," the ironic discussion between them concerning what "moral" should inform the final stanza of the voyeuristic "ballad" he will write about her tragedy. Here some semblance of what the novel might be getting at finally comes to the surface. In that "ballad"—not the deeply satiric romance Hawthorne gives us but the narrative provided by Coverdale—Coverdale presents two morals: The first moral is offered as a direct product of his analysis of Hollingsworth:

> The moral which presents itself to my reflections, as drawn from Hollingsworth's character and errors, is simply this,—that admitting what is called philanthropy, when adopted as a profession, to be often useful by its energetic impulse of society at large, it is perilous to the individual whose ruling passion, in one exclusive channel, it thus becomes. It ruins, or is fearfully apt to ruin, the heart, the rich juices of which God never meant should be pressed violently out, and distilled into alcoholic liquor, by an unnatural process, but should render life sweet, bland, and gently beneficent, and insensibly influence other hearts and other lives to the same blessed end. I see in Hollingsworth an exemplification of the most awful truth in Bunyan's book of such;—from the very gate of heaven there is a by-way to the pit![26]

However, such moralizing on the part of Coverdale is the real trip down the pit. Hollingsworth's monomaniacal desire to build a great reformatory for criminals is an emblem or parallel for Coverdale's poetic reformatory for comprehending human motivations, analyzing human weaknesses, and pronouncing moralizations. The efficacy of such moralizations is just as implausible as the redeemed and reformed criminals Hollingsworth would like to produce. As Hollingsworth lusts after the realization of criminal reform, Coverdale lusts after the realization of some deliverance from the secrets of the human heart. This monomania fuels his voyeuristic pursuit into Zenobia's past and her relationship with Westervelt, whom Coverdale has the childish temerity to believe—so long as it helps to shelter him from human involvement—is Satan. Coverdale cannot love Zenobia because she cannot be primly analyzed. She remains living and variable. He cannot face real involvement; that is, involvement with variability. Coverdale's "mystique," as it were, is simply his using intellectualization to cover up his cowardice.

Disgusted with Coverdale's "mystique," Zenobia describes to him a series of morals which mocks his voyeuristic moralizing, his intellectualization, and his inability to confront real human involvement:

> "O, a very old one will serve the purpose," she replied. "There are no new truths, much as we have prided ourselves on finding some. A moral? Why, this:—that, in the battlefield of life, the downright stroke, that would fall only on a man's steel head-piece, is sure to light on a woman's heart, over which she wears no breastplate, and whose wisdom it is, therefore, to keep

out of the conflict. Or, this:—this the whole universe, her own sex and yours, and Providence, or Destiny, to boot, make common cause against the woman who swerves one hair's breadth out of the beaten track. Yes; and add (for I may as well own it, now) that, with that one hair's breadth, she goes all astray, and never sees the world in its true aspect afterwards!"[27]

However, as Zenobia prophesied a moment or two earlier, the actual moral of Coverdale's ballad will be "distilled in to the final stanza, in a drop of bitter honey."[28]

So the novel concludes: Before pronouncing that moral, and with fiendish affectation, Coverdale asks the reader to "charitably suppose me to blush, and turn away my face:—

>   I—myself—was in love—with—Priscilla![29]

Like Hollingsworth, Coverdale is in love with the real world only so long as it suits his purposes. When it becomes apparent that Zenobia has lost her fortune, she has no usefulness for Hollingsworth. When Coverdale discovers her earlier relationship with another man (who subsequently turned out to be Westervelt), he finds he doesn't have the courage to enter human affairs. He flees from her by making her into an object of a grotesque contemplation—his own lack of manhood.

But is this being too hard on Coverdale? By engaging so deeply in our analysis are we escaping from our awareness that the exercise of such an analysis might be for ourselves merely a Coverdale-like escape act? Has our investigation become like an essay Coverdale might mediate for *The Dial*, "in which the many tongues of Nature whispered mysteries, and seemed to ask only a little stronger puff of wind to speak out the solution of its riddle"?[30]

Coverdale shows that pursuing abstractions only yields further abstractions. The world is left out of this process by being reduced to text. For the dialectical critic, this "text" is reduced to propositions which confirm some *a priori* assumption. In the process of providing *explanation*, a richer and more valuable *understanding* is lost sight of. Like Zenobia's fictitious Theodore as he sat in the lyceum hall in anticipation of the appearance of the veiled lady, the student of such a critic can do very little more than anticipate the experience of reading *The Blithedale Romance*:

> There he waited, listening, I suppose, to the stifled hum of the great audience; and no doubt he could distinguish the deep tones of the magician,

causing the wonders that he wrought to appear more dark and intricate, by his mystic pretense of an explanation.[31]

The Blithedale Romance is a text with peculiar and shifting properties. It involves the reader in a game played in a valley of echoes where explanations concerning author, character, setting, theme, reader, ideology, anti-religion, and culture call to one another in ingenious, suggestive, and ironic ways. Perhaps the greatest irony of this horrid novel is that it is so amusing.

4
Menacing the Good Baker's Oven

THE BEST READING EXPERIENCE IS EXTEMPORAL. YEARS SPENT STUDYING literary criticism can train the reader to better understand, appreciate, and describe the experience of reading a literary text. Reading itself, however, is a personal activity which no more can be reproduced by language than can the personal experience of exchanging a kiss, glancing at the sky, or cutting one's finger. These experiences, like reading, can be described, suggested, and evoked through imagery, analysis, and the artful triggering of memory. But language does not recapitulate experience in the absolute sense. Indeed, the notion of such a recapitulation is obviously nonsensical.

This point is illustrated repeatedly in Herman Melville's *The Confidence-Man* where the text is deliberately manipulated so that the only thing a reader can be sure of about the text is that he or she is reading it. Harrison Hayford has claimed that *The Confidence-Man* is a "book where by definition no person, word, thought or deed can be taken at fixed value."[1] Critics have argued about the nature of the text itself. Is it a novel, anatomy, allegory, satire, roman à clef, comedy? As John Bryant phrases it, "*The Confidence-Man* is Melville's problem novel."[2] I wonder, however, if perhaps the problem lies in trying to label the book with some sort of *a priori* generic abstraction. Never mind what the book is. What does it do? Suffice it to say that in *The Confidence-Man* Melville explores critical synoptics.

Examined at a "deep" level, *The Confidence-Man* might serve in the kangaroo court of deconstruction as exhibit number one in the case which argues that, as part of its normal process, verbal and written communication unravels and becomes meaningless. Indeed, *The Confidence-Man* can be read as a self-deconstructing text, a play of signifiers that leave fading "traces" of meaning in the minds of readers who try to construct their own fictions, narratives and interpretations based upon the vocabulary and syntax of the novel. Melville deliberately manipulates meaning throughout the novel so that very often readings become misreadings. In the style of the anatomy, Melville nests issues in circumscribing perspectives and sets himself up in the text, like a Greek chorus, to speculate on the nature and believability of his own fiction and characters. Whatever the obvious meaning of the text might be, he stands that meaning on its head, anticipating the deconstructive reading. What is to be done with a text that comes "pre-deconstructed" from its author?

Precisely because its inconsistencies are already obvious to ordinary readers, *The Confidence-Man* preempts the deconstructionist program. Since this novel's inconsistencies are deliberate, it is more than possible that these inconsistencies might in themselves convey a particular meaning, or a precisely conceived constellation of meanings. It is not the inconsistencies of language but rather the inconsistencies in the world referred to by that language which the reader should address in a text. This strategy is particularly useful in reading the *The Confidence-Man*.

Instead of focusing on the text, it is far more rewarding to examine the nature of the world the text is talking about. Like the real world Melville rigorously probes and examines, *The Confidence-Man* recapitulates a multidimensional variability. According to our established metaphor, the novel involves the reader in a game played in a "hall of mirrors," where author, character, setting, critic, ideology, and culture reflect upon each other, and usually to the embarrassment of all involved. But atop these fun and games there is a more obvious purpose. *The Confidence-Man* elaborates and qualifies the problem of religious faith, seeking a specific, case-by-case resolution of the risks inherent to the exercise of faith and philanthropy—that is, a love of humanity—in an imperfect and "fallen" world. Each of these cases represents a context against which possible mythological conceptions of "faith" can be identified. In the terms of descriptive, or synoptic analysis, Melville portrays a series of language games to examine the legitimacy of confidence-related propositions.

Chapter 3 of *The Confidence-Man*, "In Which a Variety of Characters Appear," presents an interesting inconsistency. The problem focuses on the character of the crippled black beggar, Guinea. Is Guinea, as he appears to be, a poor unfortunate cripple in need of alms? Or is he a Mississippi River operator, a white confidence man painted up with boot black who is playing a deceit upon the sympathy of the passengers aboard the steamer *Fidèle*?

At the opening of the chapter textual evidence supports Guinea's legitimacy. He is described by the narrator as a grotesque negro cripple, in tow-cloth attire and an old coal-sifter of a tambourine in his hand, who owing to something wrong about his legs, was, in effect, cut down to the stature of a Newfoundland dog; his knotted black fleece and good-natured honest black face rubbing against the upper part of people's thighs as he made shift to shuffle about, making music, such as it was, and raising a smile even from the gravest. It was curious to see him, out of his very deformity, indigence, and houselessness, so cheerily endured, raising mirth in some of that crowd, whose own purses, hearths, hearts, all their possessions, sound limbs included, could not make gay. (*CM* 7)

One of these charmed passengers accosts Guinea, and with much magnanimity makes his acquaintance. He asks Guinea where he sleeps at nights. Guinea answers:

"On der floor of der good baker's oven, sar."

The passenger inquires about this oven. What baker, he asks, bakes bread in this oven? Guinea points to the sky and answers that the sun is the baker. The floor of the oven, in fact, is the pavement of the city. Their exchange continues, becoming progressively more grotesque as the setting and Guinea's character are established. Guinea then breaks free and moves off through the crowd to gather alms—a task for which he discovers an ingenious expedient. Guinea makes of himself not only a charity but also a "*diversion.*" Guinea throws his head back like an elephant in a menagerie and makes his mouth a target in a pitch-penny game. He strikes his tambourine each time a passenger successfully lands a coin in his mouth.

The game of charity continues until the approach of the strange passenger with the wooden leg, "Canada thistle" as he has been called in Melville scholarship. He surveys the spectacle, and then casts doubt over Guinea's authenticity, calling him a "white operator, betwisted and painted up for a decoy" (*CM* 10). Up to this point textual evidence has suggested Guinea's legitimacy, so the reader is somewhat confounded by the gathered passengers who now begin to suspect Guinea might, in fact, be a fraud. A crisis in the narrative emerges. The suspension of disbelief is nearly jeopardized by what is evidently a glaring inconsistency. It seems unbelievable that the passengers could be so easily swayed in their perceptions. Again, the narration up to this point has supported Guinea's authenticity.

Along with the crowd of alms-givers, the reader can only follow the debates between the strange, one-legged passenger and the two or three passengers who intercede on behalf of the black beggar. These debates dominate the balance of the chapter. Nowhere in these debates or in the supporting narration is there any solid clue that either establishes or dismisses Guinea's authenticity. Melville has evidently altered the narrative game he is playing. Upon the advent of "Canada thistle," the chapter shifts from an omniscient third-person narrative to a sort of interior dialogue or debate in the costume of fiction, which in some way examines the problem of whether or not to place faith in humanity, as if it were a question of conscience. Departing from a veristic fiction, the chapter transforms into a vision of judgment or a mental stage play where the character of Guinea has been transported off the stage or behind the intervening screen of a painted two-dimensional piece of scenery. The reader sees the play, but can only follow the course of the debate and the reactions of the players who portray the passengers. Indeed, it is not Guinea's legitimacy, but rather the passengers' reactions which are the subject of Melville's analysis.

What preserves the suspension of disbelief at the crisis in the narrative is not merely the ingenious portrayal of the subsequent debate, but, more incisively, the outlandish character of the strange passenger. More fantastic than the black cripple, the stranger, who went on a wooden leg, is described as

> a limping, gimlet-eyed, sour-faced person—it may be some discharged customhouse officer, who, suddenly stripped of convenient means of support, had concluded to be avenged on government and humanity by making himself miserable for life, either by hating or suspecting everything and everybody. (*CM* 8)

Rather than casting doubt on his narrative, Melville opens it up into richer, more profound, and more highly comic dimensions.

The crux of the matter lies in this: the allusion to a discharged customhouse officer is too obvious to be ignored.[3] The personage of the stranger can suggest none other than Nathaniel Hawthorne, Melville's friend and artistic hero. But what kind of a Hawthorne do we find here? The description of this "sour-faced person" seeking vengeance against "government and humanity . . . by hating or suspecting everything and everybody" is hardly a complimentary caricature, particularly of a great artist and a friend. Moreover, in the passages subsequent to his entrance, this character is the source of some of the darkest observations and insinuations voiced in *The Confidence-Man*.

In the debate over Guinea's authenticity, a Methodist minister crosses swords with the angry wooden-legged passenger, urging him to bring charity to bear in judging the black beggar. The response is pure gall, and the exchange with the "discharged custom-house officer" increases in profundity as the Methodist minister becomes more deeply implicated in the former's insinuations. The minister is in fact "seeded" with distrust, a fact which is celebrated by his wooden-legged foe. The chief dynamic Melville associates with the "discharged customhouse official" is the character's ability to spread distrust. In chapter six the character again makes a brief appearance. Again, he becomes the focus of a debate over Guinea's authenticity. He departs and a discussion over him ensues. The man in gray observes he can "make truth almost offensive as falsehood." The young Episcopal clergyman calls him "the origin of my own distrust" (*CM* 31).

The timber-toed cynic is a richly comic caricature or mythic abstraction of Melville's own misanthropy, cast in the familiar accouterments of the one-legged Captain Ahab and the dark, ironic side of his friend Hawthorne. Hawthorne's darkness is well known; his morose preoccupation with sin and error; his suspicion of community; and the impatience he felt toward himself for his animosity and his own self-doubts. Like *Moby-Dick*, is *The Confidence-Man* also inscribed, after a fashion, to the genius of Nathaniel Hawthorne?

Melville scholarship seems to support an affirmative answer. Critics have encountered allusions to many of Melville's contemporaries in their readings of *The Confidence-Man*. The most famous and controversial of these allusions is certainly Egbert S. Oliver's identification of Emerson and Thoreau with the characters Mark Winsome and his "practical disciple," Egbert. Oliver has also identified the character Goneril with the actress Fanny Kemble. Harrison Hayford has identified Poe with the crazy beggar who accosts the Cosmopolitan and Winsome. Along these lines, John Bryant inventories many such allusions in *The Confidence-Man* chapter of the *Companion to Melville Studies*. John Seelye's article " 'Ungraspable Phantom': Reflections of Hawthorne in *Pierre* and *The Confidence Man*" is particularly supportive of the thesis put forward here. In light of the thoroughness of Seelye's discussion, it is curious that he fails to associate Hawthorne with the peg-leg "Canada thistle" who is also a disgruntled ex-customhouse official. Seelye's article is nonetheless very compelling. He explains the connection between Hawthorne and the shy, secretive character "Vine" in the poem *Clarel*. In *Pierre*, Seelye sees a parallel for Melville's fascination for Hawthorne in the protagonist's love for Isabel. Seelye denies that the relationship between Pierre and Isabel is a direct allegory of Melville and Hawthorne's relationship. He asserts, however, that "Melville seems to have been consciously drawing on his feelings toward Hawthorne as he wrote the story [*Pierre*].[4] Seelye argues that Hawthorne's influence is also prominent in *The Confidence-Man*. He describes the short tale of "Charlemont, the Gentleman-Madman" as a "cameo of guilt and self-imposed exile" like Hawthorne's "Ethan Brand" and "Wakefield." "Like many of Hawthorne's stories, it is quasi-allegorical, having a psychological base and moral overtones which are brought out at the end."[5] Similar comparisons could be claimed for the "Story of China Aster" which mirrors some of Hawthorne's Bunyanesque proclivities. Edwin Fussel claims the story to be a "transparent allegorical parody of Melville's disastrous literary career and of its relation to Hawthorne's."[6] It is possible that Melville was thinking about Hawthorne when he sketched the character of Orchis, the "friend" who leads China Aster to take the risk which leads to his ruin. Other critics have suggested that the loan exploit in China Aster relates to Melville's dealings with Tertullus D. Stewart. According to Seelye, the encounter in the novel between Frank Goodman and Charlie Noble is an elaborate parody of the breakdown in the relationship between Melville and Hawthorne. In this reading, Noble/Melville is mislead by Hawthorne/Goodman—"a type of impostor" who returns the former's hypocritical affection. Both men, then, are confidence men.[7] "The bosom friendship," according to Seelye, "cannot be sustained after this sudden shock of recognition, and if it can be said of the estrangement between Hawthorne and Melville that neither was 'in the wrong,' so may it be said of the parting of the two confidence-men that neither is in the right."[8]

The character of the one-legged customhouse official, "Canada thistle," adds new brush strokes to Seelye's canvas. Does Melville, perhaps humorously, identify Hawthorne as the source of his own lack of "confidence"? In the words of the young Episcopal minister, does Melville claim Hawthorne to be "the person to whom I ascribe the origin of my own distrust?" (*CM* 31).

It would seem that the resolution to this issue might lie in biography, and in an exploration of the friendship shared by Melville and Hawthorne. There could be, however, an explanation that has more to do with issues of critical synoptics: the influences of context, scenario, and syntactical precision upon the meanings of propositions and concepts. Rather than referring to the origins of Melville's "lack of faith," the passage might be read as instead alluding to the origins of Melville's theme and technique. The argumentation is rather involved, but the logic holds together remarkably well: Apropos to "the origin of distrust" we might imagine Hawthorne as a young boy reading John Bunyan. We see Hawthorne turning from the first to the second page of *The Pilgrim's Progress* and coming upon the passage where Christian tells his wife and children that he must leave them in order to relieve himself of a great burden that, he fears, "will sink me lower than the grave, and I shall fall into Tophet." Christian in fact leaves his family. How startling and dreadful this must seem to a little boy reading by the fireside! If Christianity should inspire a man to leave his family, is it not possible that this is a false and odious religion, indeed? Of course, Bunyan is speaking of a dream. Christian did not really leave his family. But the startling image and the shocking experience is filed away by young Hawthorne. What was a misreading for the child becomes a deliberate technique for the mature artist. Thus, many years later, Hawthorne might sit down to write a story such as "The Hollow of the Three Hills" and portray a young woman who has left the people who love her. She flees to nature, to loneliness and isolation, and seeks comfort in the lap of an old witch. But is this comfort damnation or salvation? Hawthorne is exploring an issue of critical synoptics; for whether or not the witch is the woman's damnation or salvation depends upon the context of the situation. But in the hollow of the three hills Hawthorne takes us outside of any such regulating context. Superseding the issue of whether or not the young woman is finding salvation or damnation, Hawthorne demonstrates that the only way that she (and the reader) can know is through the identification of a context that will define the nature of such salvation or damnation. If the scenario cannot provide such a reference frame, then the story—and the young woman—has left the realm of sense and entered the realm of nonsense. It may be that the young woman is seeking her salvation in such a realm, and her quest has become a self-destructive plunge into ideology, theory, and nonsense. She is perishing in a void without social or linguistic references. Just as Christian had feared, she has sunk lower than the grave and fallen into Tophet. If she has any hope it is only in faith, but if she has been led into this void by faith itself, then she has been led to the precipice indeed; and the devil whistles at the freak. Thus, when through the device of the young Episcopal minister Melville intimates that Hawthorne is "the person to whom I ascribe the origin of my own distrust," Melville is not referring exclusively to a moral or theological issue that was brought to his attention by Hawthorne, but rather Melville is alluding to his interest in critical synoptics and attributing the origins of this interest to Hawthorne. That this interest might be coached in theological terms, re a loss of faith, is rather the culmination of a long, drawn out joke that spans many authors, many misreadings (both deliberate and mistaken), and many texts.

Alongside the synoptic reading, the biographical reading of the passage seems pale; however, it is instructive. In the character of "Canada thistle" Melville may index a more objective or appreciative appraisal of Hawthorne's character and genius. In probing this possibility we must again turn to Hawthorne himself. According to this reading, Melville is playing against the irony Hawthorne experienced when, as an artist, he inventoried his doubts, his ambivalence to his intense loathing, and the inscrutable arabesque humor of this preoccupation. With maturation, Hawthorne's doubt, loathing, and humor were transformed from the fabric of his sensibility into the objects of an amused but serious contemplation. As the legend goes, Hawthorne, through his marriage to Sophia Peabody, surrendered some of his reclusiveness, transcended the gloom of his Werther-like sorrow, and entered a higher state of "happiness" and spiritual balance. As Hawthorne says in the introductory essay to *Mosses From an Old Manse*, "there had been epochs of my life, when I, too, might have asked of this prophet [Emerson] the master-word, that should solve me the riddle of the universe; but now, being happy, I felt as if there were no question to be put."[9] It was this process of growth which finally allowed Hawthorne to emotionally understand the joy and the strength of the skepticism he formally aspired to at an intellectual level as a bachelor writer of short philosophical allegories and conundrums.

Melville is responding in the timber-toed cynic not to the Hawthorne of biographical legend, but to the ironic Hawthorne mystique which glows sullenly behind it. Melville is acknowledging the comic genius of his fellow artist's myth; and, by giving him a false leg, joins this myth to the Ahab genius which Hawthorne helped Melville create. Again, *Moby-Dick* is inscribed to the *genius* of Nathaniel Hawthorne. And the word "genius," as I read it here, refers firstly to the poetical or mythic notion of sensibility and spirit, and then, secondly and only minimally, to the conventionally applied notions of talent and creative energy. In the third chapter of *The Confidence-Man* Melville revisits in his imagination with old mythic friends and sees how they've transformed and grown. If there is a comprehending point of view or "best" reading circumscribing the character of the wooden legged "Canada thistle," it is probably to be got at through the exercise of imagining and describing how Hawthorne—not the myth, but the real Hawthorne—might have reacted as he read the early chapters of *The Confidence-Man*. One might then detect the demure—but not too demure—laughter of a dark but "happy" sensibility. Of course, Hawthorne might also have registered the odd sensation of being the object of an Ahab-like obsession on the part of Melville who viewed Hawthorne in a mythic light. But then the exigencies of this particular masquerade expire as the world of the text intervenes. There is a story being told which traces off in different directions, though to return once more to this issue as Frank Goodman sits down with Charlie Noble.

As for the myth of Guinea: the authenticity of his blackness along with the question of his need for charity is left by Melville for the reader to decide in the privacy of his or her own conscience. Melville would have us look closely at the structure of the scenario before drawing any such conclusions. And this is more to the point. Melville's relationship to Hawthorne and the latter's influence are incidental matters to *The Confidence-Man*—roman à clef though it may be. The crucial issue in *The Confidence-Man,* as in all of Melville's best work, remains the elaboration and exercise of critical synoptics.

5
The Question of the Monster

> At last, to the East, distant about three degrees, appear'd a fiery crest above the waves; slowly it reared like a ridge of golden rocks, till we discover'd two globes of crimson fire, from which the sea flowed away in clouds of smoke; and now we saw it was the head of Leviathan; his forehead was divided into streaks of green & purple like those on a tyger's forehead: soon we saw his mouth & red gills hang just above the raging foam, tinging the black deep with beams of blood, advancing toward us with all the fury of a spiritual existence.
> —Blake, *The Marriage of Heaven and Hell*

ALTHOUGH HE WROTE IN FRANCE AND IN FRENCH, JULES VERNE'S AFFINITIES were sometimes profoundly American. His enthusiasm for the giant potentials and tragic shortcomings of democratic America, his technique of detailed verisimilitude, the manner of his wit, and the cast of his orientation toward certain social and political problems firmly locate him among the great "romantic" (or are they "satiric?") literary artists of the American Renaissance: Edgar Allan Poe, Nathaniel Hawthorne, and Herman Melville. What is often striking about Verne and these authors is that the character types they explore, although marginalized socially, are yet at the forefront of scientific, technical, and moral (or is it amoral?) progress.

Verne's debt to Poe is particularly conspicuous.[1] Like Poe, Verne exhibits strict adherence to known science or pseudo-science, a journalistic style ornamented by a wealth of technical detail, and a curiosity for radical character types existing at the fringes of conventional society. Early in *From the Earth to the Moon*—Verne's satire of a hypothetical military-industrial complex running rampant in post-Civil War America—Poe is briefly evoked. Poe is mentioned in passing by a speaker addressing the Baltimore Gun Club. The purpose of their meeting is direct physical communication with the moon. Poe, "a strange moody genius," is connected with a series of hoax newspaper reports of lunar travel. The members of the Baltimore Gun Club, electrified with patriotism, cheer for their literary countryman, "Hurray for Edgar Poe!"² . . . which can hardly be taken for anything but ironic. Just the sort of mob as filled the great hall of the Gun Club also filled the streets of Baltimore with election rioting when Poe was found dead there in 1849.

In his 1864 article, "Poe and His Works," Verne speculates on Poe's novel, *The Narrative of Arthur Gordon Pym of Nantucket*, claiming "the story of Pym's adventures breaks off in mid-air. Who will take it up again? Someone more daring than I, who does not fear to launch himself into a sphere of the impossible."³ Thirty-one years later, having through his success outgrown his awe for the impossible legacy of his master, Verne was completing his sequel to *The Narrative of Arthur Gordon Pym*, published in France as *Le Sphinx des Glaces* (*The Sphinx of the Ice-fields*).

Verne's *Twenty-thousand Leagues Under the Sea* is another work with significant antecedents directly traceable to a masterpiece of the American Renaissance: Herman Melville's *Moby-Dick*.⁴ As with Poe's novel, did Verne see in *Moby-Dick* the basis for a sequel? Both *Twenty-thousand Leagues Under the Sea* and *Moby-Dick* are set against the backdrop of the sea and the exotic forms it contains. Both works portray the odd circumstance of an educated gentleman and a super-human harpooner brought together to solve ineffable mysteries. Both works contain mad or near-mad captains obsessed with loathing, vengeance, and a quest for worldly justice. And both works feature a wonderful monster.

At the level of satire, the tenor of the first chapter of *Twenty-thousand Leagues Under the Sea* strikes directly at the heart of *Moby-Dick* for its inspiration. Readers of *Twenty-thousand Leagues Under the Sea* will remember that the year 1866 was marked by a series of strange events. These mysterious and inexplicable phenomena particularly agitated the maritime industry. "Merchants, common sailors, captains of vessels, skippers, both of Europe and America, naval officers of all countries, and the governments of states on both sides of the Atlantic were deeply interested in the matter."⁵ No one was quite aware of the very first sighting, but suddenly ships from all over the Atlantic and Pacific oceans were reporting encounters with an object referred to with awe as "an enormous thing." It was long, spindle-shaped, occasionally phosphorescent, and infinitely larger and more rapid in its movements than a whale. Initial reports varied on the size of the object, but as the frequency of sightings increased it was determined the object was approximately 350 feet long, far surpassing the dimensions of any whales admitted to by the ichthyologists of the day. Was it then a shifting reef? Might it be a moving sand bar? But the evidence indicated this thing could transport itself rapidly over vast distances; in one instance over seven hundred nautical leagues in three days. A fantastic collision with the monster was reported, leading to a very precise and methodical memorandum directed by the officers of the French frigate *Normandy*. Then a similarly accurate survey of the phenomenon was made by the staff of Commodore Fitz-James aboard the *Lord Clyde*, and "the question of the monster," as it came to be called, infected the public mind. "In every place of great resort the monster was the fashion. They sang of it in cafés, ridiculed it in the papers and represented it on the stage."[6] Politicians, bureaucrats, scientists, and even philologists joined the maritime community in the debate over the monster's nature and significance. The newspapers printed "caricatures of every gigantic and imaginary creature, from the white whale, the terrible 'Moby Dick' of hyperborean regions, to the immense Kracken whose tentacles could entangle a ship of five-hundred tons, and drag it into the dark abyss of the ocean depths . . . Controversy burst forth between the credulous and the incredulous in the societies of savants and scientific journals."[7] Finally, Verne reports, satirical writers seized upon "the question of the monster," and entreated their learned contemporaries not to admit to "the existence of Krackens, sea serpents, 'Moby Dicks,' and other lucubrations of delirious sailors."

The controversies surrounding the "question of the monster" described in the first chapter of *Twenty-thousand Leagues Under the Sea* suggest a parody of the controversies surrounding the multitude of representations of the whale juxtaposed in Melville's scholarship and imagination. The introductory section to *Moby-Dick* entitled "Extracts" comprising copious, odd, arbitrary and random allusions to whales embodies the divergent points of view on, if you will, the "question of the monster." Throughout *Moby-Dick* Melville delights in illuminating this controversy as he explores the many differing points of view people hold concerning whale anatomy, whale taxonomy, legalistic particulars of whale ownership, whales as depicted in art, whales as conceived by Christian and cannibal theologians, the etymology of the word "whale," even the psychology and personalities of whales. Contributing his own energies toward this effort and bringing to bear the considerable experience and expertise of a seasoned whaleman, Melville himself examines and probes into the whale from every conceivable vantage point. He criticizes artists' renderings of it, looks for its form in mountains and in stellar constellations, attempts to rationally define and classify it, chases it, harpoons it, eats it, examines its head phrenologically, dissects it, measures its skeleton, boils it down, and even cuts off its foreskin, which, after sartorial alterations, he triumphantly wears like a raincoat.

But along with the satirists Verne describes in the first chapter of *Twenty-thousand Leagues Under the Sea*, would Melville go so far as to admit his white whale, or even the novel *Moby-Dick* itself, to be a mere figment of delirious lucubration? Or is *Moby-Dick*, both novel and whale, even more monstrous for being this lucubratory figment, an awful articulated conglomeration of imaginative swagger, black bile, and what could only be an egomaniac's standard of scholarly attainment?

In chapter 7 of *Twenty-thousand Leagues Under the Sea*, entitled "An Unknown Species of Whale," Professor Aronnax, his servant, Conseil, and the harpooner, Ned Land, finally not only meet with but also *tred upon* the monster. To their surprise they find that it is made of riveted steel plates. Professor Aronnax discovers perhaps what Melville suspected about his own monster. Aronnax says, "There was no doubt about it! This monster, this natural phenomenon that had puzzled the learned world, and overthrown and misled the imagination of seamen of both hemispheres, was, it must be owned, a still more astonishing phenomenon, in as much as it was a simply human construction."[8]

In chapter 35 of *Moby-Dick*, "The Mast Head," Melville makes an innocuous but significant assertion about the denomination of human inventions. His topic is Captain Sleet's recent invention, the Crow's Nest. Melville says: "He called it the *Sleet's Crow's-nest*, in honor of himself; he being the original inventor and patentee, and free from all ridiculous false delicacy, and holding that if we call our own children after our names (we fathers being the original inventors and patentees), so likewise should we denominate after ourselves any other apparatus we may beget."[9] It should be noted that Melville adhered pretty closely to this principle throughout his writing career. Each of Melville's works is indeed named after himself. *Typee* is Melville as Marquesian cannibal. *Omoo*, Polynesian for "wanderer," is Melville as beachcomber in Tahiti. *Mardi*, a mythic island archipelago, is the constellation of philosophical and artistic ideals that comprise Melville's imagination. *Redburn* is Melville as a young destitute gentleman trying his hand at the merchant service. *White Jacket* is Melville as a conscientious individual coming to terms with his alienation and abhorrence at the evils of the authoritarian world of a man-of-war. *Pierre* is Melville as a naive and alienated romantic artist coming to terms with his own sexuality and the dynamics and expectations of the American aristocracy. "Bartleby the Scrivner" is Melville as frustrated artist coming to terms with the demands of the market place, the tedium of writing, and the amusing, liberating, but terrifying voice that says "I would prefer not to." "Benito Cereno" is Melville as bound, muzzled, and deposed captain unable to decry the barbarians around him. *Israel Potter* is Melville as prototypic Jeffersonian yeoman surrounded by his Revolutionary War counterparts: Benjamin Franklin, the shrewd and cunning organizer; Ethan Allan, the Rousseauean noble savage in white skin; John Paul Jones, the ruthless egocentric warrior with his corollaries, Alexander Selkirk and Juan Fernandez. *The Confidence-Man* is Melville as metaphysical masquerader and literary slight-of-hand artist. *Clarel* is Melville as pilgrim seeking his lost faith in the Holy Land. *Billy Budd* is Melville as a balance of self-destructive naiveté, human innocence, and avatar of the Prince of Peace. And of course *Moby-Dick* is Melville as ineffable mystery, the sum total of metaphysical questions about himself and the universe which will not bear scrutiny or explanation. And in this scheme Ahab is the will to force an answer to these mysteries, to the point of forming them into a tangible entity, into a monster. Ahab is the archetypical monster maker.

Melville's solution to the "problem of the monster" lies in his understanding or his realization that people are the creators of their own monsters. Although veiled in lyrical rhetoric, schoolboy parodies, working class posturing, and aristocratic condescensions, the novel *Moby-Dick* yet very neatly if not systematically explores the role of semantics and epistemology in the genealogy of human belief systems. In *Moby-Dick* Melville explores the role and effects of semantic and epistemological issues on the problem of human mythologies, rituals, and institutions.

In all its variations and permutations, only one thing has happened in human history: the reification and institutionalization through language and symbols of mythological explanations of the world. The interaction of these mythological explanations forms the dialectic which is, so to speak, the "question of the monster" that occupies the world in the beginning of *Twenty-thousand Leagues Under the Sea*, and comprises the scholarship throughout *Moby-Dick*. William Blake very clearly describes the dynamics of this phenomenon in *The Marriage of Heaven and Hell*:

5: THE QUESTION OF THE MONSTER

> The ancient poets animated all sensible objects with Gods or Geniuses, calling them by the names and adorning them with the properties of woods, rivers, mountains, lakes, cities, nations, and whatever their enlarged & numerous senses could perceive.
>
> And particularly they studied the genius of each city & country, placing it under its mental deity.
>
> Till a system was formed, which some took advantage of & enslav'd the vulgar by attempting to realize or abstract the mental deities from their objects; thus began priesthood.
>
> Choosing forms of worship from poetic tales.
>
> And at length they pronounced that the Gods had ordered such things.
>
> Thus men forgot that all deities reside in the human breast.[10]

For Blakes' ancient poets, myth and archetypes were descriptive tools used to investigate and describe the world around them. As time passed, the ancient poets' understanding of the world became more sophisticated, and the language they used to express this understanding also became more sophisticated, and more abstract. Blake describes how these mytho-poetic systems evolved into orthodox religions, but this evolution might be looked at another way as well, where what has happened is that the ancient poets were, so to speak, taken over by their own tools; the tools subjugated their masters.

The theme of humanity being taken over by its own tools is explored in Stanley Kubrick's famous film, *2001: A Space Odyssey*. The mysterious black monolith in the film has been identified as a symbol for many things: God, Christ, Original Sin, the Tree of Knowledge, the Call of Evolution. What I propose is that it is a symbol of symbols, or, more specifically, a symbol of our ability to use symbols like tools. The monolith is a symbol of our ability to think symbolically, in terms of archetypes; it is a symbol of our ability to manipulate abstractions. *Space Odyssey* explores many themes, the struggle for survival and supremacy, the triumph of corporate social organization, the conquest of space . . . but the unifying theme in the film is that of our relationship with our tools, and at the climax of the great conflict in the film, the showdown between HAL the computer and the astronaut David Bowman, Kubrick prophesies an apocalypse in which humanity must confront and overthrow the very tools we have created. The greatest tool we employ, of course, is our language, our abstract manipulation of the poetic myths and archetypes we use to understand and manipulate the world. Kubrick warns us, and we should do well to heed him, that we have to keep our tools under control, or they will seek to control us. These tools include the archetypes and myths that make up our world view and our identities.

Like Kubrick, Milton has provided us with a sort of technical knowledge that will help us to keep our tools under control. Milton in this sense is the modern purveyor of the poetics I call "Transformational Mythology." Mythological archetypes are transformational. Their significance changes depending upon how they are viewed, in relation to the altering dynamics of the myth they arise from, and in relation to the altering context in which the myth is read. An example of this transformational pattern in *Paradise Lost* can be found in the images of the fallen angels in the first book, where early they appear to be noble heroes of colossal proportions, but at the end are compared to puny bees swarming chaotically about a hive. A more intriguing example comes at the juncture of the second and third books. The second book closes with Satan emerging from chaos to gaze across the empty deeps of space where in the distance glimmer the gold and sapphire lights of Heaven and God's creation. Then at the beginning of the third book a comparative transformation has occurred as Milton describes himself peering through the night of his blindness to glimpse the inspiration that illuminates his poem. Milton thus finds recompense within the curse of darkness. For Blake, the moral—or human—correlative to this process of poetic transformation is the forgiveness of sins.

Building upon these poetics Blake sketches a dichotomy between two forms of scholarship, what he calls the Greek and Roman model as opposed to the Hebraic model. The Greek and Roman model embraces the dialectics of memory, orthodoxy, the arbitrary dictatorship of scholasticism, and, as Eric Auerbach suggests, seeks to establish and *express* reality. The Hebraic model embraces the dialectics of inspiration, the evolution of beliefs, the humanism of poetry, and, rather than expressing reality, seeks to *suggest* reality. The Greek and Roman model is based on Aristotelian and formalistic analysis which requires fundamental or "atomic" categories upon which to base its deductions. The Greek and Roman dialectic is thus fixed and cumulative, and only revisable through institutional upheaval—which explains why Blake called the Greeks and Romans "silly slaves of the sword" and declaimed "The classics, it is the classics! & not Goths or Monks, that Desolate Europe with Wars."[11] The Hebraic model is a process of continually revising these fundamental or atomic categories. This is seen in *Ezekiel* and *Revelation* where myths and imagery are revaluated, reprocessed, re-deemed, and recast into ever newer and evolving forms. In the Hebraic dialectic myths are subject to the vision and intentions of the poet. In the Greek and Roman dialectic, officers within the theocracy are subject to the mandates and standards of the myths which form and justify their institutions.

Twenty-thousand Leagues Under the Sea can be seen in this respect as a Hebraic recasting of *Moby-Dick*. Verne's mind is charged with Melville's images and his imagination has been illuminated by the example of Melville's inspiration. Verne's task as a poet in *Twenty-thousand Leagues Under the Sea* is to rework Melville's images and recast them in the forms dictated by the continuation of this inspiration. In Blakean terms, the continua of this inspiration is Christ. The ever evolving expression of this inspiration—the transformations, say, between Melville's images and those same images reworked by Verne, are inspired knowledge or gnosis. It may be that Ishmael survived the wreck of the *Pequod* and "the sharks, which glided by as if with padlocks on their mouths" (*MD* 573), because he had discovered this gnosis within himself. Ishmael rejects Ahab's mythologies, and returns to land to recast them.

Verne seizes upon this gnosis and rapidly, though not as rigorously as Melville, sets down his own new forms for Melville's icons.

Ahab makes Moby Dick a monster:

> All that most maddens and torments; all that stirs up the lees of things; all truth with malice in it; all that cracks the sinews and cakes the brain; all the subtle demonisms of life and thought; all evil, to crazy Ahab, were visibly personified, and made practically assailable in Moby Dick. He piled upon the whale's white hump the sum of all the general rage and hate felt by his whole race from Adam down; and then, as if his chest had been a mortar, he burst his hot heart's shell upon it. (*MD* 184)

However, as Ray Bradbury points out in his introduction to the Signet Edition of *Twenty-thousand Leagues Under the Sea*:

> Captain Nemo instead creates a symbol of the deep, a manifestation of God's huge wonders, submersible, long-ranging, capably destructive, submissive to Nemo's commands. Nemo will course the oceans in his monster, to spread a more personal and therefore more constructive terror in the world. Nemo will not run after Moby Dick. He will rear him whole and live in his belly and be the mystery himself.
>
> In sum Nemo skins together and rivets tight the very symbol most feared and whispered of by Ahab's mind and Ahab's crew. Casting aside any doubts, precluding any inhibitions, Nemo intrudes to the monster's marrow, disinhabits mysticism, evicts terrors like so much trash, and pro-

ceeds to police the universe beneath, setting it to rights, harvesting its strange crops, be they animal, vegetable, or mineral-gold from sunken . . . ships to be distributed to the worlds needy.[12]

Verne's solution then is to set aside his fear, examine the monster, and identify his own role within it. Ishmael says as much early in *Moby-Dick:* "Not ignoring what is good, I am quick to perceive a horror, and could be social with it—would they let me—since it is but well to be on friendly terms with all the inmates of the place one lodges in" (*MD* 7). Of all the monstrosities we lodge with, *Moby-Dick* entreats us to be on friendly terms with what can sometimes be the most horrible inmate of all—ourselves. To this end, Melville offers the metaphor of a monster within us. For Verne, we are in the monster.

The question of monstrosity can be closely tied to the production of texts, with the idea of monstrosity and text closely parallel to each other. As Ahab makes Moby Dick a monster, so he makes the text a monster. This notion of text-as-monster has significant roots in the scientific revolution of the late Renaissance. It is convenient to identify its philosophical formulation in the eighth chapter of the second book of the *Essay Concerning Human Understanding*, where Locke elaborates the notion that the apprehension of light and colors are only ideas of the mind and have no external existence in the physical world. In the argument developing here, monsters are a product of the imagination. In poetry, it is surely Milton who has penned the most famous expression of this idea:

> The mind is its own place, and in itself
> Can make a Heaven of Hell, a Hell of Heaven.

Before embracing the idea out of hand, however, the careful student would do well to consider that Milton puts these words in the mouth of Satan. But to continue: Locke's notion is central to Addison's understanding of the creation of monsters, where monstrous birth is the result of unnatural mixtures. In the creation of texts, a monstrous text will result from the unnatural combination of disparate ideas. Shakespeare plays on this notion in *The Winter's Tale* where it is asserted "This is an art / Which does mend nature, change it rather, but/The art itself is nature" (4. 4. 111–13). That is to say, nature prohibits combinations which produce prodigies. But when nature allows these combinations, then they are natural. The implications of this formulation might be inferred from Walpole's comments on the creation of his

Castle of Otranto where he describes his work in terms of an experiment in which he combined elements of ancient romance (imagination and improbability) with modern romance (a conscious intention to copy nature). The result is a fiction in which characters react "naturally" to inventive and fanciful (and impossible) circumstances. Walpole confesses that this invention was borrowed from Shakespeare. Of course the most famous literary monster maker is Mary Shelley, who in the preface to the Standard Novels Edition of 1831 refers to *Frankenstein* as "my hideous progeny." Barbara Johnson has suggested, "*Frankenstein* is the story of the experience of writing *Frankenstein*."[13] I suggest "monstrosity" in *Frankenstein* is the act on the part of Victor and the monster of dismissing their humanity and instead embracing the senses, the elements of nature that act on those senses, and an empirical, linear apprehension of time as it is perceived through memory. In *Frankenstein, or the Modern Prometheus* we see this radical interpretation of Locke's principles triumph as an essential plank of Romantic epistemology (and, interestingly enough, this emphasis is not far removed from the basis of German metaphysics or contemporary radical cultural relativism). The radical emphasis upon sense data is the fire brought to earth, as it were, by the "Modern Prometheus." And this fire was brought across the Atlantic to find further refinement—indeed, ultra-refinement when combined with the deep-seated puritanism of American literature which, whether it be in sympathy or reaction, was an important theme in any literary admixture. Surely Emerson looked over the sharp edge into the abyss of relativistic epistemology and realized how the "first person" was so important in rhetoric and yet so monstrous. Robert D. Richardson quotes a line that points to the essence of Emerson's revelation: "It is awful," says Emerson, "to look into the mind of man and see how free we are."[14] Indeed, according to the reading explored here, Melville built the great American novel on this theme. It is to Verne's credit that he could so painlessly grapple with this "monster" and introduce a guiding clarity into a discussion ("the question of the monster") which occupied literature and philosophy since Shakespeare and Locke. Indeed, Verne's solution—a combination of social activism, Byronic heroics and machine-age optimism—has dominated the positive face of Romantic discourse to the present day.

Where Ahab makes the text a monster, Nemo makes the text a machine that looks like a monster. Ahab uses the text to frighten the world for evil purposes while Nemo uses the text to terrorize the world for progressive purposes. It is interesting to note that while he shares profound affinities with the captain of the *Nautilus*, Professor Aronnax, the "narrator," firmly rejects Nemo's program of terror, and (harkening back to Blake) witnesses how Nemo's ruin is brought about by his inability to find forgiveness in his heart.

Verne shows us how we might take up the mantle of Jonah, enter the monster, and exploit the experience to positive ends. Verne—following after the pattern set by Melville—accomplishes this task by transforming prodigy into parody. And perhaps this is the solution to the "question du monstre"?

Postscript

The philosophical origins of this monstrosity are worth enlarging upon.

British philosophy divides into two traditions which Jane Austen has been kind enough to name for us: the tradition of *Sense* and the tradition of *Sensibility*. The table at the end of this chapter depicts these two traditions in juxtaposition, with authors representing common sense on the right, and authors representing sensibility on the left. The tradition of common sense might also be called the humanist tradition, while such words as *scholastic, empirical* and *ideological* are apt cognomens for the tradition of sensibility. Setting aside Bacon (who straddles both traditions), it is useful to think of Locke as the origin of the tradition of sensibility in British (and European) philosophy. It is one of the striking ironies of philosophy that Locke's empiricism became the parent of idealism. Indeed, it is tempting (and usually correct) to identify empiricism as an expression of idealism. The left column in the table traces the evolution of idealism, beginning with Locke's reification and objectification of such notions as *mind* and *matter*. By divorcing such words as "mind" and "matter" from the contexts in which they occur in every day language, Locke sets the philosophical stage for the mechanization and dehumanization of the human self concept, so that in a hundred years time William Godwin was contextualizing human experience within a sensual, quasi-solipsism that recognized strict materialistic and determinist principles, which, on one hand, yielded a vision of man as a biochemical machine, and, on the other, promoted an anarchistic and utilitarian political ethos that anticipated Hegel and Marx, and which plunged Europe into the ensuing two hundred years of radical national and class identifications, bloody revolutions, and mechanized conflicts. Mary Shelley encapsulates Godwin's utilitarian principles in *Frankenstein* when Victor says, "If our impulses were confined to hunger, thirst, and desire, we might be nearly free."[15]

5: THE QUESTION OF THE MONSTER

Traveling through Europe in the wake of the ideological revolutions that had been championed by their father/father-in-law, the Shelleys saw the grisly implications of the Promethean fire that had been touched off by Locke: The idealization, the theorization, and the mechanization of the world brings destruction, chaos, and dystopia. Here then, the notion of the monster is sown in the late-romantic imagination. And hence, at the heart of Mary Shelley's novel, we have Victor Frankenstein's monster describing his self-realization in strictly Lockean terms, with waves of sensations building upon one another and culminating in a horrified, pained, and hateful consciousness that rivals Milton's Satan as an articulation of despair, tragedy, and evil.

As she so aptly named the two major divisions in British philosophy, perhaps we might also look to Jane Austen for a solution to this question of the monster, which looms so frightfully at the line of ideological demarcation between sense and sensibility. In *Northanger Abbey* we find this solution, whereby Catherine Moreland's enthusiasm for novels becomes a satirical allegory for the scientific enthusiasms of the great philosophers of the eighteenth and nineteenth centuries. It is a devastating comparison. On the one hand we have a silly seventeen-year-old girl moonstruck by her reading in gothic romance novels; on the other hand, bombastic Kants, Hegels, Nietzsches, and Marxes constructing *a priori* dungeons with thunderbolts and hammers, while the cold wind of a hollow and amoral universe whistles a diabolic tune in their ears. Not that Catherine doesn't encounter monsters—for example, the grasping, opportunistic Thorpes, or the not-any-less opportunistic General Tilney. But where our philosophers require new metaphysics and awesome revolutions of consciousness and nation-state to solve their problems, Catherine gets by with the common sense advise of her mother and father—and, I should be happy to point out, with far more impressive results.

Sensibility

Francis Bacon,
Novum Organum (1608–20)
The New Atlantis (1624)

Sir Isaac Newton
Philosophiae Naturalis Principia Mathematica (1687)

John Locke
Essay Concerning Human Understanding (1690)
Two Treatises of Government (1690)
- All knowledge comes from experience and through our senses. We know nothing but matter. Thus matter is the material of mind.

Bishop George Berkeley
An Essay towards a New Theory of Vision (1709)
- Matter does not exist except as a form of mind. Matter is not the object of perceptions. Matter is a bundle of perceptions. We don't know matter, we know only sensations. Thus matter is a mental condition. The only reality we have direct knowledge of is mind. Thus matter is a form of the mind.

David Hume
Treatise on Human Nature (1739–40)
An Inquiry Concerning Human Understanding (1748)
- There is no such thing as "mind"; we never perceive any such entity as the "mind"; rather what we perceive is merely separate ideas, memories, feelings, smells, etc. There is no such thing as mind.

Sense

Robert Burton
The Anatomy of Melancholy (1651)

Jonathan Swift
A Tale of a Tub (1704)
Gulliver's Travels (1726)

Alexander Pope
Essay on Criticism (1711)
The Dunciad (1728–43)
Essay on Man (1733–34)

Voltaire
Philosophic Letters on the English (1733–34)
Candide (1759)

Henry Fielding
Tom Jones (1749)

Samuel Johnson
The Vanity of Human Wishes (1749)
Rasselas (1759)

Laurence Sterne
Tristram Shandy (1760–67)

5: THE QUESTION OF THE MONSTER

Thomas Reid
Enquiry into the Human Mind on the Principles of Common Sense (1764)
- The senses give us direct contact with a mind-independent reality.

Tobias Smollett
Humphrey Clinker (1771)

William Blake
The Marriage of Heaven and Hell (1790)

Mary Wollstonecraft
A Vindication of the Rights of Woman (1792)

Mary Shelley
Frankenstein (1818)

Thomas Love Peacock
Nightmare Abbey (1818)

Jane Austen
Northanger Abbey (1818)

Lord Byron
Don Juan (1818–21)
The Vision of Judgement (1821)

- Natural laws and cause and effect: We don't observe cause and effect, but only sequence. (Wittgenstein will say the same thing [early phase].)

Now, skepticism and empiricism lead to Idealism: Ideas—mind-dependent entities—are the immediate objects of our perception, memory, and thought. Hence Kant and German Idealism, and Romanticism.

William Godwin
Enquiry Concerning Political Justice (1793)
- All types of society and government are corrupt because of vested interests and prejudices of class and nationality. In place of government Godwin proposed Anarchism founded on strict utilitarian and determinist principles.

Wordsworth: Preface to *Lyrical Ballads* (1800)
1) Poetry should ground itself in the primary and simple feelings of the common man. 2) Poetry should portray "Emotions recalled in tranquility."

Late 18th century Intellectual mythology: Transcendentalism, pantheism, scientism, nature worship; Rousseau and the idea of the noble savage; scientific/romantic notions of mind-body dualism, sensual materialism, the nobility of the common man, the nature and purpose of the state.

6
Grinding the Apophatic Axe

*M*OBY-DICK SCHOLARS CAN BE DIVIDED INTO THREE GROUPS OR CATEGOries. The first category is the "Seekers and Divers." Resembling the various characters in *Moby-Dick*, these scholars stare deeply into the mystery of the great whale—both the fish and the story—and report their astonishing findings. Their writings are like the yarns told by sailors newly returned from distant seas and barbarous shores. The Seekers and Divers report on Melville's themes, symbols, and ambiguities; the influence of poets such as Milton, Shakespeare, Hawthorne, Emerson, and Burton; Melville's early experimentation with modern artistic themes and techniques; Melville's biography and his views on issues ranging from transcendentalism to racism, from struggles with faith to the bitter realities of nature's cannibalism; and they catalog in a constant flow of volumes the countless allusions to myth, philosophy, science, religion, and history that Melville pours into his great novel. Hayford and Parker's *Moby-Dick as Doubloon: Essays and Extracts (1851–1970)* collects together a representative sample of the work of the Seekers and Divers.

The second group of *Moby-Dick* scholars follows more in the lines of a professionalized class of scribes—organized, disciplined, suggesting the intelligentsia depicted in Edward Bellamy's *Looking Backward*, who are dedicated to the firm and balanced administration of their small corner of what Bellamy fondly calls the "Industrial Army." These scholars are broadly recognized as the "New Historicists." Their emphasis is upon Melville's biography and the historical circumstances that drove, directed, and guided Melville as he fulfilled, to use Michel Foucault's term, the "author function." In her introduction to the Signet edition of *Moby-Dick*, Elizabeth Renker announces the current vogue of New Historical study in Melville: "*Moby-Dick* is indeed a powerful record of 'the times' on many levels."[1] Some of the New Historicists see Melville as a half-conscious critic of history, not fully aware of the Hegelian Punch-and-Judy show in which he is a bit

6: GRINDING THE APOPHATIC AXE

player, while in Samuel Otter's study, *Melville's Anatomies* we are presented with a Melville examining his own historicization. Otter makes Melville himself a New Historicist, "a Melville fascinated with the rhetorical structures and ideological functions of antebellum discourse."[2] Where the New Historicism becomes dubious is in the way it takes a work of art and reads it against immediate, localized, and rarefied backgrounds; the effect being to cut a work out of its larger historical context and mitigate the important human traditions a work vocalizes; so that in turn readers are cut off from their heritage, cut off from their own past.

In *Strike Through the Mask: Herman Melville and the Scene of Writing*, Elizabeth Renker elevates the New Historicist program to bizarre levels. The blurb on the back of the book neatly encapsulates the germ of her thesis: "Melville's frustrated encounter with the page—characterized by illegible handwriting, chronically bad spelling, and violent manipulations of the text—is the most important source of his work's drama and power." Renker remains unsatisfied by the argument that considers Melville's confrontation with the page to be "secondary in importance to his concern with the epistemological condition of humankind . . . because it fails to attend to the intense primacy for Melville of the particular surface that he stared at and labored over."[3] Apparently Renker has hit upon a usable alternative for fulfilling the tyrant's dream of burning undesirable books—she simply teaches people not to understand them.

In his essay "*Moby-Dick* as Revolution," John Bryant represents a kinder, gentler New Historicism, mixing the geniality of the Seekers and Divers with the solid orientations and responsible concerns of a serious cultural worker. According to Bryant, Melville "makes readers read in ways that politicize and radicalize."[4] *Moby-Dick* is a stage on which Melville can "perform and work out the nation's evolving political tensions over its inchoate national identity."[5] Without suggesting parody, Bryant claims that Melville is using Shakespearean forms to further the portrayal of these mid-nineteenth-century political tensions. "The real dramatization going on is not Ahab's histrionics but Melville's guerrilla theatrics of pulling us on stage and forcing us to enact Ishmael's and Ahab's conditions of love and fright."[6] *Moby-Dick* is thus a drama of "conflicting ideologies" reflecting an "age of revolution." Readers find themselves "revolving in and out of variant worlds—pitting Ahab's fears of nihility against Ishmael's faith, the politics of supremacy rooted in sterility against the politics of inclusion rooted in sexualized community, an ontology of self against other, and the rhetoric of Shakespearean theatrics against the poetics of transcendence."[7] Bryant places political theory at the center of Melville's imagination, contributing to the fiction of some unifying transcendental zeitgeist or radical defection as the focus of the American renaissance. The New Historicism is ingenious, but unfortunately fifty centuries of humanistic understanding are left out of the formula. Melville evidently has political concerns, and his work certainly has political implications, but his *activity* remains synoptic analysis. I don't challenge Bryant's basic contention that Melville explores revolutionary themes; where I disagree is in the characterization of Melville's orientation. For me, *Moby-Dick* is a revolt against stupidity. If Melville indeed cuts a radical figure, it is not following the sage forms of Hegel, Nietzsche, Heidegger, Bakhtin, Foucault, or whoever it is the New Historicists may have in mind. I should rather look for Melville in reflections of hard-nosed western liberalism such as Milton, Swift, Byron, Nabokov, or George Carlin.[8]

I call the third group of *Moby-Dick* scholars the "Readers of *Moby-Dick*." They have difficulty with the hermeneutic discipline of the New Historicists. Beyond a certain point they become uninterested in the detailed discoveries of the Seekers and Divers. Yet they do share the Seekers and Divers' enthusiasm for faraway seas and barbarous shores. Indeed, for many of them *Moby-Dick* isn't their favorite Melville book. They much prefer the wildness of *Typee*, or the free and easy lawlessness of *Omoo*; nor are they limited to Melville's works exclusively. They can follow a theme across oceans and continents, and in the consideration of Melville they may find Jules Verne, Mary Shelley, Thomas Love Peacock, or Jane Austen to be far more relevant to their investigations than the latest breakthroughs in Melville scholarship. And, indeed, as their experience with new authors grows they formulate serious reservations concerning the vast regimented industry that Melville scholarship represents. This is not to say that the Readers of *Moby-Dick* are reactionary or anti-intellectual; rather, they are serious about their open-mindedness, and in their reading they are ever on the alert to closures that might curb the liberalized expectations they have developed gazing down the open road of literature. These readers can be painters, musicians, sculptors, architects, poets, philosophers, graduate school dropouts, health care providers, voters, tax payers, concerned parents, social workers, sailors. They don't wish to read professionally prepared and refereed explanations of *Moby-Dick*. They possess an intuitive understanding that critical insight will not be found in the haughty reiteration of theoretical fashion but in the enlargement of literary ideas. In reading as in their own lives, they don't seek explanation but self-clarification.

Wittgenstein's views on Frazer present an apt illustration of what exactly the Readers of *Moby-Dick* are looking for in this novel. Wittgenstein was unsatisfied with Frazer's reading and conclusions regarding Frazer's own anthropological findings. Wittgenstein asserted that the human rituals Frazer cataloged went beyond the simple expedient of an empirical explanation, and that, indeed, *understanding* Frazer's discoveries does not require an empirical explanation. Frank Cioffi describes this in *Wittgenstein on Freud and Frazer*. "Whatever relevance empirical method may have to the question of the nature and origin of ritual practices . . . is not the central question which Frazer raises and is not, in any case, the question which arises for us when we contemplate human sacrifice and the ritual life of mankind."[9] Wittgenstein voices the same objection to psychoanalytic explanation. Again, according to Cioffi, "Freud advances explanations when the matters he deals with demand clarification, that is, they call for an elucidation of the relation in which we stand to the phenomena rather than an explanation of them."[10] Again, as to aesthetics, "causal hypotheses are conceptually inappropriate responses to requests for the explanation of aesthetic experiences and . . . they are not what we really want."[11]

Melville also makes this distinction in *Moby-Dick*. In *Moby-Dick*, Melville is rejecting scientific, philosophical and religious explanations in favor of what he really wants, which is a kind of self-understanding, or an understanding of how he stands in relation to scientific, religious, and philosophical phenomena.

Consider the following propositions:

> Methinks we have hugely mistaken this matter of Life and Death. Methinks that what they call my shadow here on earth is my true substance. Methinks that in looking at things spiritual, we are too much like oysters observing the sun through the water and thinking that thick water the thinnest of air. (*MD* 37)

The above trope, taken from an early chapter in *Moby-Dick*, embodies the three major thrusts of Ishmael's ontological polemic. Sentence by sentence, Ishmael is saying (i) our accumulated philosophical, scientific, and religious knowledge concerning ontology contains many errors and inaccuracies; (ii) our self-ness, our personalities, our living consciousness—our identities—are strictly material and extrinsic; (iii) the epistemological problems inherent to any investigation or speculation concerning "spiritual" issues prohibits any accurate formulations or conclusions.

Apparently Ishmael has dismissed philosophical inquiry into the nature of being. However, if Ishmael neatly dismisses such questions early in *Moby-Dick*, why then does he (along with Melville) go on to elaborate them—as well as a wide variety of philosophical questions—throughout the book? The answer is to be found in accurately characterizing the type of analysis Melville is conducting in the novel. Melville's criticisms in *Moby-Dick* concerning philosophical propositions superficially resemble an orientation having affinities with empiricism, deductive logic, skepticism, and the authority of science and law. At a variety of levels Melville's empirical and parodic analyses overturn the notion of the metaphysical, the nonmaterial, and the spiritual. Taken in the synoptic aggregate, however, these analyses themselves suggest a sort of super-metaphysics or even a surreality which Melville is interested in exploring. In this view Melville appears as some Janus-faced philosopher, presenting an unlikely combination of empiricism and mysticism, much like the combination of modern logic and scientific metaphysics Wittgenstein explored and overthrew in the *Tractatus*. It is compelling to speculate that Melville came to assume this station through his Keltic cultural antecedents which embrace irony in poetry, act rather than belief in religion, description (rather than empiricism) in science and philosophy, and ornate and patterned complexity in graphics and music. Notwithstanding these wonderful antecedents, however, an even more compelling formulation considers *Moby-Dick* as an expression of apophatic theology presented in the form of Menippean satire. *Moby-Dick*, however, builds upon the tradition in an ingenious fashion, insomuch as *Moby-Dick* is a Menippean satire in search of itself. Herein lies the fiery hunt. *Moby-Dick*—successful even in its frustrations—is an essay of critical synoptics.

The central problem Melville addresses with his analysis is the nature of human creativity. The particulars of art, philosophy, science, and religion are created to satisfy human needs. Creative and imaginative activity are normally healthy processes. However, as in the case of Ahab's monomania, human creativity can sometimes go awry and take on demonological aspects. Among the worlds portrayed in *Moby-Dick* is a psychological landscape ravaged by the ever-unfolding capriciousness of Queen Mab, who comes, as Mercutio tells us:

> Drawn with a team of little atomies
> Athwart men's noses as they sleep. (1.4.)

Even the mystical undertones of Ishmael's hard-nosed empiricism, when elevated to an orthodoxy, can entail a demonological danger. The keen introspective empiricism which moves Ishmael to say his "shadow here on earth is [his] true substance" produces an illusion of some introspective consciousness divorced from materiality. The offspring of this paradoxical illusion is both a source of terror and a source of comfort for the self-destructive young whaleman. In his acceptance of materiality he is divorced from materiality. He becomes reckless and ecstatic in his freedom:

> Methinks my body is but the lees of my better being. In fact take my body who will, take it I say, it is not me. And therefore three cheers for Nantucket; and come a stove boat and stove body when they will, for stave my soul, Jove himself cannot. (*MD* 37)

The reasons Melville felt compelled to conduct synoptic analyses and pursue intellectual mythology are too complex to enter upon here. However, the question of how Melville chose satire as his intellectual vehicle leads to important insights. Why, indeed, did Melville write satire? In light of Melville's particular status, that of a novelist, satire might have been the only mode open to him to investigate and express his desire to purge the world of intellectual mythology—a mad desire, he might have playfully thought, akin to Ahab's drive to kill the white whale. The question might be asked why Melville didn't give up his writing career and frame his notions concerning intellectual mythology in the form of a dissertation and pursue a tenured academic position, as most people would do? In light of his "artistic" temperament this was perhaps the least of Melville's considerations. Indeed, as far as the book-buying public is concerned, the threads of relation extending between satire and the "real world" are far more numerous than those extending from an academic treatise (notwithstanding how brilliant and earnest that treatise might be). Also, in terms of intellectual freedom, "Melville the thirty-three year old satirist" sits in a position superior to any conceivable position he might occupy as "Melville the thirty-three year old academic." But perhaps a more crucial reason for writing satire was due to the fact that Melville was in debt to his publisher. In order to recoup his losses, Melville's publisher *had* to publish whatever the author chose to give him. At the same time, Melville wanted to draw this relationship out as long as possible in order to sustain the career of a scribbling intellectual. He was motivated to *sell* his synoptic analyses. It was necessary for him to be convincing at a level which is seldom encountered in other forms of discourse where this motivation is lacking. Rather than addressing an academy, a ladies' club or a group of dilettantes, Melville was making bold to present his arguments before the grand inquisition of the human race. Satire is the argumentative language of the human race. Satire afforded Melville a tool that was economically viable, popular, and amusing. Satire equipped Melville to de-mythologize science, philosophy, and religion to his heart's content.

The critique of science in *Moby-Dick* is perhaps most overt in the "cetology" chapter. What do we know about whales? What can we know about them? To what extent can we express this knowledge? These are the questions Melville uses as paradigms for the problems inherent to scientific inquiry on any subject. In the "cetology" chapter, Melville begins his inquiry by quoting several authorities in the study of whales, all of whom attest to the difficulty inherent to the study of their subject. Whales, because of their location, are difficult to study. Because of the incomplete and confused knowledge concerning whales, they are not to be easily divided and cataloged within taxonomic systems. Further problems exist in the mere definition of what a whale is. In his characteristic tongue-in-cheek tone, Melville suggests that "a whale is *a spouting fish with a horizontal tail*" (*MD* 137). From this axiomatic definition Melville supposititiously proceeds to the taxonomic problem, classifying whales, according to magnitude, as Folio whales, Octavo whales, and Duodecimo whales. The image of designating large books for the larger whales, medium-sized books for the medium-sized whales, and small-sized books for the smallest whales is funny because it combines terms from the business of book making with the subject that, so to speak, keeps the book business afloat; the business of book making becomes the mythological source for the terms which express the "scientific" topic of those books. The moral is that systems of taxonomic nomenclature are arbitrary, and in some cases exist only to fill up books—which are often only puffed-up market commodities. Systems of taxonomic nomenclature can serve to contrast the distinguishable characteristics of phenomena, but what really do they say about whales in, for instance, an existential sense? Do taxonomic systems accurately represent whales or fully explain what whales are from, for instance, a whale's own perspective? Do taxonomic systems tell us those ineffable things about whales, beyond sense, that we really want to know? And even once taxonomic order is established, the question of what and why we want to know about whales remains. The resolution of these problems lies in the wisdom of the synoptic overview. Those questions whose answers lie "beyond sense" are nonsense. They are questions rooted in conceptual confusion, in the idols of the cave and marketplace, and in our misuse of language. As synoptic analysis demonstrates, there is nothing beyond sense, excepting only nonsense.

In chapters 55 and 56, respectively "Of the Monstrous Pictures of Whales" and "Of the Less Erroneous Pictures of Whales, And the True Pictures of Whaling Scenes," Melville further sharpens his assertion that we cannot know the whale. He points to the numerous inaccurate representations made by people throughout history. That these representations are inaccurate is not surprising:

> The living whale, in his full majesty and significance, is only to be seen at sea in unfathomable waters; and afloat the vast bulk of him is out of sight, like a launched line-of-battle ship; and out of that element it is a thing eternally impossible for mortal man to hoist him bodily into the air, so as to preserve all his mighty swells and undulations. And, not to speak of the highly presumable difference of contour between a young sucking whale and full-grown Platonic Leviathan; yet, even in the case of one of those young sucking whales hoisted to a ship's deck, such is then the outlandish, eel-like, limbered, varying shape of him, that his precise expression the devil himself could not catch. (*MD* 263)

This inaccuracy of representation is due not only to the inaccessibility of whales, but also to their protean nature. Like the universe they inhabit, whales are variable and particular. There is no Platonic absolute which characterizes them outside the mind's ability to trick itself with its own expressive tools, and transform conjecture and myth into intellectual orthodoxy. In chapter 55 Melville explores how the medium and techniques we use to represent scientific ideas can lead to conceptual confusion that adversely affects our scientific understanding. Melville underscores how the imprecise use of language and images can confuse our understanding of the world around us. In chapter 56 Melville offers a criterion for accuracy. Rather than seeking accuracy in the images themselves, Melville suggests that the best images of whales are those that are placed in the representation of a living context:

> "[Scoresby] has but one picture of whaling scenes, and this is a sad deficiency, because it is by such pictures only, when at all well done, that you can derive anything like a truthful idea of the living whale as seen by his living hunters." (*MD* 264)

A picture of a whale in water is obviously more accurate than a whale out of water. The difference between a whale in and out of its living context is like the difference between a still photograph and a cinema film. By taking the whale's living context into consideration, the accuracy of the representation is enhanced, broadened, and deepened. In addition to obvious environmental implications, Melville's emphasis on the relationship between a living being and the living context of which it is a part underscores the remarkable ductility of synoptic analysis, as next in chapter 57, "Of Whales in Paint; in Teeth; in Wood; in Sheet-iron; in Stone; in Mountains; in Stars," Melville pursues the theme of monstrous representation further by considering the human desire to create such images. With characteristically sportive and facetious humor, Melville shows how our passion to create leads us to overlook and accept the inaccuracies evident in these images, implying that our creative instincts and our capacity to accept conceptual confusion are complementary. In a metaphor that ranges across art, science, philosophy, and religion, Melville sees an underlying barbarism that, ironically, is the seat of our most sanctified aspirations.

In *Moby-Dick* Melville thoroughly anatomizes the whale. He looks at pictures of it, defines and classifies it, chases it, harpoons it, dissects it, makes a raincoat of its foreskin, examines its head in Lockean and Kantean terms, smells it, tastes it, measures its skeleton, and boils it down. He even reads about it at the library. However, and he is wont to do so, he never presents us with a "whale."

Melville's critique of science and the epistemological problems inherent to it are neatly buttressed by whimsical tropes which suggest the absurdities which plague reasonable and informed inquiry. In one instance Melville even suggests manipulating the whale's head phrenologically. The error Melville illustrates in these passages is the ignorance people have of the creative potential of their own minds. Without knowing what they are doing, people superstitiously apply science to unscientific problems or, indeed, problems which are themselves merely belief creations. Science then ceases to be a subdued rational inquiry and becomes a code or incantation for joining the human "mind" to the universe. This error is embraced by Ahab whose ultimate science is a megalomaniacal infatuation with a mythic universe he deems real. Ahab says

> "O Nature, and O soul of man! How far beyond all utterance are your linked analogies? not the smallest atom stirs or lives in matter, but has its cunning duplicate in mind." (*MD* 312)

6: GRINDING THE APOPHATIC AXE 123

Melville's critique of science in *Moby-Dick* is for the most part wry and jocular. So is his critique of philosophy. Again, the same basic error is attacked. For Melville the dialectical consideration or intellectual entertaining of cosmic absolutes is unrealistic. He suggests that in their desire to plumb the unfathomable, metaphysicians must be flawed in some way. Ishmael says:

> So soon as I hear that such or such a man gives himself out for a philosopher, I conclude that, like the dyspeptic old woman, he must have "broken his digester." (*MD* 50)

It is an observation that Wittgenstein would certainly applaud.

When Tashtego is pulled from the sweet smelling interior of a sperm whale's head, Melville speculates upon such a death and likens it to the dark trap of philosophical idealism:

> How many, think ye, have likewise fallen into Plato's honey head, and sweetly perished there? (*MD* 344)

Melville's criticisms extend from the whimsical jest to the hysterical lampoon. Viewing the heads of a sperm and right whale hoisted over the stern of the *Pequod*, Ishmael is inspired to engage the reader directly:

> Can you catch the expression of the Sperm Whale's there? It is the same he died with, only some of the longer wrinkles in the forehead seem now faded away. I think his broad brow to be full of a prairie-like placidity, born of a speculative indifference as to death. But mark the other head's expression. See that amazing lower lip, pressed by accident against the vessel's side, so as firmly to embrace the jaw. Does not this whole head seem to speak of an enormous practical resolution in facing death? This Right Whale I take to have been a Stoic; the Sperm Whale, a Platonian, who might have taken up Spinoza in his later years. (*MD* 335)

It is evident that Melville's interest in philosophy is rather more precisely an interest in spoofing philosophy. Melville wonders how we could truly know anything about metaphysical realms or invisible ontological entities—be they constituents or coinhabitants of our bodies and our world. From where comes evidence of such phenomena beyond the confusion of our concepts, and in the faery capers and moonbeams of our imaginations? Our problems comprehending the ethereal are similar to our inability to comprehend the whale. The problem is not unlike conceptualizing the visual experience of whales, which have eyes staring out in opposite directions from either side of their heads. We simply aren't equipped to do it. Wittgenstein provides an interesting parallel in the notion of the talking lion. Even if a lion could talk we would be unable to converse with it because a lion's experience is so completely alien from our own. Still, could the exercising of the mind's eye through philosophical contemplation increase our awareness to the point of realizing such imponderables? Melville doesn't think so:

> Is it not curious that so vast a being as the whale should see the world through so small an eye, and hear the thunder through an ear which is smaller than a hare's? But if his eyes were broad as the lens of Herschel's great telescope; and his ears capacious as the porches of cathedrals; would that make him any longer of sight, or sharper of hearing? Not at all.—Why then do you try to "enlarge" your mind? Subtilize it. (*MD* 331)

Melville's appeal is to empiricism and epistemological common sense. But while Melville might urge his readers to "subtilize" their minds, the practice he engages in is more accurately termed *synoptic analysis*. His method consists of testing propositions by examining them in contexts where they will be revealed as either valid or nonsensical.

As with philosophy, in religion human beings create their own theological structures and landscapes. The theme of humans creating their own illusion-based myths and belief systems is crucial in *Moby-Dick*. The entire romance, the succession of its events is propagated through the catalyst (and the contexts) of myth, in particular those held by Captain Ahab. Our suspicion that their mythic systems destroyed the men of the *Pequod* becomes a moral lesson through the realization that these belief systems were phantasmagorical—mere creations of pitifully ignorant, superstitious, and (in the case of Ahab) insane minds. Herein lies the central tragedy of *Moby-Dick*. Ahab stands as the terrible exponent of this terrible problem. He is the dark side of the human capacity for creating beliefs. As Ishmael laments:

> God help thee, old man, thy thoughts have created a creature in thee; and he whose intense thinking thus makes him a Prometheus; a vulture feeds upon that heart for ever; that vulture the very creature he creates. (*MD* 202).

In chapter 69, "The Funeral," Melville introduces to his demonological notions the role played by random and catastrophic events in the formation of human belief systems. In this chapter the carcass of a dead whale is let go from the *Pequod*. Melville describes the corpse floating in the ocean. The image serves as the basis for a fascinating mediation:

> Desecrated as the body is, a vengeful ghost survives and hovers over it to scare. Espied by some timid man-of-war or blundering discovery-vessel from afar, when the distance obscuring the swarming fowls, nevertheless still shows the white mass floating in the sun, and the white spray heaving high against it; straightway the whale's unharming corpse, with trembling fingers is set down in the log—*shoals, rocks, and breakers hereabouts: beware!* And for years afterwards, perhaps, ships shun the place; leaping over it as silly sheep leap over a vacuum, because their leader originally leaped there when a stick was held. There's your law of precedents; there's your utility of traditions; there's the story of your obstinate survival of old beliefs never bottomed on the earth, and now not even hovering in the air! There's orthodoxy! (*MD* 309)

The demonological theme illuminating this observation has interesting archaeological correlatives. Here Melville's satire suggests the spiritual impoverishment of the ancient agricultural civilizations of Peru, Mexico, the Yucatan; and the river valleys of the Nile, the Indus, and the Euphrates. Melville's whale funeral evokes in particular the dry, demonological worldview of ancient Mesopotamia where gods are little more than stone idols to be placed in the temples of conquered cities, where the egotism of tyrants is the expression of Heaven's will, where the theme of loss, suffering, and lamentation is central to Man's spiritual experience, and where the memory of earthquake, flood, or military invasion encompasses the extent of the folk consciousness while comprising the mean and squalid prospectus of the national mythology.

The demonological aspects of unenlightened and orthodox religion often appear dreadful and awful. But Melville has the capacity to be "social" with a "horror." Again and again in *Moby Dick* Melville demonstrates the capacity to transform hopelessness into a source for wry and even spectacular amusement. The following example is satiric in the tradition of Swift. It reduces "civilized" ecclesiastical proceedings to the level of absurdity by clothing those proceedings in the costume of barbarism. In chapter 102, "A Bower in the Arsacides," Melville makes us party to a wonderful theological debate. Ishmael is in the process of measuring a whale's skeleton he discovered on a tropical island when suddenly he is beset by a horde of cannibal high priests:

"How now!" they shouted; "Dar'st thou measure this our god! That's for us." "Aye, priests—well, how long do ye make him, then?" But hereupon a fierce contest rose among them, concerning feet and inches; they cracked each other's sconces with their yardsticks—the great skull echoed—and seizing that lucky chance, I quickly concluded my own admeasurements. (*MD* 451)

Perhaps Melville's most interesting and provoking inquiry into the interrelationship between religion and the human proclivity for myth-making is found in the juxtaposition of chapter 9, "The Sermon," and chapter 10, "A Bosom Friend." Here Melville presents a series of synoptic overviews that underscore the relationship between meaning and context. In "The Sermon" Ishmael hears a powerful oration from a very passionate and pious Father Mapple. It is the story of Jonah's disobedience and repentance. The lesson of the sermon, "To preach the Truth to the face of falsehood!" (*MD* 48) is carried deep into the hearts of the congregation. The sermon is so powerful that the reader holds little doubt that Father Mapple's sermon reveals Melville's own profoundest belief.

But in the following chapter, "A Bosom Friend," Ishmael returns from his service to find Queequeg quietly and happily re-carving his little wooden idol, Yojo. Queequeg is "peering hard into its face and with a jack-knife gently whittling away at its nose, meanwhile humming to himself in his heathenish way" (*MD* 49). Just as Father Mapple has hewn his god with words so does Queequeg carve his god, Yojo, with a penknife. Later in the chapter Ishmael demonstrates his Christian piety by worshiping this very same Yojo:

> I was a good Christian; born and bred in the bosom of the infallible Presbyterian church. How then could I unite with this wild idolater in worshiping his piece of wood? But what is worship? thought I. Do you suppose now, Ishmael, that the magnanimous God of heaven and earth—pagans and all included—can possibly be jealous of an insignificant bit of black wood? Impossible! But what is worship?—to do the will of God—*that* is worship. And what is the will of God?—to do to my fellow man what I would have my fellow man to do to me—*that* is the will of God. Now, Queequeg is my fellow man. And what do I wish that this Queequeg would do to me? Why, unite with me in my particular Presbyterian form of worship. Consequently, I must then unite with him in his; ergo, I must turn idolater. So I kindled the shavings; helped prop up the innocent little idol; offered him burnt biscuit with Queequeg; salamed before him twice or thrice; kissed his nose; and that done, we undressed and went to bed, at peace with our consciences and all the world. (*MD* 52)

6: GRINDING THE APOPHATIC AXE

Viewing science, philosophy, and religion with circumspection, Melville suggests that satisfying the insatiable human appetite for illumination will rather be found in understanding the creative powers we possess as human beings. Through such knowledge we might see where we really stand in the cosmos, though this too can be a two-edged sword, itself representing a narrow formula exceeded by the larger set of exigencies represented in the human condition. The solution, such as it is, to the human condition will be found in our specific responses to particular scenarios.

Seeking general or abstract definitions of reality, like seeking such definitions in the greater cosmos or in other human beings, is a precarious enterprise. Such definitions are contextual, and when taken out of context they can be seen to be nonsensical—and hazardous. In chapter 96, "The Try-Works," Ishmael draws into himself, gazes hypnotically into the fire from the helm, and almost lets the ship reverse its course, putting the crew and ship into danger. Such perils are described in chapter 35, "The Mast-Head" where Melville warns of the dangers of succumbing to one's cosmic sensibilities while watching for whales from the top of a ship's mast:

> There is no life in thee, now, except that rocking life imparted by a gently rolling ship; by her, borrowed from the sea; by the sea, from the inscrutable tides of God. But while this sleep, this dream is on ye, move your foot or hand an inch, slip your hold at all; and your identity comes back in horror. Over Descartian vortices you hover. And perhaps, at mid-day, in the fairest weather, with one half-throttled shriek you drop through that transparent air into the summer sea, no more to rise for ever. Heed it well, ye Pantheists! (*MD* 159)

Absolute spiritual attainment and knowledge are not described in *Moby-Dick*. In fact, the argument of the novel indicates that an infusion of too much so-called "spirituality"—rather intellectual mythology—leads to destruction. The notion of a self-destroying epiphany is treated in chapters 35 and 93, "The Mast-Head" and "The Castaway." A similar epiphany might be gleaned from the end of the novel. Here, however, it is not spiritual enlightenment but a more specific comprehension of his context and his place within it that Ishmael discovers. Ishmael describes only sensuous details at the novel's end: a coffin, the sea, sharks, sea-hawks, and then the appearance of a ship, the *Rachel*, which rescues him. The only mystical innuendo is an effect of a prose style and the implementation of biblical allusions which are sublime chiefly in this: they are parodic. Melville's epilogue is sardonic, ironic, coy, playfully melodramatic, and Byronic in the best sense of facetious self-detachment and wonderful gentleness. The epilogue exhibits a quiet swagger. That Melville left out any descriptions of spiritual experience, other than "hints" of questionable experiences from other chapters, is significant to the art of the novel. The author is consistent in that he, after toppling various false belief systems, does not erect any false idols of his own. However, according to a generic Menippean reading, meaning might be pushed to a location "outside the text"—pushed from text to context, from pleasure to "texture"—where it resolves itself in quiet, but not necessarily private illumination. Such readings may be censored, but they cannot be regulated. Moreover, only synoptic analysis can adjudicate their validity.

By eschewing ontological speculation, Melville aspires to survey the material universe with thoroughness and precision. And he views this universe with circumspection. Consider Pip's experience alone and adrift on the ocean in chapter 93, "The Castaway:"

> The sea had jeeringly kept his finite body up, but drowned the infinite of his soul. Not drowned entirely, though. Rather carried down alive to wondrous depths, where strange shapes of the unwarped primal world glided to and fro before his passive eyes; and the miser-merman, Wisdom, revealed his hoarded heaps; and among the joyous, heartless, ever-juvenile eternities, Pip saw the multitudinous, God-omnipresent, coral insects, that out of the firmament of waters heaved the colossal orbs. He saw God's foot upon the treadle of the loom, and spoke it; and therefore his shipmates called him mad. So man's insanity is heaven's sense; and wandering from all mortal reason, man comes at least to that celestial thought, which, to reason, is absurd and frantic; and weal or woe, feels then uncompromised, indifferent as his God. (*MD* 414)

But Melville doesn't struggle against his indifferent universe, as does Ahab. Indeed, it might be said Ahab in his dark madness joins the indifference of the universe. It is Melville's strategy to confront the universe with a synoptic overview and express this confrontation in the terms of common sense and humor; and it is in these terms, in the medium of his jolly response where his metaphysical problems are resolved. In this way he can correctly appraise worldly peril, and—unlike Pip or Ahab—still hold on to his humanity and the quiet uniqueness of his breathing persona. The theological insights occasionally expressed by Queequeg pattern the process of this humorous strategy. On one occasion, after pulling his hand in the "nick of time" from the snapping jaws of a shark, the cannibal says: "Queequeg no care what god made him shark . . . wedder Fejee god or Nantucket god; but de god wat made shark must be one dam Ingin." (*MD* 302) According to an empirical reading, Melville here engages in a sort of macho horseplay with a frightening cosmic conception with gnostic affinities: the myth of a mad demiurge that created an imperfect "fallen" world inhabited by voracious monsters. But according to the synoptic reading, Melville here simply portrays an amusing mythopoetic remark made by a flamboyant harpooner who was almost bitten by a shark. The humor—and wisdom—in this passage lies in the synoptic reading.

A very powerful and also strangely humorous apophatic statement is to be found in chapter 54, "The Town-Ho's Story." In *Moby-Dick* Ishmael puts down the Town-Ho's story in exactly the same form as he told it to a group of Spanish companions at an inn in Lima. The story is about the role played by Moby Dick in exacting vengeance, the idea being that the white whale is an instrument of God, that God would use Moby Dick to punish evil men. The scenario Ishmael describes invites an allegorical interpretation as to the character of God's involvement in the world. The tenor of the story, and this in part explains the amazement of Ishmael's auditors, is the notion that God takes an active role in policing the world, actively pursues evil-doers and brings them to justice. In the story a sailor, Steelkilt, plots to murder Radney, a horribly abusive and evil mate. But Moby Dick intervenes and kills Radney, thus sparing Steelkilt from committing the damning deed himself. The story is moonshine, of course, a perfect example of that sort of leg-pulling characteristic of the Caledonians. When asked by his Spanish friends if he will swear to the authenticity of the story, Ishmael consents and orders someone to produce a priest and also a Bible that he may lay his hand upon it to confirm and guarantee his veracity. Standing in the moonlight, Ishmael swears to the story's authenticity, claiming that he has "seen and talked with Steelkilt since the death of Radney." This is a fib—Ishmael had learned the story from Tashtigo who, as Ishmael tells us at the beginning of the chapter, had mumbled the story in his sleep. Beyond, however, the humorous picture the chapter leaves us with—Ishmael entreating his companions to procure the largest Bible they can find—is the sobering realization that the universe is not so concerned with our affairs nor in the sort of way as we should like to believe: a perfect and very clever instance of Apophatic *via negativa*. Job's response to Zophar the Naamathite concerning the prosperity of the wicked also comes to mind (*Job* 20–21).

Moby-Dick contains a powerful critique of the dynamics of human belief. The combination of unconscious creativity and an orthodox network of social relationships within the context of a variable, dynamic, and catastrophic universe patterns the operation or presence of "evil" in the world. Synoptic analysis unveils the error in those belief systems which are to some extent determined or draw their character from this "evil." That is to say, these belief systems are myths rooted in conceptual confusion. The synoptic exploration and analysis of ontological and metaphysical propositions suggest that these propositions are not only contrived, but also serve to inhibit the cause of civilization and human happiness. These propositions assume the existence of worlds beyond sense. *Moby-Dick* demonstrates the inaccessibility, the nonexistence, and the unprofitability of these far-removed, indistinct, and alien realms.

7

Originals and Their Antecedents

Chapter 44 of *The Confidence-Man*, "IN WHICH THE LAST THREE WORDS Of The Last Chapter Are Made The Text Of Discourse, Which Will Be Sure Of Receiving More Or Less Attention From Those Readers Who Do Not Skip It," presents some difficulty in reading. Melville himself in the final paragraph calls the chapter a "dissertation" which he suggests is "prosy" and "smoky." A large measure of this difficulty involves Melville's vague use of the word "original." Melville's overt purpose in the chapter is to disabuse the reader of the belief that the cosmopolitan is, as several characters in the book suggest, "quite an original." Whether or not the cosmopolitan is an original is left for the reader to decide, but the concept of originality with all its diffuse meanings as it applies to literary characters, authors, law-givers, and religious leaders, poses important questions for Melville. By punning on the notion of "Originality," Melville embarks on a voyage of discovery where parody, philosophical conjecture, and "genial" equivocation underscore and embellish the experience of reading the novel. The purpose of Melville's smoky word play remains a matter for speculation—"Something further may follow of this Masquerade," says Melville at the end of the novel. However, an essay of the chapter can yield unequivocal insights as to Melville's identity as a satirist and the synoptic nature of his philosophy.

Ten years before the publication of *The Confidence-Man*, Edgar Allan Poe, writing on Hawthorne's *Twice-Told Tales* and *Mosses from an Old Manse*, grappled with and delineated the problem of "the original." Poe's review provides insight and background for Melville's thoughts on originality, and might possibly be a direct antecedent to the problematic chapter as well.

In developing his concepts of originality, Poe first draws a distinction between the truly original and that which is simply novel, idiosyncratic, and peculiar. This latter distinction is what Poe calls "literary originality:" "[T]he element of the literary originality is novelty." The reader's appreciation of literary originality "is the reader's sense of the new. Whatever gives [the reader] a new . . . and pleasurable emotion, he considers original, and who ever frequently gives him such emotion, he considers an original writer."[1] But this is not the true original, according to Poe, because peculiarity alone, continually sustained without variation, becomes repetitive and ceases to be original. When present, this persistence of novelty figures importantly in Poe's analysis of an artist:

> [T]he critic . . . who reads a single tale or essay by Hawthorne, may be justified in thinking him original, but the tone or manner or choice of subject, which induces in the critic the sense of the new . . . [must]—if not in a second tale, at least in a third and all subsequent ones—not only fail . . . [to induce the sense of the new, but actually] . . . bring about an . . . antagonistic impression. In concluding a volume, and more especially in concluding all the volumes of the author, the critic will abandon his first design of calling him 'original,' and content himself with styling him "peculiar."[2]

Critics who fail to draw this distinction, according to Poe, mistakenly label as original that which is actually novel. But the novel is insufficient. The end of fictitious composition being "pleasure," the best effect is "wrought . . . by shunning rather than seeking . . . absolute novelty." Literary originality "tasks and startles the intellect."[3] In addition, peculiar fictions are often allegorical or didactic, which, in combination with their uniform peculiarity, makes them unpopular. This is significant for Poe because, as he proceeds to demonstrate, popularity is a direct function of the true original.

While "[i]n great measure, to be peculiar is to be original[,] . . . true or commendable originality . . . implies not the uniform but the continuous peculiarity[,] . . . giving its own hue, its own character to everything it touches."[4] Furthermore, that which is truly original is "*self impelled to touch everything.*"[5] This true originality reveals itself by the triggering in the mind of the reader an impression of revelation, intellectual fruition, and joy:

> [T]rue originality . . . is that which, in bringing out the half-formed, the reluctant, or the unexpressed fancies of mankind, or in exciting the more delicate pulses of the heart's passion, or in giving birth to some universal sentiment or instinct in embryo, thus combines with the pleasurable effect of apparent novelty, [and produces] a real egoistic delight.[6]

A "reader . . . [confronted with a work of absolute novelty (the literary original)] . . . is excited but embarrassed, disturbed, in some degree even pained at his own wont of perception, at his own folly in not having hit upon the idea." But in the case of a work which is a true original, the reader's

> pleasure is doubled. He is filled with an intrinsic and extrinsic delight. He feels and intensely enjoys the seeming novelty of the thought, enjoys it as really novel, as absolutely original with the writer—and himself. They two, he fancies, have, alone of all men, thought thus. They two have, together, created this thing. Henceforward there is a bond of sympathy between them, a sympathy which irradiates every subsequent page of the book.[7]

Poe, "with some difficulty," admits to the existence of a species of writing which is "a lower degree of . . . the true original." He calls this lower species "the natural." "It has little external resemblance but strong internal affinity to the true original."[8] In encountering "the natural"

> we say to ourselves, not "how original this is!" [—literary originality—] nor 'here is an idea which I and the author have alone entertained' [—true original—] but 'here is a charmingly obvious fancy,' or sometimes even, 'here is a thought which I am not sure has ever occurred to myself, but which, of course, has occurred to all the rest of the world.'"[9]

In sum, Poe identifies three types of originality: "literary originality," the "true original," and "the natural." Literary originality is exhibited by works which are uniformly peculiar. Often allegorical and instructive, they are unpopular. The true original is popular because of the special relationship it creates with the reader. While pursuing the true original, the reader is privately joined with the written work in an intellectual and emotional union filled with revelation, apotheosis, and joy. An inferior species of the true original, "the natural" is a union between writer and text in which the revealed knowledge, rather than being created jointly by the reader and the author, is instead handed down unto the reader who experiences a lesser version of that joy which is engendered by being a co-creator of new knowledge.

While Poe focuses on originality as it pertains to literary works and authors, Melville focuses on original characters in fiction and history. Still, their approach and conceptions are similar. Like Poe, Melville begins his treatment of originality by drawing a distinction between what is original in a "thorough sense" and what is merely "novel, or singular, or striking, or captivating . . . [or] . . . odd." This latter distinction is akin to Poe's "literary originality." Melville adds that the impression of originality in this inferior sense is a result of inexperience, youth, and lack of education (*CM* 238). Moreover, there is something about so-called or "loosely accounted" original characters that is provincial, "prevailingly local, or of the age," which, in fact, invalidates such characters' claims to originality (*CM* 239). Their originality is "something personal . . . confined to itself," an odd trait, a distinguishing mark which sets them apart from society (*CM* 239). Such distinguishing characteristics might include a white jacket, physical beauty coupled with an ugly stammer, a black veil, a birth mark, a forbidding emblem worn proudly upon the bosom, or the odd garb of an enthusiastic young transcendentalist. Such characters are separate from their social environment and unpopular. Distinguishing characteristics, however, such as an ivory leg, or the curious circumstance of being chained to a lake of fire, can sometimes enhance popularity and enhance the appearance of originality. In the final analysis, the truly original character, or the "original character essentially such," impresses itself upon its social environment, creating, defining, and illuminating it (*CM* 239).

Melville cites Hamlet, Don Quixote, and Milton's Satan as possessing originality in the "thorough sense." In the field of fiction, Melville considers such prodigies to be as rare "as in real history is a new lawgiver, a revolutionizing philosopher, or the founder of a new religion" (*CM* 239). Within their respective cosmos, these originals are the initiators of action, the decision makers, the forces which create reaction in the characters around them. The original sheds its characteristics on its surroundings. Like a revolving search light "everything is lit by it, everything starts up to it (mark how it is with Hamlet)" (*CM* 239). As Poe says, the true original gives "its own hue, its own character to everything it touches."[10]

Novelty is secondary to Melville's "original." Melville's original is a *source*: an origin of personality, behavior, action, beliefs, and ideas. Whether it be a character in fiction, a new law-giver, a revolutionizing philosopher, or the founder of a new religion, the original is a shaper of human emotion, human understanding, and human destiny. Poe's descriptions of the "true original" and "the natural" provide insight into how Melville's original impresses itself upon the psychology of the admirer. As to the origin of original characters, Melville states that they cannot be born in the author's imagination, but are found in the world "—it being as true in literature as in zoology, that all life is from the egg" (*CM* 239). Dismissing metaphysical origins, Melville draws his characters from the physical world. Although there are rare and admirable people who do seem to possess "original instincts," there is in fact no such thing as an "original" man. The "original" is a contrivance, a scarecrow cut from the cloth of myth and sewn together with language. The authors who create such prodigies are as dependent upon the real world for their substance as are their creations. Melville emphasizes this point in *Pierre*:

> "[T]here never yet was an original man, in the sense intended by the word; the first man himself—who according to the Rabbins was also the first author—not being an original; the only original author being God. Had Milton's been the lot of Casper Hauser, Milton would have been vacant as he. For though the naked soul of man doth assuredly contain one latent element of intellectual productiveness; yet never was there a child born solely from one parent; the visible world of experience being the procreative thing which impregnates the muses; self-reciprocally efficient hermaphrodites being but a fable.[11]

Melville concludes this passage remarking, "There is infinite nonsense in the world on all of these matters; hence blame me not if I contribute my mite." Evidently Melville was familiar with and skeptical toward various discourses concerning "originality," and his posture and humor in this respect reveals deeper levels of textual activity.

Melville sounds these multiple layers through mock philosophical conjecture and humor. He equivocates over the cosmopolitan's originality. Melville's purpose and technique, which reflect each other like the distorting surfaces of fun house mirrors, both invite and describe the process of conjecture. The cosmopolitan serves as a point of departure for Melville's self-reflexive meditation, and as a locus of metaphoric activity to be appreciated by the reader. Melville can be read as casting himself in the role of the cosmopolitan. In this sense, the ambiguous quality of originality exhibited by the cosmopolitan reflects Melville's role as narrator-of-*The Confidence-Man*; as well as Melville's existential or historic roles ranging from professional novelist to Hebraic prophet-artist, with all the associated baggage of the various successes and failures these roles imply.

The cosmopolitan is at times an original character within the cosmos of the novel itself, although he very often fails to convince people of his various visions of confidence. He fails to be a real origin for change. His proselytizing for his ideology of trust and charity fails to transform and re-animate—redeem—the characters around him. Is this fortunate or unfortunate? Casting the cosmopolitan as Christ or the devil may serve as a mechanism for answering this question. Some readers might at this point be prompted to reflect upon their own sensibilities in regard to the cosmopolitan's message of confidence, going so far as to seek in the novel an insight into the nature of various forms of sacrifice, charity, and salvation. This is one of the more amusing ways in which the cosmopolitan prompts the "bond of sympathy" between writer and reader which Poe states that any true original must necessarily engender. Another consideration is the idea—or ideal—of the cosmopolite. John Bryant has shown that the figure of the cosmopolite was born out of the enlightenment. "[O]n American soil the figure became associated with . . . protean and unprincipled operators."[12] Milan Kundera has characterized the idea of the cosmopolite against the broader backdrop of Western tradition. "[E]xhiled from their land of origin and thus lifted above nationalist passions, the great Jewish figures have always shown an exceptional feeling for a supranational Europe—a Europe conceived not as a territory but as culture."[13] It should not be forgotten that Melville traveled to the Levant and Jerusalem to restore himself after he completed *The Confidence-Man*. Was this the cosmopolitan seeking out his spiritual origins?

As for the book itself—is it original? The nineteenth-century readers of *The Confidence-Man* did not feel the requisite "bond of sympathy." There have been readers since, however, who have used *The Confidence-Man* as a focus for revelation, apotheosis, and intellectual joy. In his forward to the Norton edition of *The Confidence-Man*, Hershel Parker claims that the "reader of *The Confidence-Man* is rewarded by an intensity of intellectual and aesthetic exhilaration comparable to almost nothing else in our literature except some early Swift (such as *A Tale of a Tub*) and some late Nabokov (such as *Pale Fire*)."[14] There is a universe of sensibility—taking something from Stanley Kubrick, something from Beethoven, something from Wittgenstein—which suggests that Parker has achieved the distinction of having penned the highest praise a book has ever received. I do not doubt the accuracy or the implications of Parker's overview. *The Confidence-Man* is so structured that allegory, allusion, irony, and ambiguity infuse a new significance to its form and content with each successive reading. In terms of the question of originality, the cosmopolitan is an emblem of this effect. Melville has indeed succeeded in fashioning or realizing an original star which fits into the constellation of originality hitherto featuring Don Quixote, Milton's Satan, and Hamlet (to which I can't resist adding Jesus, Achilles, and Odysseus at the first tier, and then Lucian's

Menippus, Dante's Dante, Rabelais's Panurge, Shelley's Prometheus, assorted religious heroes East and West, perhaps Voltaire's Candide, and certainly Carroll's very sane Alice, who, by remaining honest and intelligent in the adult theater of ontological deficiency, intellectual fraud, and congratulatory silliness, is the most *non*-original original of all!). It might be suggested that Melville's white whale is the most original character in his fiction, while Ishmael remains the white whale's most original interpreter. Ahab, who seems to cast his characteristics on his surroundings like a revolving search light, is a projector of the world's weirdest images focused and turned outward. A ghastly reflector, he glows with the worldly illusion of Hegelian master/slave relationships, material dialectics, and fear. Naturally, he is a tyrant.

As the white whale is a pasteboard mask for Ahab's hatred and fear (or anything else that's convenient to the purposes of his monomania), the cosmopolitan can become for the reader another mask. Certainly Melville can be seen behind both masks. As white whale, Melville presents himself to his readers (or is it to himself?) as an unsolvable metaphysical conundrum. For Merton Sealts the theme of masks and the masquerade is central to the *The Confidence-Man*, the organizing concept for which is a "single masquerading 'confidence man,' one who victimizes in turn a whole series of gullible but representative Americans."[15] Sealts is not alone in his perspective. In "Originality of Vision in the American Romantics," Warren Staebler characterizes *The Confidence-Man* as presenting a "picture of Americans as ignorant, ego-starved, money-hungry, and credulous, altogether at the mercy of cunning, ingratiating dissimulators, [and] pelican-like ego flatterers."[16] Staebler's characterization is as compelling as it is appalling. Indeed, Melville goes beyond the material gullibility of Americans and penetrates the even more ghostly spiritual and intellectual sickness which he saw around him in the great "man show" where he goes to look for characters—a veritable world's fair of *a priori* myth-making which could have challenged even Bacon's talent for characterizing and cataloging intellectual mythology.

Another approach to examining the "smoky" chapter involves the notion of the valorization of originality. In *Origin & Originality in Renaissance Literature: Versions of the Source*, David Quint describes a philosophical crisis in the conceptualization of originality. During the Renaissance there was on one hand

> a kind of epistemological anxiety, heightened by nostalgia, in the task of depicting a source which sanctioned what were otherwise "counterfeit,"

> purely man made fictions. On the other hand, Renaissance culture valorized the human creativity which it had newly come to recognize, and it could only define the individuality of the creator in historical terms . . . [Only Rabelais] appears best able to resolve these conflicting impulses of Renaissance literary creation, to reconcile the claim to participate in a source of authorized truth with full expression of authorial individuality.[17]

Like Rabelais—and Aristophanes, Lucian, Cervantes, Burton, Swift, Byron, Peacock, Carroll, Huxley, Čapek, and Nabokov—Melville finds the resolution to this problem in synoptic analysis and satiric expression. Melville traces the origin of originality to human voices and material fixtures, and expresses his findings liberally in a farrago of parody, equivocation, and music. Melville combines a sensitivity to the historic parameters and limits of his individuality with an awareness and the exercise of his spiritual liberty. Melville doesn't make a barbaric myth out of originality, but instead realizes a civilized valorization by reconciling his authority with origins in history and reality.

Thomas McFarland has written on the theme of originality in European literature, principally as the notion is conceived in the credulous transcendental machinations of Coleridge:

> The historical rise of imagination's (and originality's) importance witnessed a transfer of mental energy from the weakening concept of soul to an alternate vehicle. Imagination, and its twin Romantic ideal, originality, were then, and still are, transformations of the human intensity earlier conveyed by soul.[18]

Melville may have accepted the poetry of a new vehicle for expressing "human intensity," but he could not brook with its reformulation, idealization, and mechanization—its philosophical reification into a new prodigy of intellectual mythology. And it was just such a monster congealing around him in the miasma of transcendentalism exhaling from Germany through Coleridge and Emerson—and exhaling from half a million similar confidence men since Aristophanes portrayed them in *The Clouds*.

Jonathan Swift analyzes and ridicules modernism, modern intellectual orthodoxy, abstract necessities, "natural" laws, scientism, secular orthodoxies, and the enterprise by which phony myths are cobbled together and published to the world. The traditions of satire and common sense philosophy in which Swift and Melville write are indexed with a critical abhorrence for a scholasticism which seeks to impose mechanism upon nature. But from where comes the desire to perpetrate these myths of mechanical artifice?

According to Mircea Eliade, "the metaphysical concepts of the archaic world

> express, on different planes and through the means proper to them, a complex system of coherent affirmations about the ultimate reality of things. [In the archaic world] neither the objects of the external world nor human acts, properly speaking, have any autonomous intrinsic value.[19]

Here then is insight into the logic of barbarism, whether it be modern or archaic, western or nonwestern. As Eliade says, the opposition and dismissal of reality within the "archaic" mind "are not merely the effect of the conservative tendencies of primitive societies . . . [I]t is justifiable to read in this depreciation of history . . . and in this rejection of . . . continuous time, a certain metaphysical 'valorization' of human existence."[20] It is in this way that the myth of "newness"—the valorization of originality—suppresses and replaces reality. Although the myth of "newness" might at first appear to present a short-cut opportunity for introducing improvements to the social matrix, the depreciation of history which accompanies such "valorization" usually produces opposite results including the coercive repression of intellectual freedom and the suspension of genuine civility.

In the nineteenth century the direct appeal of transcendentalism on both sides of the Atlantic to this new valorization, abstract rite, creation-mechanism called "originality"—like Poe's detailed, sharply delineated (and very likely satirical) discussion of originality—are prime idols for Melville's iconoclastic hammer. Elsewhere I have demonstrated that Melville's concept of barbarism is predicated upon an understanding of the importance of mythic idols to barbaric individuals and groups.[21] Barbarians require symbols to define and valorize themselves. Civilized humans can make do with reality, or, indeed, can make do with only themselves and the cycles of human involvement. In chapter 44 of *The Confidence-Man*, Melville deflates the notion of originality, of something really new, by first demonstrating the unworldly and mythic nature of the thesis, and then by burying it beneath the rubble of its own jargon. In this latter sense, the chapter is a parody of the same species of intellectual fraud that it perpetrates. Swift is a master at describing such fraud while he simultaneously parodies it, *A Tale of a Tub* being a case in point.

Still, debate continues as to whether or not this is Melville's activity.

There are hermeneutic alternatives to the satirical reading of Melville's "smoky" chapter. In *Purloined Letters: Originality and Repetition in American Letters*, Joseph Riddel argues that American literature "is as Emerson said a 'critical' or self-critical literature, and addressed to a certain degree to the problematics of clearing the ground for something 'new' which has not as yet appeared, and cannot ever appear as such, that is, the *new*."[22] Melville's chapter might be a specimen of this ground clearing, although to me Melville clearly ridicules the notion by mocking it, for Melville can scarcely anticipate anything that is really *new*. The Riddel model presents an alternative to the idea that the chapter is a parody designed to ridicule the valorization of originality and originality discourse. However, Riddel's model can only qualify the form of the chapter's grammar, but not its meaning. In Riddel's model, the chapter doesn't have a satiric purpose, but rather the chapter is a "generic hybrid that instigates but does not and cannot regulate what it uncannily engenders."[23] The question, however, is not one of *regulation*, it is one of *use*. The use of a proposition determines its meaning. How is the chapter used? And how is it understood?

To answer this question we have to take on board the debate surrounding the question of whether or not Melville is a satirist. First we will review the proposition in terms of *Moby-Dick*.

Is *Moby-Dick* satire? Northrop Frye's claim that *Moby-Dick* is an anatomy has caused continuing controversy in the scholarship. Recently, Walter E. Bezanson has answered Frye, observing that "[t]hough the paradigm is useful, it should not allow us to forget that Ishmael's deepest anxieties—or are they enchantments—come from the Bible and Shakespeare; nor should one forget the profound confluences . . . with Emerson . . . and Hawthorne."[24]

In answer to Bezanson, I should point out that, firstly, according to Ishmael, the "narrator" of *Moby-Dick*, the most profound anxieties he experienced occurred some fifteen or twenty years before his voyage with Ahab, when he was put to bed without supper by his wicked stepmother. As he lay in bed, Ishmael says, he felt "a great deal worse than I have ever done since, even from the greatest subsequent misfortunes" (*MD* 26). The shrewd reader cannot fail to group among these "subsequent misfortunes" the "deepest anxieties" Ishmael experiences aboard Ahab's whaling ship. Interestingly enough, Ishmael says that at his darkest hour—confined in bed, a small boy without supper—a supernatural "silent form or phantom" came and held his hand.

Secondly, Melville's affinities to Shakespeare, Emerson, and (to a lesser extent) Hawthorne are the outcomes and paraphernalia of his poetic odysseys, themselves serving a parodic purpose, and are not representative of the persona which animates the wise and clever narrative, which itself is far more suggestive of the styles and sensibilities of Robert Burton and the young Sir Thomas Browne. Portions of *Moby-Dick* suggestive of the Bible, Shakespeare, and Emerson, while appealing to the schoolboy's easily dazzled eye, are simply not as intelligent or sensible as Melville's more prosaic or humerous passages. And indeed, Shakespeare's agenda, notwithstanding his technique, falls along Menippean lines, as does Hawthorne's. *Hamlet*, for instance, does much to ridicule the "Shakespearean flights" (Ophelia's singing, for instance, or some of Hamlet's more peculiar and manic fits and exhibitions) that some superficial critics wrongly see as the sole end of Melville's art.

Finally, the reader must not overlook the fact that Ishmael is the fictitious narrator of *Moby-Dick*. His impressions must accompany and are circumscribed by other perspectives. "Ishmael's" infatuation with the Bible, Shakespeare, Emerson, and Hawthorne are important components of Melville's vision in *Moby-Dick*, but they remain components. The text goes further than the sum of its parts—which include a preponderance of Menippean contraptions. Beginning with the "Extracts," these contraptions dominate and define the novel. The greater generic designation for *Moby-Dick* is "anatomy." By all formalistic and philosophical criteria, *Moby-Dick* is Menippean satire.

The Confidence-Man shares Menippean affinities with *Moby-Dick*, particularly in the light of synoptic analysis and Wittgenstein's vision of philosophy where the purpose of philosophy is not to answer questions about metaphysics, but rather to clear up conceptual confusion. The solutions to metaphysical problems—to problems beyond sense—lie not in the answers to the questions themselves, but in clarifying the misleading elements in the grammar and vocabulary of language that lead us to ask these questions. Meaning is determined by the use of a proposition and the way a proposition is understood, and these are affected by context. By examining similar propositions in and out of their grammatical contexts, one can create a therapy, a series of language games that reveal the true and misconstrued meanings of propositions, and thus disabuse language of conceptual confusion, that is to say philosophical propositions. The ideas holding that "mind" is like a persona, or a brain is like a computer, or that a human being is a mechanical mating of a mind and a body are typical examples of such conceptual confusion. A simple language game illustrates the point. Decide which of the following propositions provides the most accurate description of reality:

a) My mind is hungry for a big lunch.
b) My brain is hungry for a big lunch.
c) My body—my stomach—is hungry for a big lunch.
d) I am hungry for a big lunch.

The correct answer is d. The other statements are nonsense. Minds do not exist[25]; brains are only to be found in medical textbooks, or on the tables of surgeons and gourmands; and bodies are only to be found at the morgue, at the beach, in the pages of muscle magazines, or in Newton's descriptions of objects possessing mass. The cosmopolitan's overt notions of universal charity and confidence constitute another proposition rooted in conceptual confusion. Charity applies in certain contexts, and at various degrees, and does not apply at all in others. And so with philanthropy: Love is not to be found in universals, but in particulars. One can love humanity, but regard Tom and Harry with suspicion. Conversely, one can love Tom and Harry, but loathe humanity. It all depends on you, Tom and Harry, and what side of the bed you wake up on that day (or perhaps the latest projections of global population).

The poetics of synoptic analysis are central to Menippean satire and to *The Confidence-Man*. In religious terms, Melville's fictitious scenarios in *The Confidence-Man*—like scenes in a morality play—elaborate and qualify propositions of charity and faith, seeking a specific, case-by-case resolution of the risks inherent to the exercise of "confidence" in a "fallen" world populated by snakes, canines, and Homo sapiens. In the language of synoptic analysis, Melville presents a series of hypothetical scenarios or therapeutic language games that identify conceptual errors that lead to philosophical credulousness. In chapter 44 of *The Confidence-Man*, the notion of originality is a philosophical proposition resulting from conceptual confusion. By elaborating the concept in a number of guises, the possible uses of the concept are explored. This elaboration takes on the appearance of a discussion in which are nested a series of propositions or assumptions, some of which are more legitimate, or meaningful, or more sensible than others. In the end, the concept is illuminated through the identification of its legitimate and illegitimate uses; and then, just for good measure, the concept is buried under the weight of the confused jargon which engendered it. Far from exercising some ultra-modern purgation of the past in preparation for something new, as Riddle might suggest, chapter 44 annihilates the notion entirely, relegating it to the rubbish bin of intellectual mythology, where it joins such other Melville-isms as convivial bats, unaccountable rattlesnakes, virtuous boys, the Omni-balsamic Reinvigorator, the Samaritan Pain Dissuader (which "kills pain without killing feeling"), the Protean easy-chair (where even the most tormented conscience can find rest), genial hangmen, genial misanthropes, hypothetical friends, the mystical master with one eye on the invisible and the other on the main chance, and a World Charity infused with the Wall Street spirit and charged to send "ten thousand missionaries in a body and converting the Chinese *en masse* within six months of the debraktation" (*CM* 41).

Can synoptic analysis help to describe fine, incremental characteristics of Melville's technique, tone and orientation? In *Melville and Repose* John Bryant presents a formulation that neatly describes the character of Melville's humor. Bryant is confused, however, in trying to oppose his notion of humor to his notion of satire. Bryant draws a distinction between "amiable humor" and "satire," as if the two concepts are mutually exclusive because of intrinsic, *a priori* qualities of a political nature. *Amiable humor*, Bryant says, is democratic, romantic, obscure, pastoral, Arcadian, and reclusive—having antecedents in eighteenth-century English literature such as the work of Lord Shaftesbury and Sterne, in turn originating in Andrew Marvell, the idea of the English garden, and the poetry of retreat from politics and civil war. Satire, Bryant says, shares affinities with a sensibility that is elitist, aristocratic, and egotistical.[26] This is a difficult formulation at best. Champions of democracy and classic liberalism like Jefferson, Voltaire, and Byron possessed these "satiric" qualities in profusion. Another such example is Vladimir Nabokov whose father (a central leader of Russian liberalism in exile between the world wars) was shot by right-wing assassins. Are aristocrats and satirists, or their sensibilities, necessarily anti-democratic as Bryant would seem to suggest by his distinctions? Furthermore, can Bryant's characterizations of satire—egotistical, elitist, aristocratic—describe such films as *Planet of the Apes*, *Dr. Strangelove*, and *Robocop,* or television shows like *The Beverly Hillbillies*, *Gilligan's Island*, and *Batman*?

Bryant argues that although Melville worked under a repressed urge to be satirical, Melville was in fact an amiable humorist rather than a satirist. This does much to suggest the friendly timbre and bonhomie appeal of Melville's humor. But Bryant is confused in his opposed conceptions of humor and satire. Humor refers to a quality of mood or feeling usually conducive to smiles and laughter. Satire refers to various forms of diatribe and parody that ridicule folly, cruelty, and ignorance. Yes, "humor" is a name used to designate "literature that is funny," but isn't satire also sometimes funny? Humor and satire belong to different classes of phenomena and cannot be contrasted against one another as if they were separate genres, like mystery and western. Bryant is also mistaken in assuming that satire and amiability are exclusive of one another. Yes, Melville is indeed amiable, but he is *also* satirical. The two are complementary. Indeed, it is through this amiableness that Melville realizes his most effective satirical power, that is by appealing to and insinuating himself into the imagination of his reader, by being *truly original* in Poe's best sense of the concept. This is neatly illustrated in the case of Petronius, the author of *The Satyricon*. Petronius was Nero's official party orchestrater. While Nero was by no means fastidious, he was a gentleman and he appreciated amiability. There was no more amiable author in classical literature than the unconventional, charming, refined and understanding author of the *Satyricon*. However, few canonical authors have in their art been as debauched, lurid, cynical, and sordid, or so willing to graphically portray the human race in its lowest, most avaricious, most sentimental, filthiest, and vilest projections. It is indeed Petronius's amiability, his appeal, his *originality* that makes him such a devastating satirist. The ferocity of Petronius's satire, like Melville's, lies in the amiability of his sensibility and the sureness of his composition, and not in the "offensive" or "un-correct" language of criticism, diatribe, or declamation. In response to the question of whether or not Melville is a satirist, there can be no stronger affirmation than to say, "He is amiable."

III
The Synoptic Analysis of Programmed Texts

8
The Advent of Literary Dystopia

> When Scythrop grew up, he was sent, as usual, to a public school, where a little learning was painfully beaten into him, and thence to the University, where it was carefully taken out of him; and he was sent home, like a well-threshed ear of corn, with nothing in his head.
> —Thomas Love Peacock, *Nightmare Abbey*

LITERARY DYSTOPIA IS A FORM ROOTED IN MENIPPEAN SATIRE. DRAWING distinctions between the two forms is as interesting as it is problematic. Both forms are concerned with intellectual mythology, which they critique by exploring the interrelationships that exist among ignorance, intolerance, conflict, brutality, euphemism, passivity, scientism, and various modern orthodoxies. Another similarity is an authorial bookishness. Both forms are highly literary. The most obvious difference between literary dystopia and Menippean satire has to do with humor. Except in rare instances, literary dystopia is not funny. The mood of dystopia is usually dark, pessimistic, and often reflects paranoia, alarm, or hysteria. Satire locates conceptual confusion and intellectual mythology in the present and provides diagnosis. Dystopia uses fiction to portray institutions based on intellectual mythology and essays prophecy, and prognostication. The key to distinguishing the two forms is the approach they take to the analysis of intellectual mythology. Menippean satire examines the philosophical credulousness, conceptual confusion, and misapprehensions of language upon which intellectual mythology is based. The literature of dystopia examines the possible effects intellectual mythology can have on individuals and society.

Interestingly enough, the satiric antecedents of literary dystopia are not to be found in satire's analyses of brutality and human fallibility, but rather in satire's analyses of intellectual mythology and orthodoxy. In view of the overt role of brutality in representative works such as *1984* or *A Clockwork Orange*, this is at first surprising. But consider the representative example of the satiric antecedent to literary dystopia in *Gulliver's Travels*. While all the ignorance and brutality we have come to associate with *1984* and *Brave New World* are to be found in the first, second, and fourth books of *Gulliver's Travels,* it is rather to the third book that we point to as a generic forerunner of the literary dystopia. The third book portrays a dictatorship presided over by a scientific academy that parodies the utopian scientific government envisioned by Francis Bacon in *The New Atlantis*. Strictly speaking, satire doesn't portray future states based on brutality, dictatorship, or totalitarianism—these belonging to the domain of literary dystopia. Instead, satire concerns itself primarily with the roles intellectual mythology and orthodoxy play in making such dictatorships possible. Thus it is possible to identify elements in *1984* and *Brave New World* which are satiric and distinguish them from elements which are dystopian. Seen in this light, it is easy to recognize works such as Čapek's *War With the Newts* or Burgess's *A Clockwork Orange* as not being dystopias but satires.

The accompanying table lists a number of representative dystopian novels and films which exhibit satiric and dystopian characteristics. In the left column are works that tend to exhibit dystopian qualities. In the right column are works that are more properly identified as satiric. A simple test for distinguishing dystopia from satire might be as follows: If the work describes how bad things are, you have a satire on your hands. If the work describes how bad things could be, you are tangling with a dystopia. However, notwithstanding the prophetic element, the roots of dystopia are found in Menippean satire and its diagnoses of euphemism and intellectual mythology. Curiously enough—indeed, ominously—the primary foci of Menippean satire in this respect are not despots or corrupt statesmen, but rather schoolmen and academies.

An examination of various curricular debates in satire reveals a prefiguring of many of the issues that are central to literary dystopia.

Aristophanes's play *The Clouds* (423 B.C.) depicts perhaps the earliest curricular debate in literature. In the play Strepsiades, deeply in debt and plagued by creditors, sends his son off to the Academy—the "Thinkery," as it is called—to be educated by the sophists in the techniques of rhetoric and argumentation. The reason? Strepsiades believes the sophists to possess just the sort of skills he needs to argue with and evade his creditors.

Central to the play is the debate between the characters named (depending on the translation) Philosophy and Sophistry, or The Better

Dystopia and Satire

Literature

Dystopian		Satirical	
Wells	*The Time Machine*	Verne	*From the Earth to the Moon*
Zamyatin	*We*	Wells	*First Men in the Moon*
Kafka	*The Castle*	Forster	"The Machine Stops"
"	*The Trial*	Čapek	*The War with the Newts*
Huxley	*Brave New World*	Orwell	*Animal Farm*
Orwell	*1984*	Nabokov	*Bend Sinister*
Nabokov	*Invitation to a Beheading*	Burgess	*A Clockwork Orange*
Lewis	*That Hideous Strength*	"	*1985*
Golding	*Lord of the Files*	Aldiss	*Barefoot in the Head*
Bradbury	*Fahrenheit 451*	Moorcock	*The Cornelius Chronicles*

Film

Lang	*Metropolis*	Young	*From Russia With Love*
McCarey	*Duck Soup*	Kubrick	*Dr. Strangelove*
Kramer	*On the Beach*	Flicker	*The President's Analyst*
Sargent	*Colossus: The Forbin Project*	Kubrick	*2001: A Space Odyssey*
Lucas	*THX1138*	Vadim	*Barbarella, Queen of the Galaxy*
Jewison	*Rollerball*	McGoohan	*The Prisoner*
Kubrick	*A Clockwork Orange*	Schaffner	*Planet of the Apes*
Fleischer	*Soylent Green*	Lester	*The Bedsitting Room*
Jones	*A Boy and His Dog*	Boorman	*Zardoz*
Gilliam	*Brazil*	Lumet	*Network*
Verhoeven	*Robocop*	Russell	*Three Kings*

Argument and The Worse Argument, or Old Learning and New Learning.

Arrowsmith has suggested some interesting staging. Old Learning and New Learning are wheeled onto the stage in cages. Over their heads they wear the masks of fighting-cocks. Old Learning is fit and powerfully built, expressing grace, strength, and harmony with his movements. His plumage is restrained and dignified. In contrast, New Learning is emaciated with sloping shoulders and skinny arms. His plumage, like his movements, is ostentatious and defiant. An enormous tongue hangs from his beak and he sports a disproportionately large phallus.

Their cages are opened and they circle each other, scratching and spurring the ground and slinging farcical insults at each other. This goes on for several minutes until the leader of the chorus intercedes and persuades the adversaries to state the principles of their respective teachings. Old Learning cites the virtues of decorum, modesty, deference, manliness, purity, honor, obedience, athletic prowess, a small phallus, and cold baths. New Learning counter attacks by pointing out that the Baths of Herakles were hot baths, and that necessarily by the logic of Old Learning Herakles was flabby and effeminate. And from there the conversation rapidly plummets into a debate over the relative merits of being sodomized with a radish. So much for the subtlety and delicacy of Attic wit; however, it is worth noting the contempt Aristophanes and, evidently, Athens held for debates concerning pedagogy and curriculum. And while both Old Learning and New Learning are portrayed with slap-stick contempt, Aristophanes possessed little patience for New Learning's eagerness to depreciate and confuse principles of logic, truth, justice, and morality.

Petronius, writing during the decline of Rome under Nero (A.D. 54–68), took the issue more seriously. This is not to say of course that the *Satyricon* is an expression of cold, sober invective. It is, in fact, as bawdy, outrageous, and shocking as anything in Aristophanes. Hedonistic, urbane and learned, the *Satyricon* exhibits an astonishing profusion of invention more often seen in the theater than in prose narrative. Petronius's parodies are flawlessly expert, his logic is intrinsic but turned outward toward the real world. The *Satyricon* is perhaps the most biting of satires because its ferocity lies in a highly refined sensibility combined with a liberality of expression that forcefully portrays the meanest and most despicable failings of the human race.

At the beginning of the surviving fragments of the *Satyricon*, the student Encolpius, who is also the narrator and main character, takes to task his professor, Agamemnon, for the cant and inflated language which has corrupted Roman education. In his harangue Encolpius complains of the jargon, claptrap, and stilted bombast with which the minds of Roman youth are filled. Young Romans are kept ignorant of real life and the common experience. Young Romans can't distinguish between real action and language. They possess no taste. Encolpius blames the rhetoricians for strangling real eloquence. "By reducing everything to sound," he says, "you concocted this bloated puffpaste of pretty drivel whose only real purpose is the pleasure of punning and the thrill of ambiguity. Result? Language lost its sinew, its nerve. Eloquence died."[1]

Encolpius goes on to list figures of genius who wrote before the cramping advent of programmed compositions, "set-speeches," and the formalized training of rhetoric. His list includes Homer, Sophocles, Euripides, Pindar, Plato, Demosthenes, Hyperides, and Thucydides. According to Encolpius, "flatulent rhetoric" moved in from Asia to blight the minds of the young. Poetry became sick. All the literary arts died. "And in painting," he says, "you see the same decay: on the very day when Egyptian arrogance dared to reduce [painting] to a set of sterile formulas . . . great art died."[2]

Agamemnon breaks in at this point. "Young man . . . I see that you are a speaker of unusual taste and, what is even rarer, an admirer of common sense. So I shan't put you off with the usual hocus-pocus of the profession. But in all justice allow me to observe that we teachers should not be saddled with the blame for this bombast of which you complain. After all, if the patients are lunatics, surely a little professional lunacy is almost mandatory in the doctor who deals with them. Unless we professors spout the sort of twaddle our students admire, we run the risk of being, in Cicero's phrase, 'left alone at our lecterns.' "[3]

Moving forward to the early eighteenth century we find what is surely the most widely known portrait of curricular debate, Jonathan Swift's "Battle of the Books" (1704–1710). Swift shares the frustration Aristophanes felt for the debate, and at the outset declaims the vain and worldly motives he sees lying at its bottom:

> War is the Child of Pride, and Pride the Daughter of Riches . . . it very seldom happens to men to fall out [that is, quarrel] when all have enough[.] . . . [Moreover,] Invasions usually travel from North to South, that is to say, from Poverty upon Plenty[.] . . . [As in real wars,] Poverty, or Want, in some degree or other, (whether Real or in Opinion, which makes no Alteration in the Case) has a great Share, as well as Pride, on the Part of the Aggressor.[4]

Starting at first principles, Swift contextualizes the debate as a worldly struggle with material wealth as the prime motive.

"The Battle of the Books" allegorizes a dispute current in Swift's time concerning the merits of ancient vs. modern authors. The ancient and modern books in St. James Library take up the debate in the the form of an epic battle which reverts, not unexpectedly, to a Homeric pattern—the *Iliad* being the epic which captures the genius, the depravity, and the broken outcomes of human conflict. Central to Swift's vision is the discussion which takes place in the window of the library between the Spider and the Bee. Representing the ancients, the Bee points out that the structures and the inventions of the Spider—its webs—representing the modern books, may be erected with much mathematics, method, and skill; but the materials are nothing but dirt spun out of the spider's entrails. And such an edifice, says the Bee, "will conclude at last in a Cobweb." The moderns, like the spider, feed upon the insects and vermin of the age. "As for us, the Ancients," says the Bee, "we are content with our Wings and our Voice: that is to say, our flights and our Language." The ancients range through nature like the Bee and gather, without injuring the flowers, materials to make "Honey and wax, thus furnishing Mankind with the two Noblest of Things, which are sweetness and Light."[5]

Meanwhile, the battle continues as the Modern Books call upon the Goddess of Criticism to assist them. Swift describes her as a "malignant Deity." She lives in a den at the top of a snowy mountain in Nova Zembla (interestingly enough, Nabokov's Charles Kinbote, the spirit of Criticism in the novel *Pale Fire* is also from a land called Zembla). At the right hand of the Goddess of Criticism sits *Ignorance*, her husband and father; he is blind with Age; to her left sits her mother, *Pride*. She is accompanied also by her sister, Opinion, "light of foot, hoodwinkt, and headstrong, yet giddy and perpetually turning." About her play her seven children: Noise, Impudence, Dullness, Vanity, Positiveness, Pedantry, and Ill-Manners. "The goddess herself had Claws like a Cat: Her Head, and Ears, and voice resembled those of an Ass." Her teeth point straight out from her mouth. Her eyes look inward. She has a very large spleen which produces gall at a rate faster than the "crew of ugly monsters" at her breasts can suck it away. She flies down to St. James's Library to aid the Modern Books—and I leave it to you, reader, to look round your university to see how the battle came off.[6]

Perhaps the most passionate and soaring expression of curricular debate in English literature is found in the preface to William Blake's epic poem *Milton* (1800–04).

> The Stolen and Perverted Writings of Homer & Ovid, of Plato & Cicero, which all men ought to contemn, are set up by artifice against the Sublime of the Bible; but when the New Age is at leisure to Pronounce, all will be set right, & those Grand Works of the more ancient and consciously & professedly Inspired Men will hold their proper rank, & the Daughters of Memory shall become the Daughters of Inspiration. Shakespeare & Milton

were both curb'd by the general malady & infection from the silly Greek and Latin slaves of the Sword.

    Rouze up, O Young Men of the New Age! set your foreheads against the ignorant Hirelings! For we have Hirelings in the Camp, the Court & the University, who would, if they could, for ever depress Mental & prolong Corporeal War. Painters! on you I call. Sculptors! Architects! Suffer not the fashionable Fools to depress your powers by the prices they pretend to give for contemptible works, or the expensive advertising boasts that they make of such works: believe Christ & His Apostles that there is a class of Men whose whole delight is in Destroying. We do not want either Greek or Roman models if we are but just & true to our own Imaginations, those Words of Eternity in which we shall live forever in Jesus our Lord.[7]

The passage is followed by the poem known familiarly as the lyric to the hymn "Jerusalem" —"And did those feet in ancient time . . . etc." Finally in the preface Blake quotes numbers, chap. 10, v. 29, "Would to God that all the Lord's people were Prophets." Blake maintained that one could not be a true Christian without first being an artist. Although Blake accuses Greek art and religion of being a degenerate rendering of what had been originally derived from the ancient Hebrews, it is important to realize that Blake is using this formulation figuratively. The poem *Milton* itself follows after the Greek epic model beginning with the invocation of the Muses and the epic question which marks the beginning of the story. Specifically, Blake's quarrel is with poetic models and critical traditions which keep human energy and imagination in chains; he declaims the institutionalization of Platonic universals and Aristotelian categories; he declaims the intellectual rage for order that freezes myth into repressive, spectral orthodoxies. Human imagination and energy express themselves in mental war, in the visions which inspire the art of a free people. When human energy and imagination are repressed—as it is by the "class of men whose whole delight in destroying"—then human energy and imagination realizes itself in corporal warfare. And this is why at the end of the poem Blake parodies St. John the Divine and describes terrific lions and tigers in sport and play, "and all the animals upon the earth preparing in all their strength "To go forth to the Great Harvest & Vintage of the Nations."[8] Blake lived, of course, during a period which witnessed a series of highly significant revolutions, the effects of which the world is still reeling under.

    Blake's presentation differs from the culture wars portrayed by earlier authors. There is a conspicuous lack of humor. There is an increase in seriousness. Blake exhibits an appreciation for the importance of ideology and culture that was absent from the earlier authors. Blake cannot laugh at the curricular debate the way the Greeks do. He is unable to evoke the sophisticated and droll response of Petronius. Although he demonstrates an epical energy, he does not demonstrate Swift's mastery over the conflict. Blake is embroiled in the conflict. Indeed, he sees it unfolding around him in a manifestation of world-wide revolution. One might entertain the thought that Blake was overcome by the same ideological convulsions which were being felt around Europe. However, Blake is rather reacting to the fact that the violent nature of the revolution was rooted in the inability of Europe to contain the ideological battle on the mental plane. Because Europe cannot engage in mental warfare—say, as the Greeks could by portraying it on a stage—the war "breaks out" onto the physical plane.

Another perspective on this problem is presented by Voltaire in *Candide* through the device of Professor Pangloss. Rather than examine the particulars of the world around him, Professor Pangloss represses his common sense response to phenomena and imposes his famous *a priori* formulation. Be it disease, fire, famine, earthquakes, rape, or wars, Professor Pangloss insists that there is *sufficient cause* for all of these catastrophes and thus we live, regardless of our misfortunes, *in the best of all possible worlds*. The claim that we live in the "best of all possible worlds" is of course one of the greatest *non sequiturs* in all of literature. Wittgenstein neatly formulates the dynamics of this modern euphemism in the *Tractatus*:

> 6.371 The whole modern conception of the world is founded on the illusion that the so-called laws of nature are the explanations of natural phenomena.
> 6.372 Thus people today stop at the laws of nature, treating them as something inviolable, just as God and Fate were treated in past ages.
> And in fact both are right and both are wrong: Though the view of the ancients is clearer in so far as they have a clear and acknowledged terminus, while the modern system tries to make it look as if *everything* were explained.

Professor Pangloss and his deductive denial of reality bring us to the crisis in democracy punctuated in literature by the advent of the literary dystopia. Pangloss's ideology intervenes between thought and utterance. "The best of all possible worlds" epitomizes modern euphemism. It represses the truth by interposing intellectual mythology. It attributes a false mechanism to nature. It presents an *a priori* hypothesis which can explain any phenomena. And, indeed, here its use now reveals its meaning. It is a formula that valorizes and empowers Pangloss. He represents in literature the prototype of the modern ideological dictator that was anticipated in the nineteenth century by Napoleon and his imitators, and finally cumulating a century later in a variety of guises around the globe. And literature's response has been hysterical. Orwell, Zamyatin, and Huxley best caught the spirit and the thunder of this hysteria, but C. S. Lewis, Ray Bradbury, Vladimir Nabokov, and Anthony Burgess formulated clearer analyses of both the character and causes of intellectual mythology, or the modern disease.

For Lewis, the disease is brought about by the decline of traditional religion and the set of moral criteria commonly shared by cultures around the globe. Technology is the chief cause of this decline because it makes possible the concentration of power in fewer and fewer hands. The present is cut off from the past and the future is programmed by an elite. Lewis outlines these ideas in his book *The Abolition of Man* and in his novel *That Hideous Strength*. Probably the most terrifying dystopia in literature, *That Hideous Strength* describes how a faceless corporation on the path to world domination might blend science and capitalism into an intellectual mythology that will transform universities into corporate indoctrination centers.

The notion of the university-as-industrial-operation was pioneered by Jules Verne in the recently discovered *Paris in the Twentieth Century*. With bitter humor Verne names his market-driven university the "Academic Credit Union." In his description of the university's prospectus, Verne notes that "no scholar's or professor's name appeared on the Board of Directors, a matter of some reassurance with regard to the commercial prospects of the enterprise."[9]

The theme of the present being cut off from the past has its most striking expression in Ray Bradbury's *Fahrenheit 451*. As beautifully written as it is frightening, *Fahrenheit 451* takes the notion of curricular debate to its ultimate conclusion. Instead of depicting an intellectual culture conducting internecine warfare over the relative merits or moral superiority of one canon of knowledge over another, Bradbury's novel presents a world in which all recorded knowledge is banned and burned entirely. Here society embraces a most convenient myth which holds that the past is malignant and should be erased. The novel's antagonist provides a number of remarkable rationales for burning books and destroying the past, but the undercurrent cause is plainly the quest of an entire civilization for emotional and moral numbness, or escape from the human condition.

For Nabokov, the condition of dystopia is interpreted as a conflict not between the state (or corporations) and the individual, but rather a conflict between sensibility and ignorance. *Invitation to a Beheading* describes the surrealistic death-row experience of a man guilty of the crime of "Gnostical Turpitude." The novel presents an impressionistic conflict between the protagonist and a world that dissolves around him as he penetrates its unreality. This same dissolving of the false world of dystopia occurs again in *Bend Sinister* where the end of the book presents Nabokov rising from his writing desk to go moth hunting. But *Bend Sinister* does more than *Invitation to a Beheading* to analyze the role of ignorance and *poshlost*, or Philistine vulgarity, in the manifestation of the totalitarian state. The essence of this *poshlost* is the willingness of the ignorant to embrace intellectual mythology. *Bend Sinister* portrays the misfortunes of a widowed philosophy professor who is being coerced by a dictator—the leader of the "Party of the Average Man"—to support the state's philosophical position on the status of human consciousness and individuality:

> At every given level of world-time there was . . . a certain computable amount of human consciousness distributed throughout the population of the world. This distribution was uneven, and herein lay the root of all our woes. Human beings . . . were so many vessels containing unequal portions of this essentially uniform consciousness. It was however quite possible, [the dictator] maintained, to regulate the capacity of the human vessels. If, for instance, a given amount of water were contained in a given amount of heterogeneous bottles—wine bottles, flagons and vials of varying shape and size . . . the distribution of the liquid would be uneven and unjust, but could be made even and just either by grading the contents or by eliminating the fancy vessels and by adopting a standard size.[10]

Bend Sinister provides a hypothetical instance of how an intellectual myth becomes the rational for regulation, repression, and torture.

It could be argued that several more of Nabokov's novels are dystopias—*Lolita* and *Pale Fire* in particular. Both works portray American academics as boorish committee-room counterparts to a carnival culture of broken Hollywood dreams and provincial, Philistine values. Dystopia is no longer his theme, but Nabokov still retains the unsettled distaste he felt for *poshlost* in Germany during the 1930s. Although they are "funny," *Lolita* and *Pale Fire* explore a very harsh vision of academia. The assassination of Nabokov's father certainly contributed to shape this vision. The theme of assassination is present in *Lolita*, and is central to *Pale Fire* especially as a metaphor for the destruction of judgment and artistry, both of which are interdependent to one another. Throughout his work Nabokov was sensitive to the insidious ways ignorance, rigidity, and conventionality establish foundations for extremism, oppression, and cruelty.

Anthony Burgess is a figure who has made a career out of exploring the role of art in democracy. Often this exploration serves as a point of departure for understanding the patterns of corruption possible in state and administrative institutions. The novel *1985* describes a Britain taken over by syndicals. The main character is an unemployed history professor who supports himself in various ways, including tutoring alienated youths who want to know what the world was like before the trade unions took over. For speaking out against the system he is sent to camp for sensitivity training and ends up throwing himself on an electric fence. *1985* also contains a lengthy essay on Orwell's *1984*, which explores the novel as a reflection of 1940s Britain.

A special case of the Burgessean dystopia is the book-length poem *Byrne*. *Byrne* explores the relationships between art and the political climate of twentieth-century Europe, culminating in the assertion that European union could only be a fanatic's dream. Michael Byrne is a raging Anglo-Irish painter and composer who spends the 1930s living off women, exhibiting his pornographic paintings, and writing music for the cinema. He eventually sells his talents to Nazi Germany. At war's end Byrne flees to Africa, and the story shifts forward to the 1990s, as Byrne's children, now in late middle age, are variously collapsing beneath the weight of life, profound doubt, and the wickedness of the times. Through the character of Byrne, Burgess demonstrates the relationship of rampant modernism to fascism. By the end of the century, however, even the grisly constant of this formulation is mere schoolman's nostalgia. Art has devolved into frequencies still lower than fascism. Chaos reigns supreme.

Meanwhile, Burgess presses on steadily in ottava rima as he describes Byrne's offspring making operas out of the life of Calvin and Wells's *Time Machine*. They sit as "Eurodelegates" on committees for the "House of Euroculture," an exposition of "great European contributors to European thought" sans William Shakespeare. Elsewhere, Muslims riot in libraries and burn Dante for putting Muhammad in Hell.

Some readers may see in *Byrne* Neroesque fiddling or offbeat black comedy. The dizzying effect, however, is without sudden ironical upswings or jolly surprises. The poem culminates in a meeting between Byrne and his offspring. Through subjection to his art and music, his children are prepared—kneaded, softened, deadened—for his entry. The disembodied voice of John Gielgud rattles off a series of five sonnets of a dire and troubling aspect that impresses like falling lead. (One of these sonnets, in slightly different form, is presented in Burgess's autobiography as a work he composed while in the hospital in the late 1950s; it elicited a gloomy response from his physician.) Four Africans carry Byrne in on a sedan chair, as if Mr. Kurtz had been alive all these years. After two or three deathly quips from the old man, the children flee outside to an uncertain epiphany in an uncertain "filthy world" which is being consumed in the flames of terrorist bombs.

Although it is more properly classified as satire, *A Clockwork Orange* is also a very important dystopian novel because it is so closely conscious of the implications of its satiric statement. Among representative dystopian elements—matter-of-fact cruelty, intellectual mythology, corrupt bureaucracy, the portrayal of a paranoid author who, in this case, is victimized by the very forces he seeks to champion—is the amazingly structured euphemistic language of the protagonist, which is characterized by its combination of juvenile orientations and dehumanizing machine metaphors. The language reflects a society weakened by administrative corruption and physical decay, and present in the language are Russian phrases indicative of hegemonic infiltrations. It is a society exposed to an impending colonization of one form or another—the process of which the society is for the most part senseless.

Burgess was disappointed with Kubrick's film of the novel because he thought it elevated and valorized Alex, the novel's evil protagonist. But on close viewing it can be seen that the Alex of the film is even more monstrous than the Alex of the novel, precisely because the actor is so attractive. The sensitive viewer of the film will observe that it is Alex who is the work's strongest advocate of torture and conditioning as a means of control, even when he himself becomes the subject of that torture. Alex is the epitome of selfish childishness. Conditioning is the simple solution that appeals to the selfish and immature mind. The most important theme in the work—film or novel—doesn't necessarily focus upon the horror of torture and conditioning. But rather what is important is the vision it presents of a society based on selfishness and the pursuit of childish desires. This immature selfishness is at the heart of what makes the cruel, coercive society portrayed in *A Clockwork Orange* possible.

As a critique of intellectual mythology, *A Clockwork Orange* explores the ramifications of tampering with and restraining the unpredictability that makes us human. Treating nature and human beings like machines does not work. It is one of the ironies of the world that, rather than becoming more predictable and more controllable, life become in fact less predictable when subjected to programming.

In *The Confidence-Man* Herman Melville observes: "The grand points of human nature are the same to-day as they were a thousand years ago. The only variability in them is in expression, not in feature" (*CM* 71). This concludes a passage in which Melville argues that the most important feature or attribute of human beings is that they are unpredictable. This unpredictability—a complementary aspect of human adaptability—is the essential feature of what makes us human. Human beings are very similar to one another: two arms, two legs, two eyes, a sense of self counter-balanced by a hungry mouth. Satire presents a case for regarding historical and cultural variations as superficialities. Historical and cultural differences—like the myths, superstitions, and bedtime stories which support them—are demonic productions played out upon the stage of fear and ignorance. Human beings are essentially similar, and the greatest commonly shared feature or attribute of human beings is that their behavior and motives are unpredictable. Human beings thus resist definition. Great literature is the study of this unpredictability—a sweeping generalization, I grant you. But observe how such an approach illuminates the characters of Hamlet, Don Quixote, Achilles, Rabelais's Panurge, Milton's Satan, and William Blake's Christ. Once more, consider how such an approach underscores the ironies inherent in the discreet and clever character of Odysseus, whom Joyce aptly called "the first gentleman in Europe." Even more telling is this consideration in respect to Aeneas, a character completely lacking in unpredictability, a thrall to fate and loss and misery; a slave to war; a figure chained to the destiny of the imperial totalitarian state. If you take away unpredictability, then you take away the basis of human adaptability and hence our ability to survive. Again, as *A Clockwork Orange* shows, rather than becoming more predictable and more controllable, life becomes in fact less predictable and precarious when subjected to programming. It is something to think about as drug companies seek to employ management techniques that attribute disappointment and discontent to "depression," or divert ever greater numbers of unhappy children into "attention deficit disorder" programs. It is something to think about as self-appointed defenders of the oppressed seek to corral people into various victim or aggressor classifications based upon reproductive roles, skin color, or the the books they choose to read.

Menippean satire and synoptic analysis overturn the aesthetic of the programmed text and the programmed machine which "processes" it. The machine aesthetic see life as compartmental, consisting of interchangeable parts that are malleable, formable, programmable. Holding on to the old myth of Cartesian dualism, the priests of the machine aesthetic hold that the model of computer hardware and software best captures the "essence" of the human phenomenon. Like the "thinking machines" they proudly admire, the priests of the machine aesthetic offer measurement, imperatives, and programming. And like the erlkings and ogres of fable, these machine values—manifested as synthetic cultural icons, armored personal carriers, educational programs, or pharmaceuticals—will carry off the powerless.

The priests of the machine aesthetic see in literature a form much like themselves—cold, lifeless, prone to breakdowns—a programmed prodigy whose value isn't determined internally, that is, by the intrinsic value of the "text," but rather whose value is determined by the utilitarian uses to which the "text" can be put. In literature, the meaning of the text is how it is understood. But in the case of the programmed text, the use of the text is its meaning.

9
The Edge of Capital

COMPLEXITY AND THE HUMAN CONDITION

THIS IS A LESSON IN THE RELATIONSHIPS AMONG ART, SCIENCE, AND religion. There is nothing new in this lesson. The pattern is recognizable. The usual elements are present: confusion at the human condition, a startling new technology, an artistic response and mediation between the two, and then the emergence of a priest class that appropriates this mediation and shapes it into a dogma, a set of magical or scientific commandments. Finally, there is a power broker, a frowning chief who works to shepherd the whole process into a form that enhances his power and prestige.

In ancient Mesopotamia the new technology is agriculture, writing, and insurmountable brick walls. People want to know what it all means. Poets try to supply clever answers, for entertainment if for no other reason. Priests take up the answers which best preserve their position in society. The king is deified and his edicts are said to be handed down by the gods.

Today, the familiar—sometimes frightening, sometimes joyful, but mostly confused—wonder at the human condition remains. The new technology is the complex consumer society we work to maintain and the electronic systems of information manipulation which allow us to manage it. Text producers create future histories hinging upon notions of revolutions in consciousness, utopian (and dystopian) consumerisms, scientisms, and various religious, new age, and "postmodern" millennialisms. The priests in this scheme are the computer experts and the articulate explainers of culture and power. Finally, the new king is a manifold of market demands, big banks, investors, and transnational corporations whose ambitions include deconstructing nation-states and civil institutions in the name of "economic development."

An analysis of complexity theory convenes the outlines of this formulation.

Critical Patterns of Evolution

The representative figure in complexity theory is Stuart Kauffman of the Santa Fe Institute. Kauffman studied philosophy at Dartmouth and Oxford. At Oxford he developed an interest in theoretical biology and decided to embark upon a medical career. He took his MD at University of California, San Francisco. In 1987 he received a MacArthur Foundation fellowship. An emeritus professor of biochemistry and biophysics at the University of Pennsylvania School of Medicine, he now devotes his time to the Santa Fe Institute where he is a professor and member of the faculty in residence. According to the S.F.I. "Researchers in Residence" web page, which categorizes the research interests of fellows and faculty, Kauffman, along with five others, is distinguished as a "Self-Constructing Autonomous Agent."[1]

Founded in part by refugees from the down-sized Los Alamos National Laboratory, the Santa Fe Institute is an interdisciplinary "think tank" with broad undergraduate, postgraduate, and postdoctoral internships. The institute has connections with trenchant multinational financial markets. Members of the board of directors include the president and CEO of Transamerica Criterion Group, a consultant from the Fiduciary Trust Co. of New York, the managing director of the Swiss Bank Corporation, and a Citicorp vice president. Citicorp has endowed a chair at the institute known as the "Citibank Professor." The institute is dedicated to the application of complexity science to an emerging syntheses of study in fields such as biochemistry, genetics, physics, computer science, economics, industrial administration, finance, political science, and world governance. The methodology employed at the Santa Fe Institute is computer modeling, and hence reports of "life in silica" which have filtered into the mainstream press. The idea behind computer modeling is that complex interactions, from the weather to stock market activity to the intricate metabolic activities within cells, can be expressed as equations which can be solved by super computers. The mandlebrot set—the parent of fractal geometry and associated popular art images—is the best known of these silica models of the physical world. Kauffman's two books, *The Origins of Order: Self-Organization and Selection in Evolution* (1993) and *At Home in the Universe: The Search for the Laws of Self-Organization and Complexity* (1995), apply complexity science to the study of the origins and evolution of life. The former work is for scientists. The latter is for a broader audience, and it is this work I will discuss here. The book frequently lapses into a personal, journalistic style. In his own book on molecular activity and emergence, *Vital Dust: Life as a Cosmic Imperative*, Nobel laureate biochemist Christian de Duve points out that some Santa Fe Institute authors "communicate a feeling of fervor and excitement typical of new converts of some esoteric creed."[2] Indeed, Kauffman confesses that he "hold[s] the hope that what some are calling the new sciences of complexity may help us find anew our place in the universe, and through this new science, we may recover our sense of worth . . . reinvent the sacred . . . and reinvest it at the core of the new civilization."[3]

Kauffman advances a fascinating thesis. Near-chaotic complexity triggers self-organization. This is a self-ordering process of emergence which is seen again and again in nature. This penchant for self-organization is evident in complex self-catalyzing molecular systems, organisms, economic systems, technological systems and cultural systems. Kauffman's most ambitious assertion is that this "order for free," as he calls it, in the drying, molecule-rich puddles of primordial earth ignited the flame of life. Life was no accident, he claims, "we were expected." This same penchant for self-organization in complex systems went on to guide evolution, enhancing and increasing complexity near the "edge of chaos" where life is best poised for development and survival.

De Duve proposes a similar but significantly different formulation: "Life is an obligatory manifestation of the combinatorial properties of matter."[4] Complexity is a component of this combinatorial matrix, but is it significant for emergence? Kauffman insists that near-chaotic complexity is "the ultimate wellspring of the order of ontogoney." This, as he warns us himself, "is a heretical view" that diverges from the mainstream of current thinking in evolutionary biology.[5]

According to Kauffman, molecular state-spaces can either be subcritical or supracritical. In a supracritical state-space, molecular complexity is such that reactions occur spontaneously and chaotically, producing constantly increasing molecular variety. In a subcritical state-place of molecular complexity, molecular interaction is regulated. According to Kauffman, the earth's biosphere is supracritical but the organisms within it are subcritical. If organisms were supracritical, then unchecked, runaway molecular interactions would take place which would disrupt metabolism and destroy cells. Life exists at the boundary between subcritical organisms and the supracritical biosphere. The interplay of organisms and the biosphere maximizes diversification, speciation, and migration. The molecular chaos in the supracritical biosphere is necessary to promote change in the subcritical homeostatic molecular interactions within organisms. The supracritical molecular activity within the biosphere sometimes crosses the boundary into the metabolisms of subcritical organisms, resulting in bacterial and viral infections and disease.

According to Kauffman, the notion of the supracritical and the subcritical is not limited to biomolecular systems. It is yet another application of the deep rules of order which are common to all complex systems. The notion of the supracritical and the subcritical can be applied or scaled to local and global ecologies, economics, politics, culture, and linguistics. Kauffman claims this application is not metaphorical or an application of literary analogy, but is a direct application of the fundamental laws of complexity. I argue that such applications are, at best, metaphoric, and, at worst, a sham scientific whitewash for fascist world order.

Language can be seen to possess supracritical and subcritical complexity (Table 1). Like the biosphere, all language taken together—syntax, lexicon, associative contexts, families of associations, figures of speech, cognates between languages and dialects, families of languages, all languages—is supracritical. An infinite variety of systematic and nonsystematic combinations are possible which can produce the semblance of any meaning that can be suggested by the system or imagined by the auditor. Like organisms, language is sometimes subcritical. In closed contextualized exchanges, language is directed, pointed, effective, and meaningful. Poets work with language at the

Table 1
LANGUAGE REGIMES

Example	Explanation, Conversation	Poetry, Argument	Deconstruction, Euphemism
Emotion	Contemplation	Astonishment	Fear, Crisis, Confusion
Politics	Directing	Diverting	Dictating
Logic	Performative	Symbolic	Non Sequitur
Context	Workplace, Home	Entertainment, Democratic Arena	Pre-Violent Conflict, Nazi Rally
Grammar	Prescribed	Modulatory	Shifting
	Subcritical (Ordered)	**Critical (Complex)**	**Supracritical (Chaotic)**

boundary between subcritical and supracritical language, drawing from the supracritical to produce new and directed meanings which are applied in subcritical contexts. The so-called language poets have produced nonsensical, amusing, and startling effects because they present the supracritical in such a way as to cleverly mimic and disrupt subcritical contexts. Taking this further, it is possible to see how post-structuralists and deconstructionists have torn down the boundary between the supracritical and subcritical states of language and affected an incursion or an invasion of the supracritical into the subcritical.[6] In biological terms then, deconstruction is like a virus which has infected an organism. It may be that this infection can encourage the diversity of speciation in language—create new meanings—but it is important to consider that diseases can also kill. In this light, the deconstructionist is analogous to the mad geneticist who without regulation or direction combines molecules in his laboratory, indiscriminately producing new viruses, toxins, narcotics, Frankenfoods, carcinogens, and biological weapons.

The emergent science of complexity is leading us to reexamine our assumptions about historical process and the evolution of systems. Darwin's view of gradually accumulating variations is examined closely by Kauffman. The role of natural selection and historical accident is not to be replaced, but self-ordering is appreciating as an important factor in evolution. Kauffman believes further work will show that the latter is actually a complementary implication of the former, where coevolving systems actually promote catastrophe and extinction to enhance evolution. Survival of the fittest may be found to be a component of the self-ordering systemization of life. Of course Darwinism isn't the only theory of dynamic systems to come under scrutiny. The tendency for complex systems to order themselves in response to the effects of strange attractors is a discovery which leads us to reexamine Hegelian dialectics as well. The interaction of thesis and anti-thesis, according to Kauffman, "sounds more than a little bit like the evolution of the hundreds of millions of species that have come and gone, or the evolution of technologies that have come and gone."[7] Marx, Freud, and other social and psychological theoreticians are also subject to close reexamination in the light of complexity science. Possible courses this reexamination can take are discussed in the third section of this chapter.

Kauffman argues that general laws or patterns govern not only the *genesis* but also the *evolution* of complex systems, whether they be organisms, ecological landscapes, biospheres, technological artifacts, industries, economies, or civilizations. According to Kauffman, approaching critical states at the "edge of chaos" is the mechanism which orders evolutionary patterns.

The first of these patterns maps the initial proliferation of complex systems. In biology and natural history—the "Cambrian explosion" 550 million years ago is the most representative example—organisms burst into the biosphere in a variety of forms. Speciation is diverse and mutations are radical and dramatic as life forms take great leaps in design in order to explore new ways to maximize chances for survival. As fitness increases, life settles upon the forms of similar variants which are refined in more subtle ways. Kauffman argues that this same pattern governs technological evolution. The rule seems to be that "[a]fter a fundamental innovation is made, people experiment with radical modifications to that innovation to find ways to improve it. As better designs are found, so variations become progressively more modest."[8] This developmental pattern can be applied to any of the fundamental inventions we are intimately familiar with such as bicycles, cars, guns, airplanes, and helicopters. First comes a far ranging period of experimentation with a variety of forms. These forms split off into separate branches of evolution, some of which end in early extinction—the penny farthing bicycle, for example. Eventually, these evolutionary branches settle down to several prevailing lineages.

According to Kauffman, this general pattern is itself regulated by several simple laws. First, according to the principle of the "learning curve," production becomes more efficient as a factory produces more copies of a given item. Thus, assuming the break-even point is reached, it is cheaper on a per-unit basis to produce three hundred Boeing 777 aircraft than it is to produce one hundred. A million copies of Hershel Parker's new Melville biography is cheaper to produce, per unit, than a third that number. Second, according to the principle of "technological trajectories," the rate of improvement of a given technology slows with time and expenditure. Improvements in technology are initially rapid, and then slow. Typically, improvement reaches a plateau and then ceases. Lockheed has exhausted the design potential of the Constellation propeller-driven airliner and it is no longer produced. The lineage has ended. The Constellation is extinct. However, according to our understanding of the power-law relationship between cost per unit and total number of units produced, "after increasingly long periods with no improvement, sudden improvements often occur."[9] Thus, if Boeing sells enough 777's, new, specialized, re-engined, and stretched versions will appear. If students buy enough copies of a textbook, publishers produce new, revised editions. But is it human imagination and foresight or "the edge of chaos" which shapes these lineages?

These same evolutionary laws—or metaphors—can be applied to the field of literary inquiry. We can seek examples in the evolution of critical schools, philosophical orientations, or the development of theoretical ideologies. The Dada might be taken as an example. Initially within the Dada we find a wide range of dramatic early experimentation. Radically different forms are produced and presented in a wide variety of media and contexts. Later, this variety settles down to a few dominant lineages—painting and poetry, say—and these find themselves channeled into refined Dada exhibitions and readings. From regions of high complexity within Dada, emergence and speciation occur: a suicide for instance, or surrealism is born. Surrealism, in fact, becomes the dominant branch of Dada. It is the fair-haired, upmarket Cromagnon born of the undergraduate ape-ancestor. Again there is a wide range of early experimentation. Dominant branches—media and artists—emerge. The work representing these dominant branches becomes less experimental, less striking, and finds refinement in increasingly subtle ways. Dalí, for instance, abandons essays into paranoid-critical realms and explores exquisite vulgarizations of his own vain-glory. André Breton, leader of the surrealist group, seeks not to employ elaborate and clever devices to explain Dalí's turpitude but simply excommunicates him. Along these same lines, learning curve patterns, technological trajectories, and power-law relationships can be applied. Dalí makes more money, Dalí works harder, Dalí comes up with new ideas. . . .

Examples of evolutionary laws can be identified in the development of a writer's art and technique. The evolution of the subject matter and themes treated by an author, including protracted spells of low productivity and sudden innovation, can similarly be described in terms of these common evolutionary patterns. And the case also holds true for individual works themselves. It is possible to map the development of themes, characters, imagery, and plots according to evolutionary laws.

There are coevolutionary laws in effect, too. Works of art can be seen to effect each other according to established patterns. Whole landscapes of "species" interaction can be desried as works effect each other in ways which (particularly at the edge of chaos, according to Kauffman) the chances for survival, even among competing entities, is enhanced. According to Kauffman, there is a tendency for competing entities to reinforce chaos, a sort of self-organized criticality which enhances both entities' chances for survival. Thus, by way of example, British empiricism and continental *a priori* idealism might be seen to refine and reinforce each other as intellectual species in competition upon the same survival landscape.

To recapitulate: according to Kauffman, as systems approach complex states near the edge of chaos, diversification, speciation, and refinement occur. There is an emergence, a jump to a higher level of organization. This, according to Kauffman, is true for complex self-catalyzing molecular systems, organisms, technological systems, economic systems, political systems, and historical process.

Order for Free

Let's return to the Santa Fe Institute. Let's look at their "science." The methodology employed at the Santa Fe Institute is computer modeling, and hence reports of "life in silica" which have filtered into the mainstream press. The idea behind computer modeling is that complex interactions, from the weather to stock market activity to the intricate metabolic activities within cells, can be expressed as nonlinear equations that can be solved by super computers. The equations which these computers are processing have been around a long time, but it has only been recently, within the past twenty years or so, that we have had equipment powerful enough to solve them. It isn't the science that's new, just the computational instruments. The big question, of course, is whether or not these computers can accurately model the real world. They cannot. Computer models are only as good as the assumptions the models are based on. Any conclusion yielded by a computer is going to be logically consistent with the assumptions on which the model is based. This is what is known as self-consistent logic. If you don't contest your assumptions and your results cannot be refuted, then you do not run into problems.

In *Darwin's Black Box: the Biochemical Challenge to Evolution*, Michael J. Behe argues that the complexity scientists have yet to test their theories in a real world context. "No proponent of complexity theory has yet gone into the laboratory, mixed a large variety of chemicals in a test tube, and looked to see if self-sustaining metabolic pathways spontaneously organize themselves." The results of such an experiment, which has been attempted countless times in the past by frustrated, origin-of-life scientists, yields little more than "a lot of muck on the sides of a flask, and not much else."[10] Behe claims that Kauffman's work is "a mathematical analysis that leaves out all the specific features of organisms, reducing them to symbols and then manipulating the symbols . . . math is useful to science only when the assumptions the mathematical analysis starts with are true."[11] In his discussion of Kauffman's book on *The Origins of Order*, Behe states that "Kauffman discusses his ideas in a chapter entitled 'The Origin of a Connected Metabolism,' but if you read the chapter from start to finish you will not find the name of a single chemical—no AMP, no aspartic acid, no nothing. In fact, if you scan the entire subject of the book, you will not find a chemical name there either." Behe concludes by quoting John Maynard Smith (one of Kauffman's mentors in graduate school), who has suggested that Kauffman is practicing "fact-free science."[12]

Within the walls of the institute, the Santa Fe people are busy modeling universes of emergent order and competitive landscapes where organisms devour one another for the "mutual benefit of life as a whole." Self-organization and complexity theory is billed as complementary to Darwin's random forces of evolution. The net effect, however, is simply to introduce social Darwinism into administrative discourse. The institute itself might be considered a model of the way science will be done in the emerging postmodern world of complexity, horizontal organization, and life-optimizing competition for all. Indeed, Santa Fe's story provides an interesting model of the trend that sees "partnerships" forming between large research universities and private corporations. The Santa Fe people call themselves an "Institute." Perhaps this is a postmodern euphemism for what I called them earlier, a mercenary "think tank." Scientific credentials notwithstanding, they are a corporate consulting service subject to the ethos of corporate culture. I have a friend who is a corporate consultant in the six-figure bracket. He describes consulting like this: "It's a con-game. In corporate culture, the name of the game is self-promotion. Often you produce results that have a different significance than what was sought. It's all about politics—appearances—convincing people you have done something while what you're really doing is telling them what they want to hear." The Santa Fe group is a private concern which only publishes its successes. Originally, the Institute was set up to employ computer modeling to predict stock market trends. Indeed, it was an appropriate application—in the middle of the 1980s—of the "postmodern" science of complexity. A similar enterprise was undertaken in the last century by Charles Babbage with his "Difference Engine"—a computer that was programmed by Byron's daughter Ada. They wanted to use it to predict the outcomes of horse races. Their investors had a wild ride also.

However, the implications of complexity science as a template for global financial strategy are not so amusing. Complexity provides a scientific mandate for bringing crisis to managerial and labor stratums as a means of driving institutional, national, and regional economies to higher levels of complexity near the "edge of chaos." At the industrial and institutional level, downsizing and outsourcing illustrate the actions of this forced march into chaos. What emerges is a cyclical process that reinforces itself from several directions. From one such direction, banks are forcing downsizing through their loan procedures. If your company wants a loan, fire people. The shibboleth—repeated on television, in magazines, and in MBA programs across the land—says we must tighten our belts; increase efficiency; we've got to compete in world markets. Banking policy is based on the belief that if current expense is lowered, interest payments are at reduced risk. Employee costs are the most controllable of all controllable costs. To get loans, corporations let go of employees. So many are sacked that operations are stifled. The corporations have to hire consultants to keep the show running, and of course the consultants cost more than the employees who were sacked. On paper quarterly expenses appear to go down, and executives use this information to justify salary increases and bonuses. At the behest of savvy directors and administrators, this ethos has taken root in nonprofit institutions as well. Education, health, and military workers also find themselves joining the forced march into chaos. In terms of outcome, complexity "science" does little more than white wash what used to be termed "social Darwinism" and the dubious and cruel notion of Adam Smith's "invisible hand." After the 1980s, Thatcher, Reagan, and then the phenomenon of 1990s realpolitik and unchecked suburban sprawl, evidence of what the invisible hand has done to Britain and the United States is as plain as the condition of our down-sized and micro-managed business, military, healthcare, and educational systems; the increased work that must be performed for fewer benefits; the relocation of human resources across obsolete national frontiers to zones of economic development; unmarked Frankenfoods at the grocery mega-store; and the spiraling destruction of the environment.

The role of science as an articulation of such an ethos cannot be examined too closely. Complexity theory's notion of self-organization is billed as a complement to Darwin's random forces of evolution; the net effect, however, is to simply introduce social Darwinism—a legitimization of greed—into administrative discourse. And the Santa Fe people have the—is it brazen temerity or is it business acumen?—to say TQM, down-sizing and horizontal organizational structures reflect the principles of universal, emerging order—"order for free," as Kauffman calls it. I puzzled over this phrase when I first encountered it. Then it hit me. Order for *free* would appeal to S.F.I.'s patrons. A rule emerges: *In the corporate ethos, the purpose of science is to tell the client what he wants to hear.* Citicorp wanted S.F.I "to create a completely rigorous new way of doing economics based on the complex adaptive systems point of view."[13] As mentioned in a proceeding section, Citicorp has endowed a chair at the institute known as the "Citibank Professor." To what extent have Citicorp's wishes, as well as the wishes of other banks represented on S.F.I.'s board, shaped the essentials of complexity science? We have seen that complexity theory superimposes industrial, technocratic, and coarse-focus economic epistemologies—learning curves, technological trajectories, and power laws—on living systems ranging from the evolution of life to the emergence of world government. These epistemologies convene political and economic understanding to favor the emerging structure of transnational financial markets. Complexity theory boasts to have revealed a process whereby systems are responsive to minor actors at the margins and bottoms of complex systems. The fact remains, however, that the major decisions effecting the direction a system moves and the treatment of actors in the system are made at the top, in corporate boardrooms and at administrative headquarters.

Kauffman evokes the "pile of sand" model to illustrate power laws and the principle of self-organized criticality.[14] Picture sand pouring onto a table. The sand builds into a pile. As more sand is added, slides and avalanches occur along the pile's side. The sides of the pile are at "the edge of chaos" so that only a few grains of sand added to the top can create massive disturbances—avalanches—lower along the sides of the pile. As a management model the metaphor evokes images of elite actors exercising control over a broad domain of holdings through the simple tweaking of variables at the top of the pile. Catastrophic disturbances occur along the sides of the pile until self-organization—"order for free"—asserts itself, and the pile grows larger, retaining its shape. As for the individuals caught in the avalanches, their lot is doubtful. Evidently, much of this "order for free" in organizations is a result of employees living in fear of the pink slip, and so falling into line, working harder, and so on.

Another notion with disturbing applications is Kauffman's theory that coevolving systems actually promote catastrophe and extinction to enhance evolution. Could it be possible for global financial markets to promote catastrophe and extinction on local, regional, or national levels in the name of economic evolution? Reports of correlative if not indicative activities can often be found in the pages of *The Economist, Natural History, Harper's* and *The McKinsey Quarterly*.[15] Downsizing in the industrial world, the plight of Tibet, the Balkans scenario, the Asian financial crisis of the late 1990s, and much of Africa seem obvious enough examples. Would Kauffman suggest that the Holocaust was simply the activity of coevolving systems promoting catastrophe and extinction to enhance evolution?

Kauffman believes that "systems having various kinds of local autonomy, may be a fundamental mechanism underlying adaptive evolution in ecosystems, economic systems, and cultural systems."[16] Kauffman describes Peter Banks urging the Institute to find new insights into the management of complex organizations.[17] How can you manage organizations, increase their sizes, and at the same time reduce the costs of planning and administration? How can you cut off your obligations to managers and labor, maximize competition for growth, and yet maintain and exercise control over your vassals? The solution is to push organizations to the brink of chaos, that scientific Shangri-la where all good things emerge thanks to the principles of complexity science and self-ordering. The same invisible hand that created life will guide the WTO, GATT, the International Monetary Fund, the EU, NAFTA, the White House, G-8, the City of London, Tokyo, Hong Kong, Geneva, Mercosur, drug cartels, Iraq, Iran, Singapore, and China? Hong Kong's recent "phase transition" presents a good example of the "invisible hand" in action. Indeed, the third world is the "invisible hand" in action, the "edge of chaos." Kauffman relates how John Maynard Smith suggested the Santa Fe Institute was embarked upon "some kind of post-Marxist analysis of social evolution." Kauffman chafed: "Marxism has such a bad reputation."[18] Perhaps "complexity science" is a more palatable euphemism for a similar scientific justification for corrupt, arbitrary authority? Smith's criticism was spot on. Kauffman does in fact argue for the efficacy of dialectical materialism and "a place for 'law' in the historical sciences."[19]

Is history a science? The question is problematic. The most immediate answer seems to be: "That depends upon what you mean by *science*." Indeed, the question has more to do with semantics than history. Still, the quest for an answer produces interesting fruit.

In his inaugural lecture delivered in Strasbourg in 1862, N. D. Fustel de Coulanges suggests that the purpose of historical science is to understand humanity. History is a study of how "man shapes his own beliefs, how from his beliefs he derives his institutions, what path his thought and laws have followed, how much the historians of the ancient world differed from ours, and what road mankind has traversed in thirty centuries."[20]

In *The Nature of History*, chapter 4, "History, Science and Social Science" Arthur Marwick approaches the question "is history a science?" by affirming that it is. Where history differs from the traditional sciences, however, is in the nature of the subject being treated by historical science. Marwick says, "the historian is concerned with a different kind of a material, human experience in the past, from that which the natural scientist is concerned."[21]

For myself, the question is best approached by addressing the context of the particular "historical science" one is investigating, and by context here I mean the practical uses and outcomes that "historical science" is put to. Thus, to parody Wittgenstein, *the use of a "historical science" determines its meaning*.

Now, as a historical science, to what use is complexity put?

According to Kauffman, Robert Axelrod, a MacArthur Fellow and political scientist at the University of Michigan,

> has been looking at simple models in which new higher-level political "actors" could emerge. His new model is based on states that intimidate their neighbors, demand tribute, and then form cooperating alliances with those tribute states for mutual benefit. These alliances emerge as new actors.[22]

To me this suggests classic *manoeuvre*. One example springs immediately to mind: The methods by which transnational banking interests promote ecological "management," that is, suppressing local environmentalists and forcing deforestation and mining in the third world. But even more clearly in this vein, such models prompt speculation as to the roles scenarists certainly played in what happened in the Middle East in the early 1990s, and in Asia and the Balkans eight years later. It has been possible to count off the "new actors" as they "emerge."[23] There is of course nothing new in this. Using crisis as a catalyst for consolidating power and manipulating people is as old as (and forms the plots of) the stories told in the first half of the Epic of Gilgamesh. Indeed, using crisis in this way is the real "world's oldest profession."

What I find most disconcerting here is the supposition that frames the dispensation of such events in terms of a "historical science" that commingles the creation of life and underlying universal order with the outcomes of adventure, coercion, and conflict. Kauffman's "historical science" invests political and capital interests with the unassailable authority of "cosmic order" and "God." In this view, one also gets a very clear picture of the Panglossian nature of the self-ordering thesis. Kauffman's "We the expected" is interchangeable with Professor Pangloss's "Best of all possible worlds."

Kauffman strongly advocates "democracy." It reflects, he says, other types of emergent, noncentralized order revealed by complexity theory. His noble vision, however, is clouded by social Darwinism and cynicism. Democracy, according to Kauffman, is a "disjointed, opportunistic, fractured, argumentative, pork-barrel, cheat, steal-a-vote, cluttered . . . well-evolved system to solve hard, conflict laden problems and find, on average, pretty good compromises."[24] Compromise is one thing, a civil consensus undergirding good government is another; and aren't these features he lists what democracy is supposed to protect us from? Kauffman isn't describing democracy but rather transnational graft and a state-space of colonial adventure. Do his computers take into account passions, irrationality, and altruistic motives? Perhaps his definition is, in the postmodern sense, "realistic," as in "realpolitik," but the ethical superiority of the vision of democracy expressed in Pericles' funeral oration is, for want of a better adjective, *obvious*. Thomas Paine, Thomas Jefferson, and Franklin Delano Roosevelt also offer some useful ideas on the subject.

Apparently Kauffman has formulated a theory that is little more than a sophisticated "management tool" designed to support the decisions made in the board rooms of transnational development consortia, and to provide up-market management consultants with yet another argument to promote their own importance—and in the name of underlying cosmic order. There is, however, a further dynamic to be considered.

Kauffman is pursuing a grandiose ambition. He claims to be driven by a quest for an underlying cosmic order, an underlying principle of universal unity that can be perceived and described. Repeatedly in his book Kauffman speaks of a life-long quest for this order. "I have always hoped that the order in organisms would come to be understood as natural, as expected."[25] In *Artificial Life: the Quest for a New Creation*, Steven Levy quotes Kauffman: "I've always wanted the order one finds in the world not to be particular, peculiar, odd or contrived—I want it to be, in the mathematician's sense, generic. Typical. Natural. Fundamental. Inevitable. Godlike. That's it. It's God's heart, not his twiddling fingers, that I've always in some sense wanted to see."[26] Lewin and Waldrop present similar reports.[27] While Kauffman certainly works very hard to promote Santa Fe in the marketplace, he apparently has a superintendent desire to make a mark in the history of science at the level of Copernicus, Newton, or Einstein. He wants nothing less than to "reinvent the sacred." Citicorp's patronage may not be the direct object of Kauffman's personal ambition, but it enhances Kauffman's impression that he is "really on to something." Santa Fe, while it is a think tank and subject to market demands, shares Kauffman's goal and is actively carrying forward an effort to perpetrate a revolution in science. But even in this light it is evident that Stuart Kauffman's program and the Santa Fe Institute are functions of promotional ambitions.

I do not believe that Kauffman is outstanding in either motive or ambition; he is yet another expression of the failing characteristics of a commodified intellectual culture that embraces a managerial approach to knowledge as a means of self-promotion. In both character and implication, complexity is a science derived from the marketplace. But there is one final dynamic to be considered. A statement Charles Jencks made during the early 1970s in *Architecture 2000* puts the finger on it:

> The idea that man is an unconscious victim of external forces, or internal necessities, is one of the greatest intellectual orthodoxies of our time. Ever since the waning of traditional religions, men have been convincing themselves of one inevitable necessity after another, until the point has been reached where some of them have actually started to become operative in detail. Whether or not this desire to discover some omnipotent external force signifies an intellectual rage for order and understanding or rather a deep psychological drive to identify with a superhuman force and avoid responsibility is open to question: but its existence is beyond dispute. It can be seen in the Marxist appeal to inevitable laws of history, in the Freudian appeal to basic drives of the libido and most recently in the appeal to underlying forces of technology by Galbraith and McLuhan.[28]

In addressing itself to issues ranging from the origins of life to the emergence of world government, complexity has become a "science" that aspires to the level of religion. While complexity *theory* might serve as a compelling metaphor, my conclusion is that complexity *science* is not separable from the "corporate" context in which it was invented. It is a reflection of a entrepreneurial intellectual sensibility oriented in self-promotion and the programmed management of knowledge. While complexity's cousins in economics—learning curves and technological trajectories—seem to have coarse-focus descriptive applications in industry, the emphasis complexity theory places on the "edge of chaos" as necessary for emergence is factitious and quite contrary to the lessons of fifty centuries of civilization. Chaos is not haunted by a benign invisible hand. Chaos is chaos.

10

Scaling Up to the Homeric Question: The Aesthetics of Chaos, Complexity, and Cosmogenesis

"Have you guessed the riddle yet?" the Hatter said, turning to Alice again.

"No, I give it up," Alice replied. "What's the answer?"

"I haven't the slightest idea," said the Hatter.

"Nor I," said the March Hare.

Alice sighed wearily. "I think you might do something better with the time," she said, "than wasting it in asking riddles that have no answers."

THE COSMOGENIC MANIFESTO

CHARLES JENCKS IS THE AUTHOR OF OVER TWENTY BOOKS ON ARCHITECture and culture. His work is distinguished by inventiveness, remarkable lucidity, and a philosophical approach that is both rigorous and accessible. He is recognized by many as being the leading advocate and interpreter of post-modernism. *The Architecture of the Jumping Universe: A Polemic: How Complexity Science Is Changing Architecture and Culture* is Jencks's most ambitious work since his 1971 study of sociocultural prognostication, *Architecture 2000: Predictions and Methods*. In *The Architecture of the Jumping Universe,* Jencks interprets and advocates the "post-modern science of complexity" as a new philosophy of aesthetics. His philosophy is called Cosmogenesis.

According to Jencks, "Our aesthetic enjoyment and pleasure in life are deeply tied to curiosity, adaptation, the will to discover new truths; and this drive has to be put at the center of a new philosophy."[1] Jencks argues that we stand at a watershed in history where, because of our science, we know vastly more about the universe than anyone in the history of the human race. There are two sources from which we draw this new knowledge: first, astronomy and physics; second, the "post-modern sciences of complexity" including complexity theory itself, chaos science, self-organizing systems, and nonlinear dynamics. According to Jencks there is a new "post-modern paradigm" in the works, a "post-Christian synthesis of a new world view, an emergent consensus that is uniting scientists, theologians, architects, artists, and much of the general public."[2]

Cosmogenesis pulls together the numerous strands of this paradigm. Jencks's philosophy is rooted in the most recent theories of cosmological evolution and the anthropic theory which claims this process, including the emergence and development of life, is teleological. Complexity science draws these notions together through the unifying paradigm of emergence—the idea that, as systems advance toward higher levels of complexity, sudden "jumps" to new, self-ordering levels of organization occur. These startling and unpredictable "jumps" occur as complexity approaches "the edge of chaos." According to cosmogenesis, four major events or jumps have occurred in the past fifteen billion years. The first three jumps—beginning with the big flaring (Jencks prefers "flaring" to the patriarchal "bang")—demarcate the eras of Energy, Matter, and Life. The fourth jump initiates an era of Consciousness which, amongst other remarkable properties, possesses the "mysterious and uncanny" ability to reflect with astonishment upon the outlines of this process.

The spiritual implications of the cosmogenic narrative impress Jencks enough to contemplate a new religion. The universe is "a single, unfolding, creative event that is always reaching new levels of self-organization."[3] Our aesthetics and values should reflect "how the universe is always trying to organize herself in more sensitive and intelligent directions."[4] Jencks promises a more dynamic and creative world view than modernism offers. Cosmogenesis is an alternative to the modernist machine aesthetic which in art and administration seeks to represent centralized authority, "machinery, the process of building, or the minimal functional envelope."[5] Cosmogenesis introduces new dynamism and images to art which reflect the cosmogenic world view: "a language of building and design closer to nature, of twists and folds and undulations; of crystalline forms and fractured planes [and] wave motion."[6] Jencks promises "explosive" as well as subtle emergence—the full ramifications of which, in terms of global politics and the ticking population bomb, are only too apparent. While we might expect new beauty reflecting the joy and exuberance of creation as well as liberation from the rationalized machine-mind of modern

Homo economicus, cosmogenesis also promises some of the horrors of the jungle and the Old Hunter who makes his home there.

Although Jencks is a "post-modernist," he is careful to acknowledge the benefits of modernism, and aptly condemns the faults embedded in post-modernism: "ersatz, phoniness, camp, Kitsch, the lies perpetrated by an electronic society." He accepts cosmogenic post-modernism as an evolving paradigm, "a mixed blessing with developing stages, not an ideology and movement to be accepted or rejected *in toto.*"[7]

The greatest value in Jencks's philosophy is not so much the details of the scientific theories he seeks to explore, but rather the underlying question that prompts us to explore them. One is reminded of the riddle of the Sphinx. The riddle itself is not nearly so remarkable as the circumstances and the inspiration whereby Oedipus was able to answer it. For Jencks the issue isn't so much the revelation of a new science, but it is rather the process of this revelation itself. Jencks's philosophy brings us back to this important question: Where do we belong in the universe? What is the essential nature of our being? Jencks reminds us that Plato sees a world of individuals aspiring toward immortality. Freud sees in our motivations the drive to indulge our repressed and panting libidos. Nietzsche and Hegel picture us as either hammer or anvil, master or slave. Arguing along these lines, Jencks proposes another solution. While immortality, sex, and power are not without importance, what most matters to us is learning. "We are the *learning* animal."[8]

What should we be learning?

A friend of mine, a Hittitologist who declaims the history of the past two thousand years as "journalism," advocates cuneiform writing as the premier field of inquiry. I would suggest Aristophanes, Thucydides, and Homer. Drollery is not altogether my end here as my enthusiasm leads directly to what many understand to be the end of our learning—an answer to the Homeric question:

> Who, and whence, are you?[9]

I will not argue that the emerging science of complexity can answer this question to the satisfaction, say, of Wittgenstein, Hawthorne, Odysseus, Teiresias, Proteus, or myself. Complexity science, however, provides an important framework for understanding certain implications of the question. Complexity science presents a startling perspective which marks the outlines of a very compelling answer: We are evolving complexity. What is more, we are an evolving understanding of this complexity.

The mechanism described by this theory is fairly simple, and here we will review it one last time:

The theory claims that near-chaotic complexity triggers self-organization. Nature exhibits a self-ordering process of emergence which is seen again and again in different phenomena. This penchant for self-organization is evident in complex self-catalyzing molecular systems, organisms, economic systems, technological systems, and cultural systems. Once again we recall complexity guru Stuart Kauffman who has claimed that this self-ordering in the drying, molecule-rich puddles of primordial earth ignited the flame of life. Life was no accident, he claims, "we were expected." This same penchant for self-organization in complex systems went on to guide evolution, enhancing and increasing complexity near the "edge of chaos" where, according to the theory, life is best poised for development and survival. This general law or pattern governs not only the genesis but also the evolution of complex systems, whether they be organisms, ecological landscapes, biospheres, technological artifacts, industries, economies, or civilizations. As systems approach complex states near the edge of chaos, diversification, speciation, and refinement occur. There is an emergence, a jump to a higher level of organization. This is true for complex self-catalyzing molecular systems, organisms, technological systems, economic systems, political systems, and historical process.

Not surprisingly, striking emergencies can occur when these critical patterns of genesis and evolution become the subject an artist or movement seeks to explore. As we will see, however, an aesthetic analysis quietly disrupts the complexity thesis.

The Aesthetics of Complexity—Complexity as Technique

According to Charles Jencks, complexity science provides a powerful new language or set of metaphors for creating, appreciating, and evaluating art, literature, and politics. These metaphors include:

> *Scaling and Self-simularity.* Parts resemble not only each other but the whole as well. Self-simularity represents a "transformational similitude"—not exact replication.[10]

> *Strange Attractors.* A "chaotic but still ordered organization of form and movement around maxima and minima."[11]

Non-Linear Change. The universe is mostly nonlinear as opposed to linear, that is to say, it consists of random processes which often relay information back into itself. Jencks points to waves that twist, undulate, grow, and diminish continuously and abruptly.[12]

Unity in Variety. Complexity is "canonic" or universally prevalent in nature.

Folding and Catastrophe. "The fold dramatizes change and contradiction—the quick transition from one system of meaning to another—without trying to resolve them."[13]

Sudden Emergence and Phase Transitions. The outcome of complexity; when pushed from equilibrium or pressed to the "edge of chaos" systems "jump" to new levels of organization.

Jencks wishes to use these metaphors in a new language of art. The purpose of this language is to create a dialogue that communicates emergence and cosmogenesis. It is a dialogue rooted in the aesthetic value of complexity.

How is complexity appreciated? How is complexity created? To answer these questions we must examine the measure of complex value. Jencks calls this measure *organizational depth*.

Organizational depth (OD) is the basis for most appreciation, evaluation, and criticism of art. A sort of ornamental elaboration of complexity, OD creates the "resonance," "deep character," and "integrity" we perceive in art. Jencks sees it even as a quality which imputes moral value to a work. Formal depth and relationships are ultimately experienced on an ethical plane. Psychological speaking, the good, the true, and the beautiful are perceived to converge perspectively at infinity. Granted, this is a synesthetic leap of such complexity that one should wonder if all these attributes can maintain their value-ladenness as they disappear over the horizon. The notion of time being a function of organizational depth is a little clearer. In this formulation, the length of "computational time" one invests in studying a multivalent and complex work is a component of OD. The longer span of time one spends appreciating and evaluating a work, the more OD that work must possess. OD can, in this sense, "build in" time. Perhaps the best way to conceive of OD is by examining its practical limits. In a work exhibiting too much OD, complexity gives way to complication, senseless ornament, excess, and clutter. In a work exhibiting too little OD, the lack of complexity appears raw, impoverished, lacking in character, cheap, and quick.

It is desirable then for artists to be sensitive to and control the level of OD in their work.

How do artists create OD? How do they "build" time into their works? There is of course no prevailing method, but Jencks suggests the value of participatory design, plural design, eclecticism, and ad hocism. Layering, ambiguity, transparency, and juxtaposition are applications which "create" time, complexity, and, hence, OD.

There are other techniques and strategies to achieve OD. *Superposition* is a technique which "forces" complexity out of a conjunction of unrelated components: "a series of adjunct experiences which blur, contrast, complicate, and force an emergence." Jencks cites "Choral Works," a garden for the Parc de la Villette in Paris designed by Peter Eisenman and Jacques Derrida as a work employing superposition.[14] Jencks wonders in this case, however, if too much complexity results only in chaos and turbulence. Superposition can push systems to jump beyond self-organization and confute perceptual activity in a welter of irresolvable chaos.

Perhaps the best way to visualize the value of complexity is to place it on a graph. Jencks offers what he calls a "cosmic axiology" (Figure 1). Works of art which reflect and produce the cosmic process of complexity and self-ordering "are *better* than those which are poorly organized: either too simple or too entropic."[15] " 'Value' lies at right angles to these extremes." Along the X-axis Jencks plots increasing order to the left and increasing disorder or entropy to the right. "Complexity," a positive value, "the good," increases vertically along the Y-axis. An arc is described which curves up from a state of high order, appreciating along the complexity axis as it becomes more disordered. A peak is reached where disorder draws the line back down again until, at a state of complete entropy ("absolute zero" in the thermodynamic sense), complex value is lost entirely.

The veracity of this metaphysic rests on the assumption that complexity is a direct corollary of value. I have to reject this assumption. Jencks's Y-axis does not graph the "Complexity" described by complexity science.[16] His Y-axis rather describes something that is more accurately termed "Sophistication." Furthermore, value—literary value, for instance—cannot be determined arbitrarily according to a set of propositions or assumptions. Value cannot be determined *a priori*. It is a quality that exists in the "real" world. Value must be determined in the particular instance of particular phenomena within particular contexts. For example, Jencks himself argues that beauty

Fig. 1. "Cosmic Axiology" by Charles Jencks.

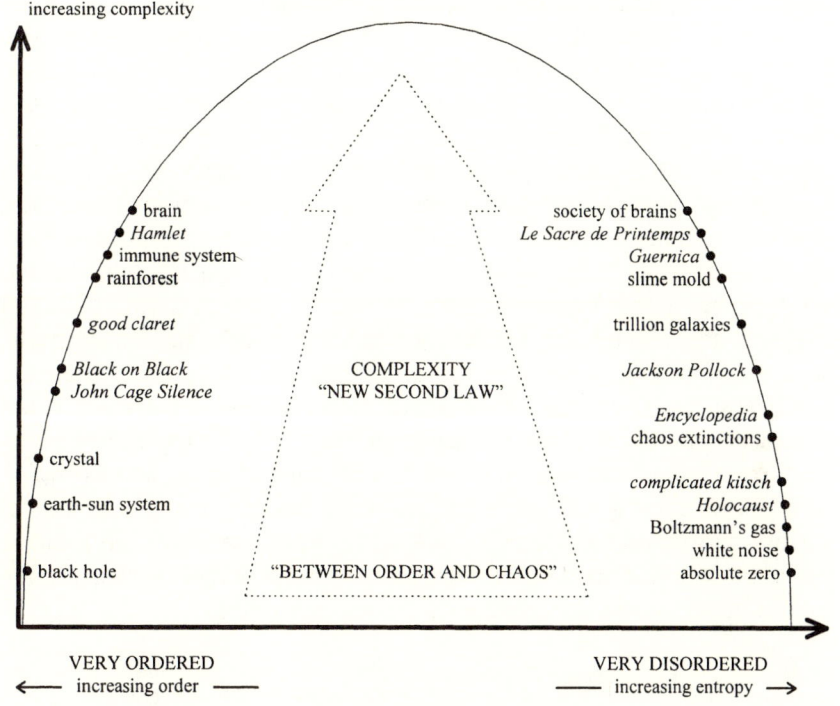

exists in the "real" world, and, in heroic defiance of Derrida, cites the example of the Bower Bird:

> Are we to deny the aesthetic intention of the Bower bird, the bird that decorates its nest to attract a mate?[17]

We must turn to the real world of particular instances to determine our criteria of artistic and literary value. This value does not arise or reveal itself through the mechanism of a world view or philosophy, but is determined by the literary works and traditions which have formulated it—the wisdom of our species. In a civilization of awakened minds, this value is measured in terms of *Cleverness* and *Integrity*. Cleverness and integrity are the parents of wisdom and knowledge. Without them, democratic civilization cannot flourish. Respectively, cleverness and integrity are beauty and truth raised to their highest pitch. Does complexity bear any relationship to these real life standards of value?

We can explore this question graphically in Figure 2, the Table of Literary Complexity. Complexity increases from left to right along the horizontal. Traditional Standards of Literary Value: Cleverness and Integrity (or the Wisdom of Our Species), increase vertically. Complexity is divided into three fields or regimes: ordered, complex, and chaotic. Jencks's discriminations among the modern, post-modern, late-modern, and ultra-modern are expressed below the graph as a function of complexity. Obviously, the relative positioning of the works on this table reflects the arbitrary and inexact factors of my personal sensitivities, learning, and taste. The mental estimations needed to adjust for organizational depth as well as solving ratios between integrity and cleverness are inexact processes at best. For example, because of its length and the scope of its vision, *Moby-Dick* obviously possesses more organizational depth than *Pale Fire*. However, when organizational depth is handicapped to provide for complexity of conception, it is easy to see why *Pale Fire* is graphed at a more complex level. Controversy will certainly erupt concerning my placement of various works and authors on the table, but I stand by the generic truths of the relations I have established. I believe the verdict of intellectual history shall signal overwhelming agreement.

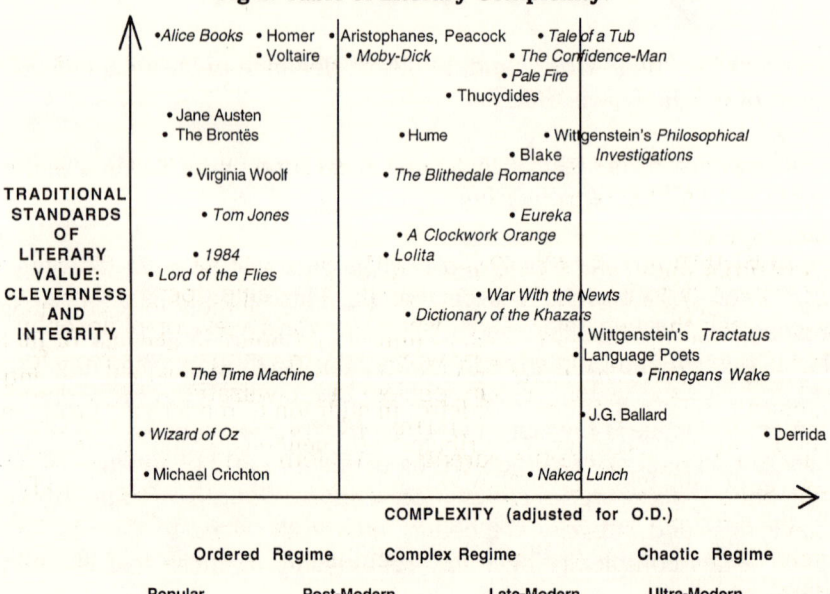

Fig 2. Table of Literary Complexity.

The graph shows there is no necessary relationship between complexity and value. Interestingly, a categorical relation emerges among certain elaborately conceived forms of Menippean satire such as are represented by various works of Swift, Melville, and Nabokov. We might expect Huxley's *Point Counter Point* to lie in this vicinity as well. However, the generic thesis erupts with the *Alice* books—in Northrop Frye's opinion, "perfect" examples of Menippean satire. The *Alice* books are situated within the ordered regime. Indeed, the presence of complexity in Menippean literature is a deliberate parodic device intended to ridicule the complexity it represents. Only within the chaotic regime is there an apparent necessary correlation between complexity and value, and that is clearly negative.

A multifaceted problem remains. We have established that complexity possesses little correlative value *in* literature, but does complexity perhaps play an important generative role? Is complexity performative or symbolic? Does complexity diminish as a work is perused and assimilated? Is complexity really necessary for creation at all? It is toward a solution to this problem that we now turn.

The Aesthetics of Cosmogenesis—The Cosmogenic Narrative

The main features of the cosmogenic narrative have by now been sketched out. The universe is a field of complexity from which self-ordering systems emerge. These emergencies take the form of dramatic jumps to higher (and sometimes lower) levels of organization, sophistication, and consciousness. Patterns of complexity, diversity, eclecticism, pluralism, variety, and bottom-up participation by co-creators of the narrative can enhance cosmogenesis and impel jumps to new levels of organization. We are built into this process, if for no other reason than to observe it.

It is not the purpose of a discussion of cosmogenic aesthetics to provide a comprehensive bibliography of cosmogenic narratives in literature. However, I should like to suggest several cosmogenic categories and, within them, discuss representative critical patterns. Then, after learning what's there, I shall examine, following the conclusion of this section, a contemporary novelized cosmogenic narrative which itself essays complexity science and emergence.

The first category of cosmogenic narrative is *mythological*. Stories about the creation of the world and human beings are called cosmogonies. The function of a mythological cosmogony is to explain how the world came to be. However, mythological cosmogonies are poetic and not necessarily believed in. People participate in myth-rituals at this level not because people necessarily believe in them but because such performances fulfill complex needs. Superstitions such as throwing spilled salt over one's shoulder or knocking on wood provide convenient illustrations. The people who practice such rituals don't necessarily believe in them; what they do believe is that in practicing the rituals certain needs will be met. We participate in these rituals and beliefs not because they provide an *explanation* of the phenomena involved, but because somehow they satisfy our need for *understanding* the phenomena involved; they help to establish our relationship to these phenomena (see chapter 6). Reading mythological cosmogonies is entertaining and fulfilling at many levels. Nobody today believes in Greek or Chinese or Native American creation stories, but they continue to sell in bookstores and are borrowed from libraries. They are satisfying because, even if you don't believe in them, they fulfill certain needs and expectations. Jencks's cosmogenic narrative fits neatly into this category because it is, at *prima facie,* very believable. It *feels* good, as if it *should* fulfill our needs and expectations. It is intelligent, and appeals to intelligence are very convincing. Once again, it seems to go beyond the complex exigencies of an explanation, and suggests something along the lines of understanding. The cosmogenic narrative encourages us to consider our relationship to the universe.

The second category of cosmogenic narrative is *religious.* A religious cosmogenic narrative is a creation story that is believed in. It fulfills a need some people have to know where the world comes from. Jencks's cosmogenic narrative runs into trouble as a religious narrative. Self-ordering implies a kind of predestination which, carried to its logical conclusion, is fatalistic. Moreover, cosmogenesis is based on a perception of the cosmos which is dependent on data from scientific measurements. If we go along with cosmogenesis, then each time a new, more powerful telescope is placed in orbit, or a new, bigger particle accelerator is built, we will have to upgrade our cosmogenic belief because of the discovery of some new particle or the detection of a still lower wavelength of background radiation in the heavens. To the people living three thousand years from now our "scientific" cosmogenic narrative will look as silly as the "scientific" cosmological beliefs of the Sumerians look to us today. And as far as that goes, the educated Sumerians didn't believe in them either.

The third category of cosmogenic narrative is *literary.* It lies somewhere between religious and mythological cosmogony. The purpose

10: SCALING UP TO THE HOMERIC QUESTION

of the literary comogony is to make a point about the human condition. For instance, the garden story expresses the angst writers felt toward the human condition. The unhappiness in the world can be explained in allegorical terms: it is *as if* the father of all humanity disobeyed the friendly creator and ate an apple which enlightened him to the fact that he (Adam) was an idiot. The spirit of the conflict between the city and the country might be explained in allegorical terms: it is *as if* the first farmer murdered the first shepherd, and thus all us inheritors of the legacy of agriculture are uprooted from the land and have to live in some dire place like Ur or Nineveh and work hard in these cities to administer the agriculture around us; wouldn't a shepherd's life be far better? How noble Abel's life must have been. It is obvious why God preferred him over his brother the farmer. The appeal of these literary origin stories has much to do with the formal brilliance they exhibit. They contain inherent ambiguities, paradoxes, and mysteries that delight, confound, frustrate, and lead, ultimately, to more stories. They cause artists to create new, increasingly refined explanations. On this track, literary cosmogonies become progressively more subtle and sometimes more complex. The course of these narratives can be kept in check by "the edge of chaos." If they become too confused, they fall apart into fragments of unintelligibility. Do "emergencies" appear at the edge of this supracritical complexity? I think so. The problem is, things emerge from commonplace and mundane regimes as well. I would suggest that emergence isn't so much a function of complexity, but simply a behavior people engage in. Art is something people do. They talk to cats too. Whether artists are bored, excited, depressed, manic, inspired, half-asleep, clinging tightly to a bucking Pegasus—something will emerge. It is the way of things. As for the cosmogenic narrative—it is very simple after all. It doesn't embody many ironic subtleties that have to be constantly re-systemized, refined, and reexpressed in increasingly clever ways. Indeed, if the cosmogenic narrative is itself simple, from where comes the critical complexity necessary to catalyze an emergent narrative? How does this normative narrative jump? I offer the following possibility.

I have suggested three categories of cosmogenic narrative. Are there others? I believe there is one (and perhaps only one). In redrafting this chapter I have used several names to designate this category, calling it magical, mystical, transcendental, romantic, paranoid-critical, poetical-critical, and "the guru." I have finally settled upon calling this category *transcendental*. In respect to the mythological, the religious and the literary categories, it is a transcendental category. In

Blake's epics, for example, all three categories are found within the same work. Poe's prose poem *Eureka* also patterns this fusion of categories. In both cases, the poetic principle that creates the poem ends the poem. A metaphysical stasis is realized; teetering at the tip-top of consciousness there is a frozen last judgment. Here the stage on which the drama of cosmogenesis occurs shifts from the real world to the stage of poetic conception. In the preceding section on the aesthetics of complexity we examined how creation can become the *object* of poetry. Here, creation becomes the *subject* of poetry. When poetry becomes the subject of its self, then the cosmogenic narrative begins to take life. However, when the cosmogenic narrative isn't based in the real world anymore, where does it find its validity? There is, I sense, something there to provide this validity, but what is it? Where is it? We have found the nothing within nothingness. With Wittgenstein's injunction on our lips—"What we cannot speak about we must pass over in silence"—we have to turn back, perhaps stopping for a good cry along the way.

GENERIC COSMOGENIC NARRATIVE—THE CHAOS POET

Michael Moorcock's work falls into three divisions. First, Moorcock was editor of the the British avant-garde magazine *New Worlds*. *New Worlds* was the epicenter of activity for "new wave" science fiction in the sixties and early seventies. The magazine was progressive, literary, and controversial. Distributors refused to carry it, and it was effectively censored out of existence. Taking cues from Joyce, Borges, and William S. Burroughs, *New Worlds* specialized in experimental narrative forms, speculative epistemologies, and hippie-ish, very often squalid antiheroes. The magazine is associated with some of the most innovative work of Brian W. Aldiss and J. G. Ballard. Consummate examples of avant-garde form such as Aldiss's *Barefoot in the Head,* Ballard's *The Atrocity Exhibition,* and Moorcock's endless *Cornelius Chronicles* originally ran as serials in the magazine. A number of other *New Worlds* authors, some of them incredibly brilliant—or mad—were never heard of again. One of the most ingenious works to appear in *New Worlds* was by one of these evaporated authors. Peder Carlsson's "Gorgias" describes the attempts of the narrator to escape beyond the meta-fields of contemporary scientific abstraction in a mental space ship on a mission to explore the nothingness of nothing. The narration

10: SCALING UP TO THE HOMERIC QUESTION 189

is configured after the decimal sentence format of Wittgenstein's *Tractatus*.

The second division of Moorcock's work is easily described as well-above-standard pulp science fiction and fantasy. Much of the money he made from this writing went to support *New Worlds*. A common theme running through this mammoth output of paperbacks concerns the conflict between Chaos and Law. The main character in each of these novels is the "Eternal Champion," a troubled, Byronic persona who is reincarnated in each volume to play a pivotal role in the "cosmic conflict" between Law and Chaos. Chaos is often portrayed as an infinite expanse of swirling colors inhabited by groans, bug-faced demons, and aristocratic archangels with a taste for pandemonium and destruction. On the other side are the ordering intelligences of Law who seek to tighten life and stiffen the spirit within a straight jacket of regulations, conventions, and forms. Depending upon the level of the Champion's sardonic wit and self-sacrifice, the cosmic balance swings toward a state of either more or less entropy. Again and again the Champion is reborn in fresh paperbacks where, with a new magic sword and a new set of physical and psychological deformities to be overcome, he participates in the struggle between Law and Chaos. Taken together, Moorcock's model worlds form a Buddhist "multiverse" of infinite, self-similar scenarios, reincarnated Byrons ("Byronsattvas"), and parallel melodramas. In keeping body and soul together at the center of psychedelic sixties London, Moorcock took generic, formula writing and molded it into a metaphysics.

The final division of Moorcock's work is characterized by a mixture of voices and narrative forms which result in a clever, audacious, and refreshing philosophical fiction. In this mode Moorcock is energetic, unpredictably inventive, and keenly sensitive to the moral implications of surreptitious irony. While he never entirely abandons pulp conventions, his self-promotion is tempered by a desire to celebrate and appreciate his independence in such a way as to further surrealism's quest for a subtle, socially insinuating integrity. One of his chief themes considers how habits, customs, and experiences become archetypical as they are passed down from generation to generation. These archetypes exercise a controlling power over our being and the configuration of our "individuality." These archetypes, whether they be parents, lovers, law-givers, or sages, take the form of "gods" which Moorcock's heroes struggle to overcome. Moorcock often explores characters who use science, political causes, romantic obsessions, and various ideologies and theories as a means to hide from the human condition. Indeed, one of the features shared by Moorcock's heroes is a need for shelter and insulation from a hostile, deforming landscape. His satire of the South of England in *The Cornelius Chronicles* is some of the most compelling reporting I have come across of the obtuseness, waspishness, and vampirism which yet governs, in some ruinous and unquenchable last gasp, the heart of the decayed empire.

William Blake Meets the Corsairs of the Second Ether

Blood: A Southern Fantasy, is Moorcock's first post-Gleick essay into complexity and cosmogenesis. Mandlebrot sets, super computers, self-simularity, nonlinear bifurcating functions, turbulence, strange attractors, chaos theory, and more, have elevated Moorcock's theme to a position of enhanced importance and new respectability. Because of his position as the paperback professor of the cosmic struggle between Law and Chaos, it seems natural that his pulp background should figure into this new work. Moorcock claims to be the editor of the new volume. Like much of the work he compiled for *New Worlds, Blood* was put together from a collection of typescript and handmade magazines. In this case, the evaporating author is "Edwin Begg, the famous Clapham Antichrist," whom Moorcock had ostensibly known since the 1960s. Moorcock describes the material: "It looked like the remains of a psychedelic undergraduate project which very properly had been abandoned . . . [h]owever, as I worked on the manuscript I began to perceive its coherence. A complex and intriguing story emerged as all the disparate elements came together to form an unfamiliar whole."[18]

Blood is set along the Gulf Coast and the Mississippi River. Pools of "color" have been discovered. Like the crude oil and the waxy, plastic industrial culture it allegorizes, the color is a cheap and apparently limitless source of electronic energy. But when prospectors drill into the color they create a metaphysical "fault"—a tear in space-time which alters the ontology of the novel and the language in which it is written. Chaos-stuff spews from the fault, engulfing the region in webs of conceptual distortion. Rivers change course in mid-stream, zombie policemen bubble like burning plastic, guns shoot carcinogenic projectiles, and meat boats steam through phantom dimensions.

Jack Karaquazian and Sam Oakenhurst are riverboat gamblers who occupy themselves playing "the game." Moorcock is shifting and ambiguous as he describes their profession. Do they play with cards?

Video games? Complex fantasy role-playing games? Moorcock describes the players dealing each other subsets of intellectual history, the trajectories of hypothetical civilizations, the exotic metaphysics of ten-dimensional matrices—"whole universes, species and nations were created, sometimes down to the most ordinary individual, and then manipulated in a game which sometimes took decades of subjective time, yet only a few minutes of real time."[19] Are they writers at their word processors? Computer scientists modeling fitness landscapes of lifelike, self-ordering systems? Something about their profession suggests literary theorists manipulating synthetic culture codes or telepathic wizards exciting the neuroses of their dissolving opponents. The stakes they play for are psychic. Karaquazian and Oakenhurst live according to a strict code of conduct marked by chivalry, a taste for dueling, and a genteel dislike for whites. They are black. In *Blood* the stereotypic racial roles of nineteenth-century America are reversed.

Into the lives of Karaquazian and Oakenhurst come two women, Colinda and "the Rose." Colinda brings Karaquazian an unconditional love which he is not quite ready to understand or accept. The Rose brings both men into contact with the "Second Ether," the ulterior mythological cosmos which Oakenhurst follows in the hand-made magazines he collects.

In his enthusiasm for these magazines, Oakenhurst falls in with an invisible empire known as the Machinoix. Mysterious custodians of Second Ether scholarship, the Machinoix suggest something falling between an ashram of ecstatic, self-abusing monks and a graduate school faculty. They are a scientific mafia who inflict tortures so exquisitely cruel that their acolytes come to view the Second Ether as a window into the afterlife. Oakenhurst disappears from time to time to learn the secrets of the Machinoix. Each time he returns he bears the signs of a progressive ritualized surgical scarring so that by the end of the book he represents some martyred monster with the "cadaverous appearance of a long-dead goat."[20] His cheeks have been scraped from the sides of his skull. His broken and elongated fingers are embedded with jewels. Moorcock describes Karaquazian greeting Oakenhurst after one of his sojourns with the Machinoix. "It was like shaking hands with the Old Hunter himself."[21]

Chapters from the *Corsairs of the Second Ether* are presented and interspersed throughout *Blood* in irregularly staggered chronological order. The beings which inhabit the Second Ether are divided between two competing groups, the "Singularity" and the "Chaos Engineers."

Captain Billy-Bob Beg, Fearless Frank Force, Little Rupoldo, Pearl Peru, Professor Pop, Kapitan Kaos, Manly Mark Male, Little Fanny Fun, Corporal Pork, Karl Kapital, Capricorn Schwartz (banker to the Homeboy Tong), and others crew and skipper the various space ships which, at different fractal levels, they themselves blend and transform into. These ships go by such names as *I Don't Want to Go to Chelsea, The Right Choice For Recovery, The Smollettsphere,* and *Now The Clouds Have Meaning.* Traveling through space and time and scaling up and down through fractal levels, the ships and their crews resemble mental states, moods, motivations, and passions.

The Rose wants Karaquazian and Oakenhurst to play the *Zeitsjuego,* the game of time. She intends to bring them to the edge of chaos, to "that precise moment in time between the death of the old multiverse and the beginning of the new" where they shall play for the power to change the human condition. Karaquazian is interested, but senses arrogance in her ambition and criticizes her "visionary abstraction." Her reply converts him:

> "The answer is to create what you seek. You triumph over nature by winning at the Game. Every time you beat the odds, Jack, you add further substance to your own individuality. Ultimately you will resemble nothing but yourself yet you will recognize others like you. Self-discipline and self-knowledge are the key. An individual becomes a unique universe, able to move at will through all the scales of the multiverse—potentially able to control the immediate reality of every scale, every encountered environment."
>
> She looked up into the darkening sky. "We are magicians and ghosts, Jack. We are goblins and visitations. We are future and past. We are memory and we are forgetfulness. Yet we achieve a kind of psychic density so that we remain coherent as we travel up and down the scales, back and forth across the multiverse, walking between the worlds on the silver roads people call moonbeams."[22]

Karaquazian "scales up" to the Second Ether (the Rose flies him there in a Dornier flying boat) where he assumes a central role as a subject-observer in the conflict between the chaos engineers and the singularity. Karaquazian is absorbed into the personae of the corsairs—now psychical archetypes—who arrange themselves into an epical last judgment, an apocalypse of contraries, syntheses, and metamorphoses which is highly suggestive of William Blake's ever-evolving, redemptive (as in re-deeming, or re-designating) mythology. Both Blake and Moorcock express their religious beliefs in the form of epics that depict and examine unending cycles (Moorcock would say "branches") of mythological transformations. Blake's epics were printed and colored with watercolors by the poet himself. In this light, Oakenhurst's "hand-made" magazines gain new significance. Not surprisingly, and also deeply in the vein of Blake, Karaquazian learns to forgive, trust in himself, and love.

Rather like Professor Pop broadcasting through his omniphone, Moorcock's voice dissipates and concentrates signifier and signified through a fractal "multiverse" of permutations. His language is a post-post-structuralist pidgin of Christian humanism, transformational mythology, fractal geometry, and pulp science fiction that increases in profundity as it becomes more ridiculous. *Blood* translates meaninglessness into epiphany.

Complexity theory and cosmogenesis readily describe the narrative and thematic dynamics of this novel. The technique of superposition intensifies complexity while real and implied patterns of self-similarity enhance organizational depth, propelling the narrative to the edge of chaos where a phase transition occurs. There is an emergence, a jump to a new order and morality. One should remark, however, that *Blood* is a faery tale. Like a computer program that mimics reality, a novel is a controlled, synthetic model of the world. At best, a novel is a metaphor; at worst, a deception and a delusion. The "self-ordering" phase transition in *Blood* is realized not by the "edge of chaos" but by artifice. Self-ordering has been "programmed" into the narrative.

Let's scale up to the second Table of Literary Complexity (Figure 3). This time I have plotted *Blood* on the table. Note that it occupies two positions. On the right, low in the zone of the Chaotic Regime is *Blood* as it first appears to the reader: a collection of scrambled tenses, unfamiliar settings, and cluttered, multivalent allusions expressing a field of unexplained, shifting, and grotesque scenarios. As the plot unfolds, however, and the story emerges, the novel's position moves across the graph upward and to the left, as indicated by the vector, to a higher position in the Ordered Regime. The ordering of the narrative reflects the ordering which takes place in the life of the character Karaquazian. Notice that as a function of this ordering, the novel has appreciated according to the criteria of Traditional Standards of Literary Value: Integrity and Cleverness. It may be that the vector should be averaged at its center, just to the left of the center of the Complex Regime in a nine o'clock position relative to J. G. Ballard. Note that here averaging has the net effect of reducing the novel's literary value. But is this the only direction this averaging can take? I think not. Might

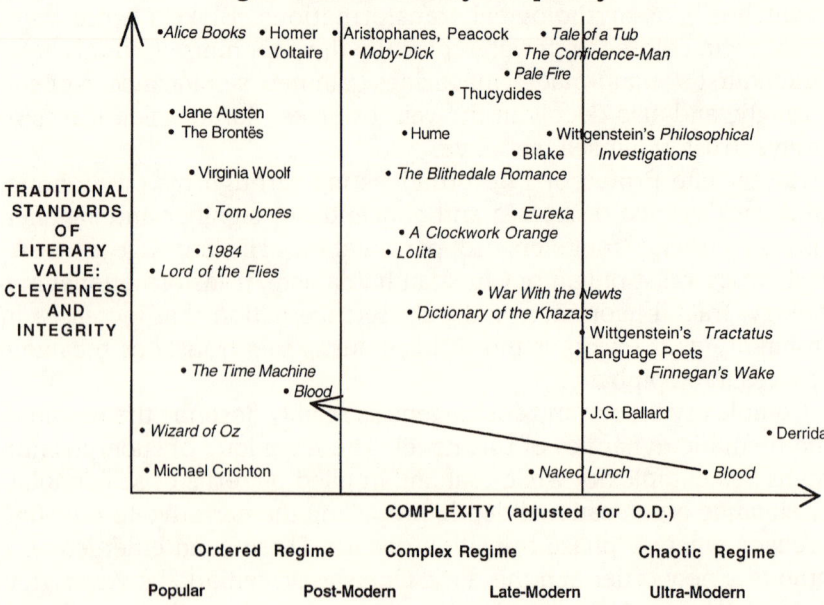

Fig. 3. Table of Literary Complexity.

it not be possible, because of the novel's radical emergence and transposition from chaotic to ordered regimes, that the averaging should move from *Blood's* position in the Ordered Regime, again toward the Complex Regime, but this time at an upward angle, on a vector directed toward Blake? Average now this new vector, and it appears that *Blood* belongs near the center of the Complex Regime in the vicinity of Čapek's *War With the Newts,* Nabokov's *Lolita,* and Pavic's *Dictionary of the Khazars.*

Moreover, like Billy-Bob Begg, captain of *Now the Clouds Have Meaning* and virtual maintype of all the chaos engineers, you can order this vector to any position on the map of cosmic complexity you desire. The only limit upon such movement is your own wit.

Performative or Symbolic?

A good test for any new philosophy or religion—even a scientific religion—is to identify its performative and symbolic aspects, place these in the pans, and see which way the scale tips. The symbolic aspects of cosmogenic art are, at this time, easier to ascertain. The cosmogenic narrative is compelling, encouraging, interesting and, in the case of Moorcock's fable, both self-satirizing and memorable. The cosmogenic buildings Jencks describes in his book are striking and thought-provoking. Whether or not this interest is created simply by the novelty represented by these buildings remains to be seen. The question, too, of whether or not they will inspire further cosmogenic art can only be answered in the fullness of time. We must wait and see what emerges.

What remains is the performative value of cosmogenic art. Will it further the cause of civilization? Can it unify in the next century the diverse perceptions of the ten billion human beings which will be walking around with mouths to feed, desires to flatter?

While the metaphors of complexity provide amusing applications in the realms of poetry and myth, the emphasis complexity science places on the "edge of chaos" as necessary for emergence is factitious and quite contrary to the lessons of fifty centuries of civilization. Chaos is without virtue. This conclusion is clearly supported by an aesthetic analysis of the question. Cosmogony, cosmology, cosmocracy, even cosmetology can be a catalyst of art. But inspiration—emergence—can just as easily be realized in spying a distant sail, hunting for chanterelles, opening a volume of Hokusai's *Thirty-six Views of Mt. Fuji,* or accepting a cup of tea from a generous hostess who then asks, "Who, and whence, are you?"

Transformations

The best aspirations of Western culture are rooted in the understanding that mythology should reflect true knowledge as well as bring peace and dignity to individual human beings. As conceived by the ancient poets, mythology was transformational, a tool for expressing ever finer and more subtle responses to human experience and the human condition. Mythology must be allowed to flow, transform, congeal, and flow again according to the unfolding of the poetic consciousness. The metaphysical and scientific attempts—conveniently marked by Plato and Aristotle—to freeze mythology into inviolable archetypes and institutions aptly represent the eclipse of the light of poetic understanding, the light of reality, the light of life. Whatever may befall, the practice of critical synoptics is the reassurance of that light.

Notes

Preface

1. This course can be descried in the work of other authors as well. The first masterpieces of Swift, Carroll, Huxley, and Nabokov, respectively, *A Tale of a Tub*, *Alice's Adventures in Wonderland*, *Antic Hay*, and *Lolita*, employ allegory and parody as critical devices. These performances were followed with second masterpieces, which are characterized by a more refined technique that addresses issues of scenario, context, and linguistic precision; again respectively, *Gulliver's Travels*, *Through the Looking Glass*, *Point Counter Point*, and *Pale Fire*. It would be interesting and somewhat gratifying to observe this evolution in Jane Austen, but she is way ahead of the game.

Chapter 1. What is Menippean Satire?

1. P. M. S. Hacker, *Wittgenstein's Place in Twentieth-century Analytical Philosophy* (Oxford: Blackwell, 1996), 100.
2. Ray Monk, *Ludwig Wittgenstein: The Duty of Genius* (New York: Free Press, 1990), 451.
3. William Blake, *The Complete Writings of William Blake*, ed. Geoffrey Keynes (New York: Random House, 1957), 738.
4. Ibid., 462.
5. Ibid., 453.
6. Ibid., 459.
7. Ludwig Wittgenstein, *Tractatus Logico-Philosophicus*, trans. D. F. Pears and B. F. McGuinness (London: Routledge & Kegan Paul, 1961). Citations in text follow Wittgenstein's decimal notation.
8. Jorn K. Bramann, *Wittgenstein's Tractatus and the Modern Arts* (Rochester: Adler, 1985), 87.
9. Bertrand Russell, "The Philosophy of Logical Atomism; Lectures Delivered in London in 1918," *Monist* 28 (October 1918), 7. Quoted in Bramann, 110–11.
10. Quoted in Will Durant, *The Story of Philosophy* (Garden City: Garden City Publishing, 1933), 282.
11. Francis Bacon, *Novum Organum* (New York: Liberal Arts Press, 1960), 50.
12. Ibid., 47–49.
13. Hacker, *Wittgenstein's Place*, ix.
14. Ibid., 1.

15. Ibid., 98. The abbreviations "Z" and "PI" refer, respectively, to Wittgenstein's *Zettel*, trans. G. E. M. Anscombe (Oxford: Blackwell, 1967) and *Philosophical Investigations*, trans. G. E. M. Anscombe (Oxford: Blackwell, 1958).
16. Ibid., 111.
17. Ibid., 98–99.
18. Ibid., 110.
19. Ibid., 125.
20. Ibid., 123.
21. Herman Melville, *The Confidence-Man: His Masquerade* (Evanston and Chicago: Northwestern University and the Newberry Library, 1984), 71. The abbreviation "CM" designates this work in subsequent citations.
22. C. S. Lewis, *They Asked for a Paper* (London: Geoffrey Bles, 1962), 150.
23. "Maimonides," *The Oxford Dictionary of World Religions*, 1997.
24. See Denys Turner, *The Darkness of God: Negativity in Christian Mysticism* (Cambridge: Cambridge, 1995). The winter 1998 issue of *Christianity and Literature* is devoted to articles treating negative theology.
25. Quoted in Charles Jencks, *The Language of Post-Modern Architecture* (New York: Rizzoli International, 1977), 36–37.
26. Ibid., 37.
27. Charles Jencks, *Architecture 2000: Predictions and Methods* (New York: Praeger, 1971), 16.
28. Quoted in Jencks, *Architecture 2000*, 24. In his last sentence Fuller seems to have caught sight of the "end of history."
29. Le Corbusier, Mies, and Pevsner are quoted in Jencks, *Architecture 2000*, 22.
30. Ibid., 24.
31. Lionel Trilling, "The Last Lover—Vladimir Nabokov's 'Lolita'" *Encounter* 11, no. 4 (1958): 14.
32. Alfred Appel, Jr. "*Lolita*: The Springboard of Parody" *Wisconsin Studies in Contemporary Literature* 8 (1967): 224.
33. Vladimir Nabokov, *Lolia* (New York: Putnam's, 1955), 7–8.
34. Fredric Jameson, *Postmodernism, or the Cultural Logic of Late Capitalism* (Durham: Duke, 1991), 76–77.
35. Brian W. Aldiss, "As to Our Fatal Continuity," *New Worlds Quarterly, Number 3* (New York: Berkeley Medallion, 1972), 42.
36. Quoted in Jencks, *Architecture 2000*, 118.
37. Quoted in Charles Jencks, *The Post-modern Reader* (New York: St. Martin's Press, 1992), 178.
38. Quoted in Jencks, *The Post-modern Reader*, 22.
39. Ibid.
40. I have taken some liberties with the plot. The episode in the bar ended the original epic. The search for eternal life and the flood story were added by scribes in later versions and placed *after* the bar scene.
41. M. H. Abrams, *A Glossary of Literay Terms* (New York: Holt, Rinehart and Winston, 1981), 169.
42. Northrop Frye, *Anatomy of Criticism* (Princeton, 1957), 311–12.
43. Eugene P. Kirk, *Menippean Satire: An Annotated Catalogue of Texts and Criticism* (New York and London: Graland, 1980), 227.
44. Theodore D. Kharpertian, *A Hand to Turn the Time: The Menippean Satires of Thomas Pynchon* (London and Toronto: Associated University Presses, 1990), 31–32.

45. Joel C. Relihan, *Ancient Menippean Satire* (Baltimore and London: Johns Hopkins University Press, 1993), 6.

46. F. Anne Payne, *Chaucer and Menippean Satire* (Madison: University of Wisconsin Press, 1981).

47. W. Scott Blanchard, *Scholar's' Bedlam: Menippean Satire in the Renaissance* (London and Toronto: Associated University Presses, 1995), 26–27.

48. Duatin Griffin, *Satire: A Critical Reintroduction* (Lexington: The University Press of Kentucky, 1994), 4.

49. Mikhail Bakhtin, *The Dialogic Imagination*, trans. Caryl Emerson and Michael Holquist (Austen: University of Texas Press, 1981).

50. Jane Austen, *The Complete Novels of Jane Austen* (New York: Modern Library), 1078.

51. Samuel Otter, *Melville's Anatomies* (Berkeley: University of California Press, 1999), 5.

52. I am not insensitive to the fact that Cook and Otter help to validate my own treatment of the subject. They come close to recognizing the centrality of the Menippean tradition in American literature, but either don't see the implications of their own thought, or deliberately veer away from it, pursuing other game. It is a reflection of our scientific age that *empirical explanation* is offered by such critics, when what is appropriate to the material under investigation is something rather in the nature of *understanding*. In the case of this kind of material, humor is necessary to reflect full understanding. Cook and Otter are not funny, at least not deliberately.

53. John M. Bullitt, *Jonathan Swift and the Anatomy of Satire* (Cambridge: Harvard University Press, 1953), 124.

54. Ibid.

55. Frank Zappa, *Joe's Garage Acts II and III*, Zappa Records, SRZ-2–1502, 1979.

56. Robert Burton, *The Anatomy of Melancholy* (New York: Tudor, 1927), 175–76.

Chapter 2. Games Critics Play

1. Ken Binmore, *Fun and Games* (Toronto: Heath, 1992), 3.

2. Ibid.

3. Lauri Carlson, *Dialogue Games* (Dordrecht: D. Reidel, 1983), xiv.

4. Ludwig Wittgenstein, trans. A. J. P. Kenny *Philosophical Grammar* (Oxford: Blackwell, 1974), 60.

5. T. S. Eliot, "Hamlet and His Problems," *Critical Theory Since Plato*, ed. Hazard Adams (New York: Harcourt, 1971), 788.

6. Loyd M. Daigrepont, "Ichabod Crane: Inglorious Man of Letters," *Early American Literature* 19 (Spring 1984): 68.

7. Ibid.

8. Ibid., 78.

9. Ibid., 79.

10. Ibid., 78.

11. Washington Irving, *The Sketch Book* (Boston: Twayne, 1978), 296.

12. Ibid.

13. Ibid., 297.

14. Ibid., 295–96.

15. Ibid., 272.
16. Quoted in P. M. S. Hacker, *Insight and Illusion* (Oxford: Clarendon, 1972), 21.
17. P. M. S. Hacker, *Wittgenstein's Place*, 125.

Chapter 3. Hawthorne's Arcadian Reality Test

1. Frederic Crews, *The Critics Bear it Away: American Fiction and the Academy* (New York: Random House, 1992), 14–15.
2. George Bernard Shaw, *Complete Plays with Prefaces* Vol. III (New York: Dodd, Mead and Company, 1963), 642.
3. R. W. B. Lewis, *The American Adam* (Chicago: The University of Chicago Press, 1955), 9.
4. Ibid., 5.
5. Ibid., 6.
6. Ibid., 7. Ibid., 8.
8. See Darrel Abel, *The Moral Picturesque: Studies in Hawthorne's Fiction* (West Lafayette, IN: Purdue University Press, 1988); Agnes McNeill Donohue, *Hawthorne: Calvin's Ironic Stepchild* (Kent: Kent State University Press, 1985); Milton R. Stern, *Contexts for Hawthorne: The Marble Faun and the Politics of Openness and Closure in American Literature* (Urbana and Chicago: University of Illinois Press, 1991). Abel, Stern (briefly), and Donohue offer useful contemporary readings of *The Blithedale Romance*. Brook Farm, historical figures upon which the novel's characters might be based, utopianism, pseudo-science and spiritualism, mid-nineteenth-century American culture, autobiographical elements in Coverdale, and the themes implicit in Hawthorne's problematic narrative are treated in these studies. Where my reading differs is in tracing various thematic, synoptic and analytical elements which locate Hawthorne in the philosophical mainstream of Menippean tradition.
9. Nathaniel Hawthorne, *The Blithedale Romance* (New York: Thomas Y. Crowell & Company, 1899), 11.
10. Ibid., 13.
11. Ibid., 17.
12. Ibid., 158.
13. Ibid., 23.
14. Ibid., 29.
15. Ibid., 158.
16. Ibid., 47.
17. Neither should the reader fail to consider Mary Shelley's response in *Frankenstein* to her father's utopianism. See chapter 5.
18. Hawthorne, *The Blithedale Romance*, 187.
19. Ibid., 185.
20. Ibid., 24.
21. Ibid., 93–94.
22. Crews, *The Critics Bear it Away*, 6–12.
23. Hawthorne, *The Blithedale Romance*, 212.
24. Ibid., 98.
25. Ibid., 196.
26. Ibid., 239.

27. Ibid., 207–208.
28. Ibid., 207.
29. Ibid., 231.
30. Ibid., 92–93.
31. Ibid., 103–104.

Chapter 4. Menacing the Good Baker's Oven

1. Melville, *The Confidence-Man*, 207.
2. John Bryant, "*The Confidence-Man*: Melville's Problem Novel," *A Companion to Melville Studies*, ed. John Bryant (New York: Greenwood Press, 1986), 330.
3. Other discharged custom house officers in Melville's orbit include his own Cousin Leonard.
4. John Seelye " 'Ungraspable Phantom:' Reflections on Hawthorne in *Pierre* and *The Confidence-Man*." *Studies in the Novel* 1 (winter 1969): 439. See also Edward G. Lueders, "The Melville-Hawthorne Relationship in *Pierre* and *The Blithedale Romance*," *Western Humanities Review* 4 (1940): 323–34; and Marjorie Kimball McCorquodale, "Melville's Pierre as Hawthorne," *University of Texas Studies in English* 33 (1953): 97–102.
5. Ibid., 441.
6. Edwin Fussel, *Frontier: American Literature and the American West* (Princeton: Princeton University Press, 1965), 314.
7. See Brian Higgens and Hershel Parker, "Reading *Pierre*," *A Companion to Melville Studies*, 232. Higgins and Parker provide examples of Melville's "diddling" the public and his publishers. "[I]t appears that he even deceived the Hawthornes, face to face, in the fall of 1850 when he said that he wrote the essay on Hawthorne (just published . . . in the *Literary World*) with no thought that he would ever meet the author of *Mosses From an Old Manse*."
8. Seelye, "Ungraspable Phantom," 442.
9. Nathaniel Hawthorne, *Mosses From an Old Manse* (Columbus: Ohio State University Press, 1974), 31.

Chapter 5. The Question of the Monster

1. Poe's influence on Verne has been studied repeatedly. See Lucette Desvignes, "De Poe a Jules Verne et du Mystere au gouffre," *Acts du VIIe Congress de l'Association Internationale de Litterature Comparée* (Stuttgart: Bieber, 1979); Mariella Di Maio, "Jules Verne et le voyage au second degre ou un avatar d'Edgar Poe," *Romantisme: Revue du Dix Neuvieme Siecle*19 (1900) 67, 100–109; David Meakin, "Like Poles Attracting: Intertextual Magnetism in Poe, Verne, and Gracq," *Modern Language Review* 88 (July 1993) 566–611; Gwenhael Ponneau, "Edgar Poe et Jules Verne: Le Statut de la science dans la literature fantastique et dans la litterature de science-fiction," *Acts du VIIe Congress de l'Association Internationale de Litterature Comparée* (Stuttgart: Bieber, 1979); J. M. Santraud, "Dans le sillage de la baleiniere d'Arthur Gordon Pym: Le Sphinx des Glaces Dan, Yack," *Etudes Anglaises: Grande Bretagne, Etats Unis* 25

(1972) 353–66; Monique Sprout, "The Influence of Poe on Jules Verne," *Revue de Littérature Comparée* 41 (1967) 37–53; Jules Zanger, "Poe's Endless Voyage: The Narrative of Arthur Gordon Pym," *Papers on Language and Literature* 22 (Summer 1986): 276–83.

2. Jules Verne, *From the Earth to the Moon* ((New York: Thomas Y. Crowell, 1978), 13.

3. Jules Verne, *An Antarctic Mystery* (Boston: Gregg, 1975), v.

4. Ray Bradbury's essay " The Ardent Blasphemers," *Stanford French Review* 3 (1979): 5–15 (reprinted as an introduction to the Bantom edition of *Twenty-thousand Leagues Under the Sea*) is the only article comparing Verne and Melville I've found. While Bradbury's insights concerning Ahab and Nemo as well as the whale and the *Nautilus* are valuable (and discussed toward the end of this chapter), much of Bradbury's reading is deeply flawed because he too closely (and painfully!) identifies Melville with Ahab. Bradbury also neglects to mention or discuss the references to the white whale in Verne's text. The first excerpts of *Moby-Dick* translated into French (a summary of *Moby-Dick* interspersed with translated passages) appeared in France in 1853; see E. D. Forgues, *Revue de deux mondes* 23 (January–March 1853): 491–515. An abridged version of *La Cachalot blanc* was published by Gedalge in 1928. See Pierre-André Touttain, "Vingt Mille Ronds De Fumé," *Grand Album Jules Verne* (Paris: Hachette, 1982): 45–84. According to Touttain, the first French translation of *Moby-Dick* was not published until 1941. Touttain points out in a footnote that Verne mentions the white whale in *Twenty-thousand Leagues Under the Sea*, but Touttain does not discuss or explain the possible implications.

5. Jules Verne, *Twenty-thousand Leagues Under the Sea* (New York: Thomas Y. Crowell Co., 1979), 1.

6. Ibid., 3.

7. Ibid., 4.

8. Ibid., 44.

9. Herman Melville, *Moby-Dick* (Evanston and Chicago: Northwestern-Newberry, 1988), 157. The abbreviation "MD" refers to this volume in subsequent parenthetical citations.

10. Blake, *The Complete Writings*, 153.

11. Ibid., 778.

12. Bradbury, 7.

13. Barbara Johnson, "My Monster/My self," *Diacritics* 12 (1982): 7. This is a fine cocktail party remark, and works as a point of departure for discussing the exigencies Mary Shelley faced putting her manuscript together, but the novel goes far beyond these issues.

14. Robert D. Richardson, Jr., *Emerson: The Mind on Fire* (Berkeley. University of California Press, 1995), 127.

15. Mary Shelley, *Frankenstein, or, the Modern Prometheus* (New York: Bantam Books, 1991), 81.

Chapter 6. Grinding the Apophatic Axe

1. Herman Melville, *Moby-Dick* (New York: Signet, 1998), xv.
2. Samuel Otter, *Melville's Anatomies*, 4.

3. Elizabeth Renker, *Strike Through the Mask: Herman Melville and the Scene of Writing* (Baltimore: Johns Hopkins University Press, 1996), xii.

4. John Bryant, "Moby-Dick as Revolution," *The Cambridge Companion to Heman Melville*, ed. Robert S. Levine (New York: Cambridge University Press), 71.

5. Ibid., 81.

6. Ibid., 85. Are "love" and "fright" the only emotions experienced by these characters?

7. Ibid., 88.

8. For a summary of the basic tenets of hard-nosed liberalism, see Thomas Love Peacock's *The Misfortunes of Elphin*, chapter 6, "The Education of Taliesin."

9. Frank Cioffi, *Wittgenstein on Freud and Frazer* (Cambridge: Cambridge, 1998), 2.

10. Ibid., 3.

11. Ibid.

CHAPTER 7. ORIGINALS AND THEIR ANTECEDENTS

1. Edgar Allan Poe, *Edgar Allan Poe, Essays and Reviews* (New York: Library of America, 1984), 144.

2. Ibid., 145.

3. Ibid.

4. Ibid., 143.

5. Ibid.

6. Ibid., 146.

7. Ibid.

8. Ibid., 147.

9. Ibid., 146.

10. Melville says this about Hawthorne in his essay on "Hawthorne and His Mosses."

11. Herman Melville, *Pierre; or, the Ambiguities* (Evanston and Chicago: Northwestern Newberry, 1971), 240.

12. John Bryant, "*The Confidence-Man*: Melville's Problem Novel," *A Companion to Melville Studies*, ed. John Bryant (New York: Greenwood Press, 1986), 331.

13. Milan Kundera, *The Art of the Novel*, trans. Linda Asher (New York: Harper and Row, 1988), 157.

14. Herman Melville, *The Confidence-Man: His Masquerade* (New York: Norton, 1971), xi.

15. Merton M. Sealts, Jr., *Melville's Reading: Revised and Enlarged Edition* (University of South Carolina Press, 1988), 99.

16. Warren Staebler, "Originality of Vision in the American Romantics, *The Origins and Originality of American Culture*," ed. Frank Tibor (Budapest: Akedemiai Kaido, 1980; Atlantic Highlands: Humanities Press, 1984), 99.

17. David Quint, *Origin and Originality in Renaissance Literature: Versions of the Source* (New Haven: Yale University Press, 1983), x.

18. Thomas McFarlane, *Originality and Imagination* (Baltimore: Johns Hopkins University Press, 1985), xii.

19. Mircea Eliade, *Cosmos and History: The Myth of the Eternal Return* (New York: Harper and Row, 1959), 3.
20. Ibid., xi.
21. Carter Kaplan, "The Coriolanus of the Sea Encounters the Crag of Ailsa," *Melville Society Extracts* 73 (May 1988): 14–15. See also Michael Tournier, *The Ogre* (New York: Doubleday, 1972) for an account of this process in Nazi Germany; and also "The Revolutionists Handbook and Pocket Companion by John Tanner, M.I.R.C. (Member of the Idle Rich Class)" from G. B. Shaw's *Man and Superman*, *Complete Plays with Prefaces*, vol. 3 (New York: Dodd, Mead and Company, 1963), particularly the section on "Idolatry," 731.
22. Joseph N. Riddel, *Purloined Letters: Originality and Repetition in American Letters*, ed. Mark Bauerlein (Baton Rouge: Louisiana State University Press, 1995), 21.
23. Ibid., 159.
24. Walter E. Bezanson, "Moby-Dick: Document, Drama, Dream," *A Companion to Melville Studies*, ed. John Bryant (New York: Greenwood Press, 1986), 191.
25. It is not an easy thing to give up one's mind. If this concept is still difficult, you need more therapy. Consider the following propositions: a) My mind is thinking about Plato. b) My brain is thinking about Plato. c) I am thinking about Plato. d) You would do well to keep Plato in mind for the exam. e) An Idea just crossed my mind. f) The idea went in my right ear and out my left, crossing my mind along the way. g) Some bees dance. h) Some bees exist. i) The dinosaurs no longer exist. j) On my day off I am going to sit in the park and exist. Propositions c, d, e, g and i are valid. The rest are nonsense. They exhibit conceptual confusion rooted in the misapprehension of language.
26. John Bryant, *Melville and Repose: The Rhetoric of Humor in the American Renaissance* (New York: Oxford, 1993).

Chapter 8. The Advent of Literary Dystopia

1. Petronius, *The Satyricon*, trans. William Arrowsmith (New York: Mentor, 1959), 21–22.
2. Ibid.
3. Ibid.
4. Jonathan Swift, *A Tale of a Tub: With Other Early Works* (Oxford: Basil Blackwell, 1957), 141.
5. Ibid., 151.
6. Ibid., 153–54.
7. Blake, *The Complete Writings*, 115.
8. Ibid., 156.
9. Jules Verne, *Paris in the Twentieth Century*, trans. Richard Howard (New York: Ballantine, 1997), 6.
10. Vladimir Nabokov, *Bend Sinister* (New York: McGraw Hill, 1973), 227–28.

Chapter 9. The Edge of Capital

1. "Santa Fe Institute: Researchers in Residence." Santa Fe, New Mexico [cited November 1,1997]. Available from http://www.santafe.edu/sfi/research/residents.html

2. Christian de Duve, *Vital Dust: Life as a Cosmic Imperative* (New York: HarperCollins, 1995), 349.

3. Stuart A. Kauffman, *At Home in the Universe: The Search for the Laws of Self-Organization and Complexity* (New York: Oxford, 1995), 4–5.

4. de Duve, *Vital Dust*, xiv.

5. Kauffman, *At Home*, 99.

6. The terms *supracritical state-space, critical state-space* and *subcritical state-space* are interchangeable with, respectively, chaotic regime, complex regime, and ordered regime. The former terminology, I believe, is best used in paleo-biological applications of complexity theory. The latter designations seem better fitted to applications in the humanities, economics, and the social sciences.

7. Kauffman, *At Home*, 299.

8. Ibid., 202.

9. Ibid., 204.

10. Michael J. Behe, *Darwin's Black Box: the Biochemical Challenge to Evolution* (New York: The Free Press, 1996), 190.

11. Ibid., 179.

12. Ibid., 156.

13. M. Mitchell Waldrop, *Complexity: The Emerging Science at the Edge of Order and Chaos* (New York: Simon and Schuster, 1992), 244.

14. Kauffman, *At Home*, 28–29.

15. The McKinsey Global Institute produces a series of reports on the competitiveness of various countries.

16. Kauffman, *At Home*, 264.

17. Ibid., 266.

18. Ibid., 299.

19. Ibid., 299–300.

20. N. D. Fustel de Coulanges, "An Inaugural Lecture," *The Varieties of History: From Voltaire to the Present*, ed. Fritz Stern (London: Macmillan, 1970), 188.

21. Arthur Marwick, *The Nature of History* (London: Macmillan, 1970), 103.

22. Kauffman, *At Home*, 270.

23. See Lowell Bryan, *et al.*, *Race for the World: Strategies to Build a Great Global Firm* (Boston: Harvard Business School Press, 1999), 97–98. With glowing enthusiasm Bryan celebrates the recent market capitalization of Asia.

24. Kauffman, *At Home*, 270.

25. Ibid., 98.

26. Steven Levy, *Artificial Life: the Quest for a New Creation* (New York: Pantheon, 1992), 128.

27. Roger Lewin, *Complexity: Life on the Edge of Chaos* (New York: Macmillan, 1992).

28. Jencks, *Architecture 2000*, 20.

Chapter 10. Scaling up to the Homeric Question

1. Charles Jencks, *The Architecture of the Jumping Universe: A Polemic: How Complexity Science is Changing Architecture and Culture* (London: Academy Editions, 1995), 51.

2. Ibid., 9.
3. Ibid.
4. Ibid., 13.
5. Ibid.
6. Ibid., 9.
7. Ibid., 15.
8. Ibid., 51.
9. *Odyssey* 1. 170, 7. 238.
10. Jencks, *Jumping Universe*, 43.
11. Ibid., 44.
12. Ibid., 47.
13. Ibid., 55.
14. Ibid., 84.
15. Ibid., 13.
16. Looked at in another way, Jencks's Y-axis does graph the emergence of new order described by complexity *theory*; but of course this order is yet to be produced outside the confines of a computer program. For further discussion see Paul Davies, *The Fifth Miracle: The Search for the Origin and Meaning of Life* (New York: Simon and Schuster, 1999), 264–70. Also, see Stephen Jay Gould, *Life's Grandeur* (Jonathan Cape, 1996), 167, 216.
17. Jencks, *Jumping Universe*, 148.
18. Michael Moorcock, *Blood: A Southern Fantasy* (London: Millennium, 1995), 1.
19. Ibid., 30.
20. Ibid., 159.
21. Ibid.
22. Ibid., 177–78.

Select Bibliography

Abel, Darrel. *The Moral Picturesque: Studies in Hawthorne's Fiction*. West Lafayette, IN: Perdue University Press, 1988.

Abrams, M. H. *A Glossary of Literary Terms*. New York: Holt, Rinehart and Winston, 1981.

Adams, Hazard, ed. *Critical Theory Since Plato*. New York: Harcourt, Brace, Jovanovich, 1971.

Addison, Joseph and Richard Steele. *The Spectator*, vol. 3. Edited by Donald F. Bond, 544–47. London: Oxford University Press, 1965.

Aldiss, Brian W. "As to Our Fatal Continuity." In *New Worlds Quarterly, No. 3*, ed. Michael Moorcock, 36–42. New York: Berkley Medallion, 1972.

———. *Barefoot in the Head: A European Fantasia*. London: Faber, 1969.

Aristophanes. *Four Plays by Aristophanes*. Translated by Arrowsmith, Lattimore, and Parker. New York: Meridian, 1994.

Auerbach, Erich. *Mimesis: The Representation of Reality in Western Literature*. Princeton: Princeton University Press, 1974.

Austen, Jane. *The Complete Novels of Jane Austen*. New York: Modern Library, [n.d.].

Bacon, Francis. *Essays Civil and Moral*. Danbury: The Harvard Classics, 1980.

———. *Novum Organum*. New York: Liberal Arts Press, 1960.

Bakhtin, Mikhail. *The Dialogic Imagination*. Edited by Michael Holquist, Translated by Caryl Emerson and Michael Holquist. Austin: University of Texas Press, 1981.

Barth, John. "The Literature of Replenishment." In *The Post-modern Reader*, edited by Charles Jencks, 172–80. New York: St. Martin's, 1992.

Behe, Michael J. *Darwin's Black Box: The Biochemical Challenge to Evolution*. New York: The Free Press, 1996.

Bezanson, Walter E. "*Moby-Dick*: Document, Drama, Dream." In *A Companion to Melville Studies*, edited by John Bryant, 169–210. New York: Greenwood, 1986.

Binmore, Ken. *Fun and Games*. Toronto: Heath, 1992.

Blake, William. *The Complete Writings of William Blake*. Edited by Geoffrey Keynes. New York: Random House, 1957.

Blanchard, W. Scott. *Scholars' Bedlam: Menippean Satire in the Renaissance*. London And Toronto: Associated University Presses, 1995.

Bowker, John, ed. *The Oxford Dictionary of World Religions*. Oxford: Oxford University Press, 1997.

Boyd, Brian. *Vladimir Nabokov: The American Years*. Princeton: Princeton University Press, 1991.

Bradbury, Ray. "The Ardent Blasphemers," *Stanford French Review* 3 (1979): 5–15.

———. *Farenheit 451*. New York: Ballantine Books, 1996.

Bramann, Jorn K. *Wittgenstein's Tractatus and the Modern Arts*. Rochester: Adler, 1985.

Bryan, Lowell, et al. *Race for the World: Strategies to Build a Great Global Firm*. Boston: Harvard Business School Press, 1999.

Bryant, John. "*The-Confidence-Man*: Melville's Problem Novel." In *A Companion to Melville Studies*, edited by John Bryant, 315–50. New York: Greenwood Press, 1986.

———. *Melville and Repose: The Rhetoric of Humor in the American Renaissance*. New York: Oxford University Press, 1993.

Bullitt, John M. *Jonathan Swift and the Anatomy of Satire*. Cambridge: Harvard University Press, 1953.

Burgess, Anthony. *Byrne*. London: Hutchinson, 1995.

———. *A Clockwork Orange*. New York: Norton, 1963.

———. *1985*. Boston: Little, Brown, 1978.

Burton, Robert. *The Anatomy of Melancholy, vvhat it is. VVith all the kindes, causes, symptomes, prognostics, and severall cures of it. In three maine partitions, with their severall sections, members, and subsections. Philosophically, medicinally, historically, opened and cvt vp. By Democritus Iunior. With a Satyricall preface, conducing to the following discourse*. Oxford: Printed by I. Litchfield and I. Short for H. Cripps, 1621.

———. *The Anatomy of Melancholy*. New York: Tudor, 1927.

Byron, George Gordon Byron, Baron. *The Complete Poetical Works of Byron*. Edited by Paul Elmer More. Boston: Houghton Mifflin, 1933.

Čapek, Karel. *The War with the Newts*. Translated by M. and R. Weatherall. Evanston: Northwestern University Press, 1996.

Carlson, Lauri. *Dialogue Games*. Dordrecht: D. Reidel, 1983.

Carlsson, Peder. "Gorgias." In *New Worlds #5*, Edited by Michael Moorcock and Charles Platt, 169–78. New York: Avon, 1973.

Carroll, Lewis. *Alice's Adventures in Wonderland*. New York: Random House, 1946.

———. *Through the Looking Glass, And What Alice Found There*. New York: Random House, 1946.

Casti, John L. *Would-be Worlds: How Simulation is Changing the Frontiers of Science*. New York: John Wiley and Sons, 1997.

Cioffi, Frank. *Wittgenstein on Freud and Frazer*. Cambridge: Cambridge University Press, 1998.

Connery, Brian A. and Kirk Combe, eds. *Theorizing Satire: Essays in Literary Criticism*. New York: St. Martin's Press, 1995.

Cook, Jonathan A. *Satirical Apocalypse: An Anatomy of Melville's The Confidence-Man*. Westport: Greenwood Press, 1996.

Crews, Frederic. *The Critics Bear it Away: American Fiction and the Academy*. New York: Random House, 1992.

———. *The Sins of the Fathers: Hawthorne's Psychological Themes*. Berkeley: University of California Press, 1966.

Daigrepont, Loyd M. "Ichabod Crane: Inglorious Man of Letters."*Early American Literature* (Spring 1984): 68–81.

Damon, S. Foster. *A Blake Dictionary*. Providence: Brown University Press, 1965.

Davies, Paul. *The Fifth Miracle: The Search for the Origin and Meaning of Life*. New York: Simon and Schuster, 1999.

Di Maio, Mariella. "Jules Verne et le voyage au second degre ou un avatar d'Edgar Poe." *Romantisme: Revue du Dix Neuvieme Siecle* 19 (1900): 100–9.

Dimic, Milan V. and Eva Kushner, eds. *Acts du VIIe Congress de l'Association Internationale de Litterature Comparée*. Stuttgart: Bieber, 1979.

Donohue, Agnes McNeill. *Hawthorne: Calvin's Ironic Stepchild*. Kent: Kent State University Press, 1985.

Drury, M. O'C. *The Danger of Words*. London: Routledge, 1973.

Durant, Will. *The Story of Philosophy*. Garden City: Garden City Publishing, 1933.

Duffy, Bruce. *The World as I Found It*. New York: Ticknor and Fields, 1987.

de Duve, Christian. *Vital Dust: Life as a Cosmic Imperative*. New York: HarperCollins, 1995.

Eagleton, Terry. *Saints and Scholars*. London: Verso, 1987.

Eco, Umberto. *Foucault's Pendulum*. Translated by William Weaver. San Diego: Harcourt, 1989.

———. *The Name of The Rose*. New York/London: Harcourt, Brace, Jovanovich, 1984.

Eliade, Mircea. *Cosmos and History: The Myth of the Eternal Return*. New York: Harper and Row, 1959.

Falk, Richard. *Explorations at the Edge of Time: The Prospects for World Order*. Philadelphia: Temple University Press, 1992.

Forgues, E. D. "Moby-Dick." *Revue de deux mondes* 23 (January–March 1853): 491–515.

Forster, E. M. *The Collected Tales of E.M. Forster*. New York: Knopf, 1947.

Frye, Northrop. *Anatomy of Criticism*. Princeton: Princeton University Press, 1957.

Fussell, Edwin. *Frontier: American Literature and the American West*. Princeton: Princeton Univerity Press, 1965.

Fustel de Coulanges, N. D. "An Inaugural Lecture." In *The Varieties of History: From Voltaire to the Present*, edited by Fritz Stern, 179–88. London: Macmillan, 1970.

Gleick, James. *Chaos: Making a New Science*. New York: Viking, 1987.

Glock, Hans-Johann. *A Wittgenstein Dictionary*. Oxford: Blackwell, 1996.

Godwin, William. *The Adventures of Caleb Williams*. New York: Oxford University Press, 1970.

———. *An Inquiry Concerning Political Justice, and its Influence on General Virtue and Happiness*. Dublin: Printed for Luke White, 1793.

Golding, William. *Lord of the Flies*. New York: Putnam, 1964.

Gould, Stephen Jay. *Life's Grandeur*. London: Jonathan Cape, 1996.

Griffin, Dustin. *Satire: A Critical Reintroduction*. Lexington: The University Press of Kentucky, 1994.

Hacker, P. M. S. and G. P. Baker. *Wittgenstein: Understanding and Meaning, Volume 1 of an Analytical Commentary on the Philosophical Investigations*. Oxford: Blackwell, 1980.

———. *Wittgenstein: Rules, Grammar and Necessity, Volume 2 of an Analytical Commentary on the Philosophical Investigations.* Oxford: Blackwell, 1985.

Hacker, P. M. S. *Wittgenstein: Meaning and Mind, Volume 3 of an Analytical Commentary on the Philosophical Investigations.* Oxford: Blackwell, 1985.

———. *Wittgenstein: Mind and Will, Volume 4 of an Analytical Commentary on the Philosophical Investigations.* Oxford: Blackwell, 1986.

———. *Wittgenstein's Place in Twentieth-century Analytic Philosophy.* Oxford: Blackwell, 1996.

———. *Insight and Illusion.* Oxford: Clarendon, 1972.

Hamilton, William. *Melville and the Gods.* Chico: Scholars Press, 1985.

———. *Reading Moby-Dick and Other Essays.* New York: Peter Lang, 1989.

Hawthorne, Nathaniel. *The Blithedale Romance.* New York: Thomas Y. Crowell & Company, 1899.

———. *Mosses from an Old Manse.* Columbus: Ohio State University Press, 1974.

Hayford, Harrison, and Hershel Parker, eds. *Moby-Dick as Doubloon: Essays and Extracts (1851–1970).* New York: Norton, 1970.

Hayford, Harrison. "Poe in *The Confidence-Man.*" *Nineteenth Century Fiction* 14 (December 1959): 207–18.

Higgens, Brian and Hershel Parker. "Reading *Pierre.*" In *A Companion to Melville Studies,* edited by John Bryant, 211–39. New York: Greenwood Press, 1986.

Homer. *The Odyssey.* Translated by Richmond Lattimore. New York: Harper and Row, 1967.

Hooke, S. H. *Middle Eastern Mythology.* Harmondsworth: Penguin, 1966.

Howard, Leon. *Herman Melville: A Biography.* Berkeley: University of California Press, 1951.

Huxley, Aldous. *Brave New World.* New York: Harper Colophon, 1965.

———. *Point Counter Point.* New York: Modern Library, 1930.

Idol, John L. and Melinda M. Ponder, eds. *Hawthorne and Women: Engendering and Expanding the Hawthorne Tradition.* Amherst: University of Massachusetts Press, 1999.

Irving, Washington. *The Sketch Book.* Boston: Twayne, 1978.

Irwin, John T. *American Hieroglyphics: The Symbol of the Egyptian Hieroglyphics in the American Renaissance.* New Haven: Yale University Press, 1980.

Jameson, Fredric. *Postmodernism, or, the Cultural Logic of Late Capitalism.* Durham: Duke University Press, 1995.

Jencks, Charles. *Architecture 2000: Predictions and Methods.* New York: Praeger, 1971.

———. *The Architecture of the Jumping Universe: A Polemic: How Complexity Science Is Changing Architecture and Culture.* London: Academy Editions. 1995.

———. *The Language of Post-Modern Architecture.* New York: Rizzoli International, 1977.

———, ed. *The Post-Modern Reader.* New York: St. Martin's Press. 1992.

———, and Karl Kropf, eds. *Theories and Manifestoes of Contemporary Architecture.* Chichester: Academy Editions, 1997.

Johnson, Barbara. "My Monster/My Self," *Diacritics* 12(1982) 2–10.

Johnson, Samuel. *The History of Rasselas, Prince of Abissinia, a Tale*. Oxford: Clarendon Press, 1927.

Kafka, Franz. *The Castle*. New York: Modern Library, 1969.

———. *The Trial*. New York: Modern Library, 1956.

Kaplan, Carter. "The Coriolanus of the Sea Encounters the Crag of Ailsa." *Melville Society Extracts*, 73 (May 1988): 14–15.

Kauffman, Stuart A. *The Origins of Order: Self-Organization and Selection in Evolution*. New York: Oxford University Press, 1993.

———. *At Home in the Universe: The Search for the Laws of Self-Organization and Complexity*. New York: Oxford University Press, 1995.

Kern, Alexander C. "Melville's *The Confidence-Man*: A Structure of Satire." In *American Humor: Essays Presented to John C. Gerber*, edited by O. M. Brock, Jr., 27–41. Scottsdale, Arizona: Arte Publications, 1977.

Kharpertian, Theodore D. *A Hand to Turn the Time: The Menippean Satires of Thomas Pynchon*. London and Toronto: Associated University Presses, 1990.

Kirk, Eugene P. *Menippean Satire: An Annotated Catalogue of Texts and Criticism*. New York and London: Garland, 1980.

Kondo, Ichitaro. *Hokusai's Thirty-Six Views of Mount Fuji*. Translated by Charles S. Terry. Tokyo: Heibonsha, 1966.

Lee, A. Robert. "*Moby-Dick* as Anatomy." In *Herman Melville: Reassessments*, edited by A. Robert Lee, 68–89. Totowa, N.J.: Barnes and Noble, 1984.

Leuders, Edward G. "The Melville-Hawthorne Relationship in *Pierre* and *The Blithedale Romance*." *Western Humanities Review* 4 (1940): 323–34.

Levine, Robert S., edited by *The Cambridge Companion to Herman Melville*. Cambridge, 1998.

Levy, Steven. *Artificial Life: the Quest for a New Creation*. New York: Pantheon, 1992.

Lewin, Roger. *Complexity: Life on the Edge of Chaos*. New York: Macmillan. 1992.

Lewis, C. S. *The Abolition of Man; or, Reflections on Education with Special Reference to the Teaching of English in the Upper Forms of Schools*. New York: Macmillan, 1947.

———. *Of This and Other Worlds*. London: Collins, 1982.

———. *That Hideous Strength*. New York: Macmillan, 1970.

———. *They Asked for a Paper*. London: Geoffrey Bles, 1962.

———. *Perelandra*. New York: Macmillan, 1965.

Lewis, R. W. B. *The American Adam: Innocence, Tragedy, and Tradition in the Nineteenth Century*. Chicago: University of Chicago Press, 1955.

Lichtman, Maria. "Negative Theology in Marguetite Porete and Jacques Derrida." *Christianity and Literature* 47, no. 2 (Winter 1998): 213–28.

Lipow, Arthur. *Authoritarian Socialism in America: Edward Bellamy and the Nationalist Movement*. Berkeley: University of California Press, 1982.

Lucian of Samosata. *Lucian's Dialogues, namely the Dialogues of the Gods, and of the Dead; Zeus the Tragedian, the Ferryboat, etc.* Translated by Howard Williams. London: G. Bell and Sons, 1888.

Luckhardt, C. G., ed. *Wittgenstein: Sources and Perspectives*. Ithaca: Cornell, 1979.

Maimonides, Moses. *The Guide for the Perplexed*. New York: Dover, 1956.

Matthiessen, F. O. *American Renaissance: Art and Expression in the Age of Emerson and Whitman*. New York: Oxford University Press, 1941.

Mawick, Arthur. *The Nature of History*. London: Macmillan, 1970.

McCarthy, Paul. "Elements of Anatomy in Melville's Fiction." *Studies in the Novel* 6 (1974): 38–61.

McCorquodale, Marjorie Kimball. "Melville's Pierre as Hawthorne." *University of Texas Studies in English* 33 (1954): 97–102.

McFarlane, Thomas. *Originality & Imagination*. Baltimore: Johns Hopkins University Press, 1985.

Meakin, David. "Like Poles Attracting: Intertextual Magnetism in Poe, Verne, and Gracq." *Modern Language Review* 88 (July 1993): 599–611.

Melville, Herman. *The Confidence-Man: His Masquerade*. Edited by Hershel Parker. New York: Norton, 1971.

———. *The Confidence-Man: His Masquerade*. Evanston and Chicago: Northwestern-Newberry, 1984.

———. *Moby-Dick* New York: Norton, 1967.

———. *Moby-Dick*. Evanston & Chicago: Northwestern-Newberry, 1988.

———. *Moby-Dick*. New York: Signet, 1998.

Micklethwait, John and Adrian Wooldridge. *The Witch Doctors: Making Sense of the Management Gurus*. New York: Random House, 1996.

Milligan, Spike and John Antrobus. *The Bedsitting Room*. Walton-on-Thames: Margaret and Jack Hobbs, 1970.

Milton, John. *The Portable Milton*. Edited by Douglas Bush. New York: Penguin, 1977.

Mintz, Beth and Michael Schwartz. *The Power Structure of American Business*. Chicago: University of Chicago Press, 1985.

Monk, Ray. *Ludwig Wittgenstein: The Duty of Genius*. New York: Free Press, 1990.

Moorcock, Michael. *Blood: A Southern Fantasy*. London: Millenium, 1995.

———. *The War Amongst the Angels*. London: Millenium, 1996.

———. *The Cornelius Chronicles*. New York: Avon, 1977.

Morgan, Ellen E. "The Veiled Lady: The Secret Love of Miles Coverdale," *Nathaniel Hawthorne Journal* (1971): 169–81.

Mushabac, Jane. *Melville's Humor: A Critical Study*. Hamden, Conn.: Archon Books, 1981.

Nabokov, Vladimir. *Bend Sinister*. New York: McGraw Hill, 1973.

———. *Invitation to a Beheading*. New York: Putnam, 1959.

———. *Lolita*. New York: Putnam, 1955.

———. *Pale Fire*. New York: Putnam, 1962.

———. *The Real Life of Sebastian Knight*. Harmondsworth: Penguin, 1982.

———. *Speak, Memory*. New York: Vintage, 1989.

———. *Strong Opinions*. New York: Vintage, 1990.

Nuttall, A. D. *The Alternative Trinity: Gnostic Heresy in Marlowe, Milton and Blake*. Oxford: Oxford University Press, 1998.

Orwell, George. *Animal Farm*. New York: Harcourt Brace, 1954.

———. *1984*. New York: Harper and Row, 1983.

———. *The Road to Wigan Pier*. London: Penguin, 1989.

Otter, Samuel. *Melville's Anatomies*. Berkeley: University of California Press, 1999.

Pavic, Milorad. *Dictionary of the Khazars*. New York: Knopf, 1988.

Parker, Hershel and Harrison Hayford, eds. *Moby-Dick as Doubloon: Essays and Extracts (1851–1970)*. New York: W. W. Norton, 1970.

Payne, F. Anne. *Chaucer and Menippean Satire*. Madison: University of Wisconsin Press, 1981.

Peacock, Thomas Love. *The Novels of Thomas Love Peacock*. London: Rupert Hart-Davis, 1963.

Petronius. *Satyricon*. Translated by William Arrowsmith. New York: Mentor, 1959.

Perkins, David, ed. *English Romantic Writers*. New York: Harcourt, Brace & World, 1967.

Perloff, Marjorie. *Wittgenstein's Ladder: Poetic Language and the Strangeness of the Ordinary*. Chicago: University of Chicago, 1998.

Poe, Edgar Allan. *Edgar Allan Poe, Essays and Reviews*. New York: Library of America, 1984.

Quint, David. *Origin & Originality in Renaissance Literature: Versions of the Source*. New Haven: Yale University Press, 1983.

Quirk, Tom. *Melville's Confidence Man: From Knave to Knight*. Columbia: University of Missouri Press, 1982.

Rabelais, François. *Gargantua and Pantagruel*. New York: Norton, 1991.

Relihan, Joel C. *Ancient Menippean Satire*. Baltimore and London: Johns Hopkins, 1993.

Richards, I. A. *Principles of Literary Criticism*. London: Routledge and Kegan Paul, 1924.

Richardson, Robert D., Jr. *Emerson: The Mind on Fire*. Berkeley: University of California, 1995.

Roth, Phyllis. *Critical Essays on Vladimir Nabokov*. Boston: G.K. Hall, 1984.

Sandars, N. K., trans. *The Epic of Gilgamesh*. Harmondsworth: Penguin, 1972.

"Santa Fe Institute: Researchers in Residence." Santa Fe, New Mexico [cited November 1,1997]. Available from http://www.santafe.edu/sfi/research/residents.html

Santraud, J. M. "Dans le sillage de la baleiniere d'Arthur Gordon Pym: Le Sphinx des glaces Dan, Yack." *Etudes Anglaises: Grande Bretagne, Etats Unis* 25 (1972): 353–66.

Schultz, Donald Deidrich. *Herman Melville and the Tradition of the Anatomy: A Study in Genre*. PhD dissertation, Vanderbilt University, 1969.

Sealts, Merton M., Jr. *Melville's Reading: Revised and Enlarged Edition*. Columbia: University of South Carolina Press, 1988.

Seelye, John. " 'Ungraspable Phantom': Reflections of Hawthorne in *Pierre* and *The Confidence-Man*." *Studies in the Novel* 1 (Winter 1969): 436–43.

Shakespeare, William. *The Complete Works*. Edited by G. B. Harrison. New York: Harcourt, Brace and Company, 1952.

Shaw, George Bernard. *Man and Superman*. Harmondsworth: Penguin, 1978.

Shelley, Mary. *Frankenstein, or, the Modern Prometheus*. New York: Norton, 1995.

Smollett, Tobias. *The Expedition of Humphry Clinker*. New York: Norton, 1983.

Sprout, Monique. "The Influence of Poe on Jules Verne." *Revue de Littérature Comparée* 41 (1967): 37–53.

Stern, Milton R. *Contexts for Hawthorne:* The Marble Faun *and the Politics of Openness and Closure in America Literature*. Urbana and Chicago: University of Illinois Press, 1991.

Stevick, Philip. "Novel and Anatomy: Notes towards an Amplification of Frye." *Criticism* 10 (1968): 153–65.

Stoehr, Taylor. *Hawthorne's Mad Scientists: Pseudoscience and Social Science in Nineteenth-century Life and Letters*. Hamden, Conn.: Hamden, 1978.

———. "Art vs. Utopia: The Case of Nathaniel Hawthorne and Brook Farm," *Antioch Review* 36 (1978): 89–102.

Swift, Jonathan. *Gulliver's Travels*. New York: Norton, 1970.

———. *A Tale of a Tub: With Other Early Works*. Oxford: Basil Blackwell, 1957.

Tamir-Ghez, Nomi. "The Art of Persuasion in Nabokov's *Lolita*." *Poetics Today* 1 (1979): 65–83.

Tharpe, Coleman W. "The Oral Storyteller in Hawthorne's Novels." *Studies in Short Fiction* 16 (1979): 205–14.

Tarnas, Richard. *The Passion of the Western Mind*. New York: Ballantine, 1991.

Thucydides. *History of the Peloponnesian Wars*. New York: Harper and Brothers, 1880.

Tibor, Frank, ed. *The Origins and Originality of American Culture*. Budapest: Akedemiai Kaido, 1980. Atlantic Highlands: Humanities Press, 1984.

Touttain, Pierre-André. "Vingt Mille Ronds De Fumée." In *Grand Album Jules Verne*, 45–84. Paris: Hachette, 1982.

Trotsky, Leon. *Culture and Socialism and a Manifesto: Art and Revolution*. London: New Park, 1963.

Turner, Denys. *The Darkness of God: Negativity in Christian Mysticism*. Cambridge: Cambridge University Press, 1995.

Verne, Jules. *An Antarctic Mystery*. Boston: Gregg, 1975.

———. *From the Earth to the Moon*. New York: Thomas Y. Crowell, 1978.

———. *Paris in the Twentieth Century*. Translated by Richard Howard. New York: Ballantine, 1997.

———. *Twenty-thousand Leagues Under the Sea*. New York: Thomas Y. Crowell, 1979.

Voltaire. *Candide*. Translated by David Gordon. Boston: Bedford/St. Martin's, 1999.

Waldrop, M. Mitchell. *Complexity: The Emerging Science at the Edge of Order and Chaos*. New York: Simon and Schuster, 1992.

Walpole, Horace. *The Castle of Otranto*. New York: Oxford, 1996.

Wells, H. G. *Seven Science Fiction Novels*. New York: Dover, 1950.

Wenke, John. *Melville's Muse: Literary Creation and the Forms of Philosophical Fiction*. Kent: Kent State University Press, 1995.

White, Morton. *The Age of Analysis*. New York: Houghton Mifflin, 1955.

Winslow, Joan D. "New Light on Hawthorne's Miles Coverdale," *Journal of Narrative Technique* 7 (1977): 189–99.

Wittgenstein, Ludwig. *Philosophical Grammar*. Ed. R. Rhees, translated by A. J. P. Kenny. Oxford: Oxford University Press, 1974.

———. *Philosophical Investigations*. Ed. G. E. M. Anscombe and R. Rhees, translated by G. E. M. Anscombe. New York: MacMillan, 1958.

———. *On Certainty*. Ed. G. E. M. Anscombe and G. H. von Wright, translated by D. Paul and G. E. M. Anscombe. Oxford: Blackwell, 1969.

———. *Remarks on Frazer's Golden Bough*. Translated by J. Beversluis. Atlantic Highlands: Humanities Press, 1979.

———. *Tractatus Logico-Philosophicus*. Translated by D. F. Pears and B. F. McGuiness. London: Routledge & Kegan Paul, 1961.

———. *Zettel*. Edited by G. E. M. Anscombe and G. H. von Wright, translated by G. E. M. Anscombe. Oxford: Blackwell, 1967.

Wollstonecraft, Mary. *A Vindication of the Rights of Woman: with Strictures on Political and Moral Subjects*. London: Printed for J. Johnson, 1792.

Zamyatin, Evgenii Ivanovich. *We*. Translated by Gregory Zilboorg. Boston: Gregg Press, 1975.

Zanger, Jules. "Poe's Endless Voyage: *The Narrative of Arthur Gordon Pym*." *Papers on Language and Literature* 22 (Summer 1986): 276–83.

Zappa, Frank. *Joe's Garage Acts II & III*. Frank Zappa Records, 1979.

Index

Abrams, M. H., 47
Addison, Joseph, 108
Aldiss, Brian W., 41, 149, 188
Alice books, 48, 137, 177, 184–85, 194, 196 n
American Revolution, 74
Aneid, The, 159
Apophatic theology, 31–32, 55, 129
Appel, Alfred, 39
Aristophanes, 46, 63, 138; Old Learning versus New Learning, 148–50
Aristotle, 153, 195
Auerbach, Erich, 106
Aurelius, Marcus, 45
Austen, Jane, 34, 63, 116, 184, 194, 196 n; philosophical traditions of sense and sensibility, 22, 110–13; views on criticism, 50
Axelrod, Robert, 173

Babbage, Charles, 169
Bacchic festival, 46
Bacon, Francis, 34, 66, 110, 112, 137, 148; abstract necessities and four idols, 25–26
Bakhtin, Mikhail Mikhailovich, 48–51, 116
Ballard, J. G., 184, 188, 193
Barbarella, Queen of the Galaxy, 149
Barth, John, 43
Batman, 143
Bedsitting Room, The, 149
Beethoven, Ludwig van, 136
Behe, Michael J., 168–69
Bellamy, Edward, 114
Berkeley, Bishop George, 21, 112
Beverley Hillbillies, The, 143
Bezanson, Walter E., 140
Binmore, Ken, 59

Blake, William, 26, 100, 110, 113, 159, 188, 190; Greek and Roman versus Hebraic models of poetic discourse, 106–7, 152–54; minute particulars, 23; transformational mythology and John Milton, 104–6; transformational mythology and Michael Moorcock, 192–93
Borges, Jorge Luis, 63
Boy and His Dog, A, 149
Bradbury, Ray, 107, 149, 155–56, 201 n
Brazil, 149
Breton, André, 167
Browne, Sir Thomas, 141
Bryant, John, 91, 95, 115–16, 136, 143–44
Bullitt, John M., 52, 54
Burgess, Anthony, 85, 147–49, 155; dystopia and human programming, 157–60
Burroughs, William S., 43, 184, 188
Burton, Robert, 34, 48, 51, 56–58, 112, 114, 138, 141
Butler, Bishop, 22
Byron, Ada, 170
Byron, George Gordon, Lord, 34, 48, 63, 109, 113, 116, 138, 143, 189
Bunyan, John, 96–97

Capek, Karel, 48, 63, 138, 148–49, 194
Capella, Martianus, 45
Carlin, George, 116
Carlson, Lauri, 61
Carlsson, Peder, 188
Carroll, Lewis (Dodgson, Charles Lutwidge), 63, 137, 138, 196 n
Cartland, Barbara, 44
Cervantes, Miguel, 34, 63, 134, 136, 138, 159

Chaucer, Geoffrey, 57
Cioffi, Frank, 117
Clairvoyance, 84–85
Coleridge, Samuel Taylor, 65, 67, 138
Colossus: The Forbin Project, 149
Conrad, Joseph, 35
Cook, Jonathan, 51, 198n
Copernicus, Nicolaus, 175
Cosmogenesis; cosmogenic aesthetics, 177–83; cosmic axiology table, 183; generic cosmogenic narrative, 188–93; literary cosmogenic narrative, 186–87; mythological cosmogenic narrative, 185–86; religious cosmogenic narrative, 186; tables of literary complexity, 184, 194; transcendental cosmogenic narrative, 187–88
de Coulanges, N. D. Fustel, 173
Crews, Frederick, 79, 86

Dada, The, 167
Daigrepont, Loyd M., 66–67
Dalí, Salvador, 167
Dante Alighieri, 137, 157
Darwin, Charles, 165, 169–70
de Duve, Christian, 163
Derrida, Jacques, 32, 182–84, 194
Descartes, René, 127, 160
Dial, The, 89
Dr. Strangelove, or How I Learned to Stop Worrying and Love the Bomb, 143, 149
Drury, M. O'C., 11
Duck Soup, 149

Eco, Umberto, 43–44, 47
Eckhart, Johannes, Meister, 32
Einstein, Albert, 175
Eisenman, Peter, 182
Eliade, Mircea, 139
Eliot, T. S., 36–37, 65
Emerson, Ralph Waldo, 58, 80–81, 95, 109, 114, 138, 140–41
Ezekiel, 106

Fernandez, Juan, 104
Fescenine verse, 47
Fielding, Henry, 63, 112
Forster, E. M., 149
Foucault, Michel, 114, 116

Frazer, Sir James G., 117
Frege, Gottlob, 26
French Revolution, 74, 111
Freud, Sigmund, 79, 117, 165, 175, 179
From Russia with Love, 149
Frye, Northrop, 30, 48, 140, 185
Fuller, Buckminster, 37
Fuller, Margaret, 84

G-8, 172
Galbraith, John Kenneth, 175
Gilgamesh, Epic of, 44, 47, 63, 197n
Gilligan's Island, 143
Godwin, William, 110, 113
Goethe, Johann Wolfgang von, 65, 67
Golding, William, 149
Graduate Record Examination, 74
Gregory of Nyssa, 32

Hamlet, 65, 141
Hawthorne, Nathaniel, 11, 34–35, 48, 63, 100, 114, 132, 179, 199n, 200n; *The Blithedale Romance*, 81–90; and Bunyan, 96–98; and Melville, 94–99, 140–41, 200n; "The Hollow of the Three Hills," 97; and Poe's notions of originality, 140–41; visions of dystopia, 84–85, 88
Hayford, Harrison, 91, 95, 114
Hegel, G. W. F., 110–11, 114, 116, 137, 165, 179
Hertz, Heinrich, 70
Hokusai, Katsushika, 195
Homer, 151, 159, 179
Hume, David, 21, 24, 26, 112
Huxley, Aldous, 35, 47, 48, 63, 138, 148, 149, 155, 196n

IMF, 172
Imagism, 36
Irving, Washington, 64, 66–67

Jameson, Fredric, 40–43
Jefferson, Thomas, 143, 174
Jencks, Charles, 186, 195, 205n; cosmic axiology table, 183; cosmogenic aesthetics, 177–83; describes postmodernism, 42–44, 179; modernism and industry, 36–38; and the Homeric

question, 179; intellectual orthodoxies, 175; metaphors of complexity, 180–81; organizational depth, 181; refutes Derrida, 182–83; superposition, 182
Job, 129–30
Johnson, Samuel, 112
Jonah, 63, 110, 126
Joyce, James, 159, 188

Kafka, Franz, 149
Kant, Immanuel, 122
Kaplan, Carter, 203n
Kauffman, Stuart, 162–76, 180
Kirk, Eugene P., 48–49
K-Mart, 74
Kubrick, Stanley, 136, 158; *2001: A Space Odyssey* and Milton, 105–6
Kundera, Milan, 136

Lawrence, D. H., 47
Le Corbusier (Charles Édouard Jeanneret), 37
Levy, Steven, 174
Lewis, C. S., 31, 149, 155
Lewis, R. W. B., 80–81
Locke, John, 21, 54, 108–12, 122
Logical Positivism, 27
Lucian, 45–46, 137, 138

Maimonides, Moses, 32
Marwick, Arthur, 173
Marx, Karl, 60, 110–11, 165, 172, 175
Marvell, Andrew, 143
McLuhan, Marshall, 175
McKinsey Quarterly, The, 172, 204n
Meleager, 45
Melville, Herman, 30, 35, 48, 51–53, 55, 58, 63, 81, 91–104, 107–8, 110, 114–44, 159, 166, 185; accuracy in representation, 121–22; and Burton, 51–52, 56–58, 141; Byronic facetiousness of, 128; demonological pantheism, 125; and Hawthorne, 94–99, 140–41, 200n; and Job, 129–30; influence on Jules Verne, 101–4, 109–10, 201n; ironic notion of piety, 126; and liberalism, 116; on Milton's originality, 134–36; monstrosity and myth,103–10; and the New Historicism, 51–52, 114–16; on orthodoxy, 125; compared to Petronius, 144; on Platonism, 120, 122–25, 127–28; Queequeg's mythopoetic remark, 129; "The Town-Ho's Story," 129–30; compared to Swift and Nabokov, 136; and Swift, 138–39; Wall Street and China, 143; and Wittgenstein, 9–11, 117, 121–24, 141–43
Menippus of Sinope, 45–46, 63
Mesopotamia, 44, 125, 161
Metrocles, 45
Metropolis, 149
Milton, John, 106, 108, 114, 116, 159; originality of, 134–36; transformational mythology, 106
Modern Language Association, 71
Monk, Ray, 12
Moorcock, Michael, 47, 54, 149; transformational mythology 188–95

Nabokov, Vladimir, 39–40, 43–44, 63, 85, 116, 138, 143, 149, 155, 185, 194, 196n; and dystopia, 156–57; compared to Melville and Swift, 136
NAFTA, 172
Negative theology, 32
Network, 149
New Historicism, 52, 114–16, 198n
New Worlds, 188–89
Newton, Isaac, 112, 175
Nietzsche, Friedrich Wilhelm, 111, 116, 179

Oliver, Egbert S., 95
On the Beach, 149
Orwell, George, 84, 147–49, 155
Otter, Samuel, 51, 115, 198n
Ovid, 53

Paine, Thomas, 174
Parker, Hershel, 114, 136, 166
Pavic, Milorad, 194
Peacock, Thomas Love, 48, 63, 113, 116, 138, 147; tenets of liberalism, 202n
Pericles, 174
Perloff, Marjorie, 13
Petronius Arbiter, 45–46, 144, 149–51
Philo, 32

Plato, 121, 123, 151, 153, 179, 195
Planet of the Apes, 143, 149
Plotinus, 32
Poe, Edgar Allan, 11, 63, 81, 136, 139; and Blake, 188; on Hawthorne's originality, 131–34; influence on Jules Verne, 100–101, 200–201n; and Wittgenstein, 27
Pope, Alexander, 43, 112
Porte, Marguerite, 32
Pound, Ezra, 36
President's Analyst, The, 149
Prisoner, The, 149
Professor Pangloss, 154–55, 174
Pseudo-Dionysius the Areopagite, 32
Pynchon, Thomas, 49

Queen Mab, 118
Quintilian, 45

Rabelais, François, 34, 63, 137–38, 159; and Bakhtin, 48–50
Ray, John Jr., 40
Reagan, Ronald, 170
Reid, Thomas, 21, 113
Renker, Elizabeth, 114–15
Richards, I. A., 42
Riddel, Joseph, 140, 143
Robocop, 143, 149
Rohe, Ludwig Meis van der, 38
Rollerball, 149
Roosevelt, Franklin Delano, 174
Russell, Bertrand, 12, 24
Russian Revolution, 74

Sant Elia, 36
Santa Fe Institute, 162–63, 168–76
Saturae, 47
Sealts, Merton, 137
Seelye, John, 95–96
Selkirk, Alexander, 104
Seneca, 45
Shakespeare, William, 34, 108–9, 114, 140–41, 157, 159
Shaw, George Bernard, 35, 80, 203n
Shelley, Mary, 109–11, 113, 116, 199n, 201n
Shelley, Percy Bysshe, 137

Smith, Adam, 170
Smith, John Maynard, 169, 172
Smollett, Tobias, 113, 192
Social Darwinism, 169–71
Soylent Green, 149
Spinoza, Baruch, 123
Sterne, Laurence, 63, 112, 143
Surrealism, 167, 189
Swift, Jonathan, 48, 63, 112, 125, 148, 185, 196n; "Battle of the Books," 151–52; and British philosophy, 54–55; corruption of learning and religion, 33; exponent of Western liberalism, 116; limits of language and reason, 34; rejection of mechanism in nature, 52–53; compared to Melville and Nabokov, 136; and Melville, 138–39
Synoptic technique, 21, 74–76

Thatcher, Margaret, 170
Theophrastus, 45
Thoreau, Henry David, 95
Three Kings, 149
Thucydides, 151, 179
THX1138, 149
Today's theoretical issues, 59
Trilling, Lionel, 39
2001: A Space Odyssey, 105–6, 149

Varro, Marcus Terentius, 45, 63
Verne, Jules, 11, 100–104, 107–9, 116, 149, 155, 200n
Virgil, 159
Voltaire (François Marie Arouet), 48, 112, 137, 143, 149, 184, 194

Walpole, Horace, 108
Wells, H. G., 149, 157
Wittgenstein, Ludwig, 12–13, 26–30, 55, 59, 63, 70, 81, 136, 173, 179, 188, 189; clarification of propositions, 29; on Freud, Frazer and aesthetics, 117; and Poe, 27; logical positivism and other miscomprehensions of, 27; early versus later thought, 27–30; therapy and games, 30, 59, 142, 203n; and Heinrich Hertz, 70; and Melville, 9–11, 117,

121–24, 141–43; modern euphemism and Professor Pangloss, 154; nothingness and nonsense, 27–28,188; and Russell, 12, 24; and superstitious modernity, 23, 26, 154; usable synoptic technique, 21, 75–76
Wollstonecraft, Mary, 113
Wordsworth, William, 113
WTO, 172

Zamyatin, Evgenii Ivanovich, 84, 149, 155
Zappa, Frank, 55–56
Zardoz, 149